P9-AEY-376

ILINC
C_____67 1984
North,   1653-1734
General pre_____ Life of Dr
John North
3 5057 00614 2961

Roger North, *General Preface* and *Life of Dr John North*

EDITED BY PETER MILLARD

FÉDÉRATION CANADIENNE DES ÉTUDES HUMAINES
CANADIAN FEDERATION FOR THE HUMANITIES
151 Slater St., Suite 415
Ottawa, Ontario
K1P 5H3

This volume contains two important works by Roger North (1651?–1734): his *General Preface* and *Life of Dr John North*. The *General Preface* is a remarkable discussion of the theory of lifewriting, in which North works towards a revolutionary new kind of biography that combines practical, ethical, and scientific uses. It is a plea for a personal biography that will entertain its readers, teach them valuable moral and practical lessons, and at the same time add to the store of data available on human nature. North is led to consider such matters as the use of a subject's own works, the separation of the private life from the public, the unreliability of memory, and the unlikely combination of qualities needed in a biographer; he goes on to discuss the ethical responsibilities of the 'historiographer' and meditates on the folly of devoting oneself to public service. The *General Preface* is a landmark in the history of biographical theory. It includes almost every point to be raised by Johnson and Boswell several decades later, and introduces issues that were not to receive full critical attention until our own day.

Following the *General Preface* is the *Life of Dr John North*, one of three biographies of North's brothers. The *Life* is beautifully focused on the neurotic Master of Trinity College, who lived for his Greek studies, kept spiders in glass jars, looked like a *madame en travestie*, and was at continual war with his students and Fellows. The biography contains fascinating glimpses of the Cambridge of Barrow and Newton in the period when Cartesian doctrines were still in the ascendant. It ends with a moving account of John North's collapse and final illness.

Roger North's brilliant use of anecdotes to reveal personality and his unflinching recording of the facts both pleasant and unpleasant make the life of his difficult brother an excellent example of what he conceived biography to be: an entertaining source for lessons in living, and a document in the 'natural history of mankind, which is everyone's interest to know.'

PETER MILLARD is a member of the Department of English of the University of Saskatchewan.

Portrait of Roger North by Sir Peter Lely, inscribed on the reverse 'aetat. 30'

ROGER NORTH

General Preface & Life of Dr John North

edited by Peter Millard

UNIVERSITY OF TORONTO PRESS

Toronto Buffalo London

© University of Toronto Press 1984
Toronto Buffalo London
Printed in Canada
ISBN 0-8020-2420-3

Canadian Cataloguing in Publication Data
North, Roger, 1651?–1734.
General preface and Life of Dr John North

Includes index.
ISBN 0-8020-2420- 3

1. Biography (as a literary form) – Early works to
1800. 2. North, John. 3. College teachers –
England – Biography. I. North, Roger, 1651?–1734.
Life of Dr John North. II. Millard, Peter, 1932–
III. Title. IV. Title: Life of Dr John North.

CT77.N67 1984   920   C83-098922-6

Publication of this book is made possible by grants from the Canadian Federation for
the Humanities, using funds provided by the Social Sciences and Humanities Research
Council of Canada, the University of Saskatchewan, and the Publications Fund of the
University of Toronto Press.

Contents

Acknowledgments

Dr Clarence Tracy first led me to Roger North and I am grateful to him. Dr Tracy was acting on a suggestion from the late Professor James Clifford, that most stimulating of scholars, whose articles on Roger North re-awakened interest in the biographer and pointed out ways in which research might go.

Through the kindness of Mr and Mrs Roger North I was able to consult manuscripts and books that gave invaluable help, and I am particularly grateful to them for permission to reproduce the portraits of Roger North and John North. I am also indebted to the late Honourable Dudleya North for much kind hospitality and for the chance to see many North treasures. The following individuals are among those who answered appeals for help, often at considerable trouble to themselves: M Al. Cioranescu, Mrs M. Clapinson, Mr J.M. Farrar, Mr N. McCloskey, Mr A. Mitchell, Mr D. Neill, Mr J.C.T. Oates, Mr N. Richards, Mr M. Swan, Mr T. Webb, and Mr J. Wilson. I must also thank the Reverend G. Midgley and Dr D. Fleeman for their friendly and expert guidance of the thesis on which part of this book is based.

The librarians of Jesus and Trinity Colleges in Cambridge were most helpful and I am especially indebted to the Cambridge University Library. Above all I must record my gratitude to the staff of the Bodleian Library.

I am most grateful to the Master and Fellows of St John's College, Cambridge, for permission to print the manuscript of the *General Preface*, and to the Trustees of the British Library for permission to reproduce the manuscript of the *Life of Dr John North*.

The University of Saskatchewan has provided generous funding to help defray the costs of this book. Finally, I acknowledge with deep gratitude the generous grants given me by the Canadian Federation for the Humanities – a civilizing agency which I think Roger North would have approved of.

PM
Saskatoon 1983

Abbreviations

Roger North's biographical works are referred to as *Francis, Dudley, John*, his autobiography as *Auto*, and the *General Preface* as *Gen. Pref.* In the case of *John* and *Gen. Pref.*, reference is to the present edition; for the other works, reference is to Augustus Jessop's edition: *The Lives of the Right Hon. Francis North, Baron Guilford; the Hon. Sir Dudley North; and the Hon. and Rev. Dr. John North. By the Hon. Roger North, together with the Autobiography of the Author ... in Three Volumes*, Bohn's Standard Library (1890). Roger North's *Examen: or, an Enquiry into the Credit and Veracity of a Pretended Complete History* ... (1740) is referred to as *Examen*.

Alum. Cant. *Alumni Cantabrigienses, a Biographical List of All Known Students, Graduates and Holders of Office at the University of Cambridge* ... Compiled by John Venn and J.A. Venn. *Part I, from the Earliest Times to 1751.* Cambridge: Cambridge University Press 1922-7. 4 volumes

Athen. Oxon. *Athenae Oxonienses* ... by Anthony à Wood ... a new edition ... by Philip Bliss. F.C. Rivington, etc. 1813-20. 5 volumes

BL The British Library, London

Cal. S.P. Dom. *Calendar of State Papers, Domestic Series ... Preserved in the Public Record Office.* Various dates

C.P. *The Complete Peerage of England, Scotland, Ireland, Great Britain and the United Kingdom* ... by G.E.C.[okayne]. New Edition ... the Hon. Vicary Gibbs [et al.] St Catherine's Press 1910-40. 13 volumes

D.N.B. *Dictionary of National Biography.* Edited by Leslie Stephen and Stephen Lee. Smith Elder & Co. 1908–9

The place of publication throughout the notes, unless otherwise stated, is London. Dates given in the notes are New Style.

Introduction

Roger North

... and now I am a grum sir in a country farm and spend my time partly moving to and fro, partly reposing in a hole by the chimney corner with a round window called a closet, when like an old bird in an hollow tree I ruminate my note of the general perfidy but more inexpressible folly of all the feathered kind in yon forest.[1]

So wrote Roger North towards the end of his long life, with the humour, self-awareness, and easygoing disgust with the world that are a mark of his mature years.

The 'country farm' was actually the estate of Rougham in Norfolk, which he had purchased in 1691, and the room which he describes was in the mansion whose construction he had himself planned and supervised. When he bought the estate he was almost forty years old, with a successful career at the bar already behind him, but with a future that did not look very promising. He was an adamant non-juror, and there was no question of compromise with the new regime that came in with William and Mary. Although he kept his chambers in the Middle Temple, he withdrew more and more from active affairs and gave himself up to his two passions, improving his estate and writing. During the last decade of the seventeenth century and the first two or three of the eighteenth he wrote, revised, and brought to a final state an astonishing array of works – essays, treatises, and histories – most of which were never published. Foremost in his concern were the biographical works that remain his most remarkable achievement: the enormous life of his elder brother Francis North, the more moderately sized lives of his brothers Sir Dudley and Dr John, a long discussion of the theory of biography entitled *A General Preface*, and, finally, an autobiographical account of the first half of his life entitled *Notes of Me*.

Although there have been several editions of the *Lives of the Norths*,[2] not one gives the text as Roger North intended it, and the *General Preface* has never been published in full. North's original plan, apparently, was to publish the preface with the three lives, 'beginning with the youngest, Dr John North, then the second, Sir Dudley North, and come at last to the Lord Guilford, Lord Keeper of the Great Seal of England' (*Gen. Pref.*, section 44). In accordance with the last part of North's intentions, this book now presents the *General Preface* complete, together with the first of the biographies, the *Life of Dr John North*, based on the final manuscript versions.

Enough material exists to supply a relatively full account of Roger North's life. The biographer would have at his disposal not only the revealing *Notes of Me* but also one or two other autobiographical fragments in manuscript. In addition, he would be able to consult dozens of letters written by and to Roger, a huge mass of North family papers, and the three lives of his brothers, each of which reveals something about Roger. Such a biography would throw many interesting sidelights on the domestic, political, and intellectual life of England from the mid-seventeenth century to the early decades of the eighteenth, and would also capture one of the more engaging minor personalities in English literature. But, for the moment, a brief outline of his life must suffice.[3]

Whether Roger North was born about 1651, as a recent scholar suggests, or 1653, as Augustus Jessop claims, seems impossible to decide now.[4] We do know that Roger was the youngest of seven sons in a family of fourteen children, four of whom died young. The Norths were a distinguished family which had first come into prominence in the early sixteenth century as a result of the efforts of Edward North. He managed to retain the favour of four successive monarchs and received a large fortune and a barony for his service; one of his sons was the Sir Thomas North who translated *Plutarch's Lives*. The family prospered until the advent of Dudley, third Lord North, who was Roger North's grandfather. Dudley squandered most of his fortune at the court of James I and then retired, in a sour frame of mind, to Kirtling in Cambridgeshire, where he made life miserable for his family and servants and forced his eldest son, Roger North's father, to pay a ruinous rent. Unreasonable to the last, he refused to die until 1667, by which time his eldest son had almost completed raising his family and was too old fully to enjoy his freedom.

Roger North's father, Dudley, fourth Lord North, did his best to pull the estate together and to provide for his huge family. They had many happy times. The children seemed to be fond of each other, and they certainly loved and respected their parents. They were united, too, by a devotion to music, and some of the liveliest passages in *Notes of Me* recount the household concerts on the Cambridgeshire estate. But they did not enjoy the luxurious ease that families of their rank might ordinarily expect. The harassed parents could make ends meet only by practising strict economy, and it was clear that Lord North could do little for the younger sons beyond providing them with a decent education. For the rest, they were on their own. Lord North explained the situation clearly and simply: "Wee saw what was to be had,' Roger North recounted later, 'and knew there was no more, and so were forc't to be contented' (*Auto*, 3:6).

This point is worth emphasizing, for this one admonition of Lord North gave rise to so many of the events of Roger North's life as well as of the lives of the three brothers whom he selected as the subjects of his biographies. As Roger North tells it, all four men were permanently anxious about getting on, and in each case this anxiety drove them on to material success which they paid for with unhappiness and stress. In the case of John North, who was to become Professor of Greek at Cambridge and Master of Trinity College, the anxiety reached almost morbid proportions, as Roger reveals so vividly in *John*. Dudley North, who in his maturity was an extremely able, energetic, and robust merchant, suffered less, but he too worked assiduously to amass his fortune. He endured a long exile in the Levant and found it necessary to observe a most unaristocratic canniness, hoarding his cash despite the taunts of his more extravagant companions because, as Roger North explained, there was no advantage in spending among strangers; 'he must at length come away and leave all that froth behind; but experience at home had a lasting influence, and was seasoned with the joy of participating with his relations and acquaintance; all the while cultivating a mutual esteem and lasting friendship amongst them' (*Dudley*, 2:38). One thing the Norths learned well was the necessary relationship between love and money.

It was Francis North who paid the highest price, as he gained the largest rewards. After Cambridge he rose rapidly through the various ranks in the legal profession until he became chief justice, a post which he found congenial and extremely lucrative. When he was offered the onerous position of Lord Keeper of the Great Seal, he did his best to decline, but his family urged him on. Admittedly, Roger argued on the grounds that Francis was needed by the king and could not decently refuse after everything Charles had done for him. 'But he might think,' reflected Roger, 'and not without reason, that we regarded our own advantage by his promotion: so there was self-interest in persuading him so much to his inconvenience' (*Francis*, 1:253–4). With heavy reluctance Francis accepted the post. The rewards followed as expected, but the burden of office helped to kill him: 'it was the decadence of all the joy and comfort of his life; and, instead of a felicity, as commonly reputed, it was a disease like a consumption which rendered him heartless and dispirited, till death came which only could complete his cure' (*Francis*, 1:253).

Roger North himself, as a child, learned the lesson of husbandry well and carried it with him to school. Some of the most durable memories of his early schooldays at Thetford Free School concerned the management of money. He remembered the 'several manufactures' he had going, 'as lanterns of paper, balls, and thread purses, which brought in some money' (*Auto*, 3:10), and he would never forget the occasion when he was cheated of some hard-earned cash which he invested in a calf that was never delivered. It was at school, also, that he learned a horror of debt. His fondness for apples had led him to run up a debt of 2s. 6d., 'which was a burden so heavy to a little man of honour, that he declined ever after to be in like circumstances' (*Auto*, 3:12). The practice of 'economy' runs as a theme throughout his whole life.

One senses that Roger derived considerable satisfaction from making-do, but there was another side of him that suffered from the constant need to establish himself. Roger North was a thoroughgoing dilettante with a zestful curiosity about almost everything, and he would have liked nothing better than to give his undivided attention to a host of delightful studies. There were early signs at Thetford. The 'several manufactures' mentioned above, for instance, included experiments with fireworks. He managed to make satisfactory 'serpents,' although he never mastered the trick of making rockets that would rise from the ground successfully. He then went on and 'got acquainted with artificers, and learnt to turn, which was a great diversion to me, because it produced somewhat neat, and well accommodated to several of the plays we had' (*Auto*, 3:11). What could be more satisfying than to spend his time in the pursuit of such skills and, later, in the mastering of more abstruse subjects? But time and again throughout his life North would have to drag himself unwillingly from his hobbies to face the irksome realities of the legal profession.

After school there was an interval of about a year, spent at home, during which time his father prepared Roger for the university by teaching him logic. At Cambridge, in 1667, he joined Jesus College, under the somewhat desultory tutorship of his brother John. During his brief stay at Cambridge he became acquainted with the two subjects that, together with music, were to engage his attention to the very last: natural science and mathematics. Mathematics ravished him from the moment he first mastered Euclid's forty-seventh proposition which, in his own words, 'entered me alive, as I may say, and I digested it with great satisfaction' (*Auto*, 3:16). Mathematics led him inevitably into science, and he was fortunate enough to enter Cambridge at the beginning of one of the most exciting periods in its history. The theories of Descartes were circulating in the university, but an interest in them was still considered rather scandalous. This fact, of course, whetted the young student's appetite and made him read the sensational new theories. He soon became convinced. He was to live to see the Cartesian system firmly entrenched in the university and became himself one of those who resisted the attempts to replace it with Newton's description of the universe.

Roger North remained at Cambridge a very short time. At some point it had been decided that he should make his career in law, and so in April 1669 he was admitted to the Middle Temple. Once he was called to the bar, in 1675, success came rapidly. In 1678 Archbishop Sancroft appointed him steward to the see of Canterbury, and during the next eight years he became successively king's counsel, solicitor general to the Duke of York, and attorney general to Queen Mary. He made money.

Later, in 1685, Roger entered parliament as member for Dunwich, and played a moderately conspicuous part in house affairs. According to his own account he promoted a bill to prevent subdivision of the fens, and later he played a prominent part in the introduction of a bill to establish a registry of estates and titles – a pet project of his. Later still he was chairman of a Committee of the Whole House formed to consider ways of increasing the supply of money to the king (*Auto*, 3:180–7). Throughout his legal and political activities North was guided by a fierce royalism; he took the king's side in most disputes. The cynic might say that this was only to be expected in a man who owed his fortune, and that of his entire family, to court favour. Yet there is no doubt that North was sincere in his attachment to the royalist cause, and he was buttressed in his beliefs by the conviction that the whole tendency of the law was towards the king's authority. His integrity is proved by the fact that he refused to follow James in everything. While in parliament, for instance, he joined in the refusal to recognize Catholic officers or to supply the king with funds to maintain a standing army. At another time, when asked by Lord Chancellor Jeffreys for his opinion on the king's dispensing power in the case of military officers, he went on record as saying that in this matter the king was not above the law.[5]

Although the London years provided some of the happiest and richest moments in North's life, there was also considerable strain. His description of this period is full of uneasiness, as a result of both a natural hatred of political machinations and his habitual feeling of insecurity. As an important lawyer and brother of the Lord Keeper, he was close to the centre of power in what was, after all, one of the most tumultuous and precarious periods of England's modern history. Although he tried to keep aloof from the broils, he could not escape them altogether and often found himself involved in some tiresome and dangerous fight when he longed only for peace. He escaped whenever possible, and the best moments were when he and Francis could shut the door, for a moment, on all the turmoil: 'And most of the conversation we had was familiar and easy, rather about arts and sciences than court brigues;[6] and at times when we were retired, and cared not for repetitions of such uneasy matters, oh! how pleasant and agreeable were those days, when in the midst of storms we lay safe and fearless in retired harbour, and never so well pleased as when we were escaped from the billows, if I may term crowds such' (*Gen. Pref.*, section 43).

The situation was made worse by the fact that he had no high opinion of his own abilities. He was always conscious that he owed his position to his brother's eminence, and he was ill at ease among the bewilderingly complicated and troublesome affairs that his brother's position led him to. Indeed, Francis North was mentor, patron, and a tower of strength to Roger, so that his death in 1685 left Roger feeling exposed. He was now in his early thirties, and he could not have been left alone at a worse time. The Lord Keeper's death coincided with the ascension of James

II and then, as Roger discovered, the times began to grow sour' for Protestants (*Auto*, 3:179). At first, it is true, Francis North's successor, Judge Jeffreys, was embarrassingly friendly. 'But I had such holy water from him, such elaborate speeches of encouragement, as I never hope to, or rather hope never to hear again' (*Auto*, 3:195). He was not surprised when Jeffrey's favour turned to hostility and insult. He held on as long as he could, drawing some comfort from a closer friendship with another brother, Sir Dudley North, but spending more and more time alone. He found peace now in the house of the late Sir Peter Lely in Covent Garden. Before his death in 1680 the painter had been a close friend of the Norths, and Roger was his executor. North devoted himself to 'philosophy, music, mechanics, and study' (*Auto*,3:196), and probably it was at this time that he began to produce the enormous collection of essays to which he would return over and over again throughout the rest of his life. Many of the thoughts that had occupied his leisure hours since his Cambridge days now began to take more substantial form. He pondered the problems of smoke, mechanics, and etymology. He was particularly interested in the barometer, and his speculations on this subject resulted in a book-length essay. Rewriting, he discovered, was a wonderful aid to clarity of thinking, so he produced revision upon revision of almost everything he wrote. He returned to the study of Descartes, and became increasingly aware of Newton's dazzling system, which was completely contrary to that of his beloved Descartes. The subjects came crowding in. He decided to collect notes for a history of law. He had something useful to say about architecture (the entrance to the Middle Temple was built to his design). He also had a modest contribution to make to the 'physics' of sound. Then there were pictures to be studied, and, above all, there was music. He had been surrounded by music from early childhood and he now found it entirely absorbing. He wrote many hundreds of pages upon the subject, historical, analytical, and critical, and he spent many hours practising and performing.[7]

North worked away quietly in the house of his old friend and watched the political upheavals with increasing disgust. The odious Jeffreys met an ignominious end, the king fled the country, and now an illegal succession, as North saw it, demanded an allegiance that his conscience would not allow him to give.

A retreat to the country was inevitable. About 1691 North purchased the small estate of Rougham in Norfolk and made enthusiastic plans for rebuilding its crumbling old mansion. Rougham was the perfect antidote to London, and North spent more and more time in this remote and beautiful part of England. The house that he began building took shape slowly, and was not ready for occupancy, it appears, until about 1695. The years during the building of Rougham must have been extremely busy ones for Roger. Not only were there the multitudinous details of construction to attend to, but he found himself in charge of an increasing number of orphaned relatives. At Francis North's death in 1685 Roger had become guardian of his three children. Then in 1691 his eldest brother, Lord North and Grey, died, leaving another three children to be cared for. In the same year yet another brother, Sir Dudley North, left two sons to Roger's care. He took his responsibilities seriously. He oversaw the affairs of his wards in scrupulous detail, and wrote them long and patient letters of advice. He was helped in these tasks by his brother Montagu. After a somewhat chequered career, including a time as a Turkey merchant interrupted by three and a half years' imprisonment at Toulon on suspicion of being a spy, Montagu had joined Roger at Rougham, and was to spend the last years of his life there. He seems to have been a kindly man, but rather infirm, and perhaps a little tetchy, as the result of a dangerous bout of the plague in Constantinople that had almost taken his life.

The troubles were endless, and it was necessary to keep alert in a naughty world where heiresses might marry adventurers or fools, and where older brothers could prove mean and intractable in the execution of wills. Towards the conclusion of the *General Preface*, when Roger North was recording details of the lives of his many brothers and sisters, he had congratulated his father on the remarkable fact that 'of a flock so numerous' there was 'no one scabby sheep in it' (*Gen. Pref.*, section 48). Alas, it was not so with the next generation, and occasionally he was troubled with problems of a rather sordid nature. One of the sons of Sir Dudley North, for instance, gave particular trouble. In 1704 'Nephew Roger' was sent to Roger North's sister Ann Foley at Stourbridge in Worcestershire. She must keep an eye on young Roger, her brother Montagu warned her; 'he is a little amorously given, and at the North's in Cambridgeshire were apt to run at mutton ... your maids must not be too coming.' Roger caused nothing but grief at Stourbridge, culminating in tangible disaster less than a year later: 'I am very sorry you had so clear, but withall so dirty a proof of his manhood,' another relative wrote to Ann Foley's son. The youth was bound to come to a bad end, which Montagu duly reported to his sister the next year: 'I am now only to tell you the final end of Roger's follies. He had got a very bad clap with some of his London whores, which in compassion of him we had a good surgeon to care and take care of him, but in the midst of the operation, he went out four days since and is not yet returned, and we hear is married to a poxed whore, of whom I have so often given him warning. So there is the end of him.' However, a month later Roger has been sent 'into the country to stay there until we can get things ready for him to send him to the Indies, where [we] hope he may yet do well.'[8]

Meanwhile, Roger North was busily forming a family of his own. In 1696 he had decided to marry and chose Mary, the daughter of an uncompromising Jacobite, Sir Robert Gayer of Stoke Poges, and by her he eventually produced seven children, one of whom died in infancy. Work on the estate continued. There were avenues of trees to plant, fields to enclose, a fishpond to construct, experiments to be conducted with new crops, and there were always the legal affairs of neighbours to attend to.

Gradually life became more peaceful. As Roger's numerous wards came of age and his own children grew up, his burden was progressively lightened, although to the very end he acted as adviser to the North family generally. He now had the leisure to put the final touches to the multifarious written works that he had begun many years before. Some very substantial bundles of manuscripts took their place on his shelves alongside the shorter treatises on scientific subjects. There was the bulky *Examen*, which was Roger North's attempt to answer a Whig history of the period in which his brother had played a prominent part, and there were the biographies of his brothers, of which the largest was the *Life of Francis North*. With its appendices this work had now swelled to many hundreds of pages. Almost as impressive was the pile of manuscript pages on music, and it is probable that there were many more works, or at least versions of works, than are now extant, for it appears that a large number of manuscripts disappeared in a general dispersal of the papers in the early nineteenth century.[9] Had he been able to know of this catastrophe, Roger North would have been very distressed. The writings were dear to his heart, as we know from a letter written to his son Montagu, at Cambridge, to whom he had entrusted some of the papers: 'I hope you have a strict care of the MSS., which I would not have miscarry in any respect, being a sort of writing slight and slovenly as it is (such a fool I am) pleaseth me to peruse better than any books' (*Auto*, 3:278).

As Roger North made revision after revision of his precious works, polishing and shaping them, so his estate slowly formed itself as he had envisaged. The chestnut trees that he had planted came into maturity, his orchards produced fruit, and his fishponds gave him fresh fish. He did not want his experience to go for nothing. He wrote a treatise on architecture based on his Rougham renovations, recently published, and in 1713 he published *A Discourse of Fish and Fish-Ponds* which quietly and directly recorded what he had learnt on that matter. 'I wish any Gentleman,' he declares in the preface, 'who hath employed his Money and Pains in cultivating Waters in Countries that are blessed with Springs and Rivers, would, for the Benefit of his Posterity and Neighbours, as I have done, set down his Experience, and communicate it to such as have a Mind to divert themselves with the most reasonable Employment of beautifying and improving their own Estates.' In the next year he brought out another little book called *The Gentleman Acomptant* which showed how a system of 'Merchants Accounts' could be modified to serve the 'Concerns of the Nobility and Gentry of England.'[10]

North's constant desire for self-improvement extended beyond his own estate. For most of his life he had been an avid collector of books, and in the early part of the eighteenth century he decided to share his collection. In 1709 Roger began building a new parochial library adjacent to Rougham Church and he deposited in it a selection of books (*Auto*., 3:303-4, 309-10). A catalogue of the library has been discovered among the Norwich episcopal records. It is dated 1714 and lists about

1,150 volumes, of which more than 800 are theological.[11] In 1712 North added to the library the collection of his bluestocking niece, the Honourable Dudleya North (whose death presented North with yet another responsibility when he took on the executorship for his nephew, Lord North and Grey).

Neither North's house nor his library survived the eighteenth century, and to tell the full story of his last years would, in a small way, compensate for the sadness of seeing his work perish. Living quietly at Rougham, doing what he could for his family and neighbours and, through his writings, for society in general, he tried to make of his own mind, as well as of his estate, a place of order, usefulness, and beauty. In doing so he displays elements of what is sometimes regarded as an empty Augustan dream – the ideal country gentleman. The most familiar description of the type is Steele's in *Tatler*, no. 169:

> He is father to his tenants, and patron to his neighbours, and is more superior to those of lower fortune by his benevolence than his possessions. He justly divides his time between solitude and company, so as to use the one for the other. His life is spent in the good offices of an advocate, a referee, a companion, a mediator, and a friend.[12]

Of course, Roger North was not quite so languidly noble, not so polished, as Steele's model. He was much more robust, and capable often of startling naïveté, not to mention the frequent broadside against human stupidity, particularly stupidity of Whig origin. Through his later years, too, there ran a twist of bitterness as he recalled what he thought were the injustices to his brothers, and as he reflected on the pointlessness of self-sacrifice. Some of his writings, and certainly his correspondence with non-jurors like George Hickes, reveal a fatalistic disgust understandable in a man rapidly being marooned because of his refusal to compromise politically. Indeed, Roger North's name appeared in the papers of the captured Jacobite spy Christopher Layer, implicating him in the scheme to support the Pretender. Whether North had in fact gone that far is not certain, although such action seems most uncharacteristic of him. However, it is clear that North was a committed member of the small group of High Church, Tory Jacobites who saw the oath of allegiance as a denial of divine right and hereditary succession. His conservatism even affected his scientific outlook, so that he regarded Newtonianism as a part of the new heterodoxy, carrying with it dangerous implications for religion.[13]

To the ordinary inhabitant of Rougham, however, such matters were too abstruse. When he died in March 1734, Roger North was something of a patriarch. He was in his eighties, and was looked up to throughout the neighbourhood as a man of wisdom, vivid character, and experience. Surveying his entire life, one remembers North not as the retired landowner in the role of guardian and sage, not as the stubbornly loyal non-juror, nor even as the lawyer with an entrée to the centres of power. The passages in the autobiography that stay in the mind are those that tell of his pleasures, for then he relaxes, the almost boyish enthusiasm shines through, and the writing becomes alive. And so one remembers the devoted virtuoso, one moment teasing his mind with the cosmic systems of Descartes and Newton, the next speculating on the minute particles of matter that constitute smoke. Or one remembers him busily learning an air by Ferrabosco on his bass-viol in preparation for an amateur concert. Most vivdly of all, one visualizes him in his small yacht on the trip to Harwich, which he describes with such exhilaration and freshness, being overtaken by the large colliers, 'with topsails out, full-bunted, and bows rustling' (*Auto*, 3:31).

North and the Theory of Biography

Roger North built his Rougham walls solid and he planted trees that he knew would last for many generations, but he was aware always of the terrible impermanence of things, especially of people. When his brother Dudley died in 1691, he had felt particularly desolate. Both parents had been gone for some time; John North was dead, so was Francis, and now Dudley. 'No loss is like mine,' he wrote to his brother-in-law Robert Foley, 'that am left alone, scarce able to go alone, in an afflicted family.'[14] As the years went by, he was alarmed at how rapidly his brothers seemed to slip from memory. They had been brilliant men, he reflected, both in intellect and in character, and had played no small part in the affairs of the nation. Yet who remembered them, even after so short a time? In the case of the Lord Keeper, it was true, the oblivion was due to a conscious endeavour on the part of biased historians 'to suppress all memory of his lordship's name and worth, to the end that his character and behaviour in the course of his great employments should be utterly unknown to aftertimes, as if no such person had ever lived in the world' (*Francis*, 1:10). And to some extent John North had only himself to blame because he had made sure that all of his writings were destroyed immediately after his death. But even under the best conditions, as Roger remarked in the *General Preface*, memory is notoriously frail, and lives that are important and useful pass away as if they had never been. In part, North's three biographies are an attempt to defy that impermanence and to rescue his brothers from the oblivion into which they seemed to be sinking with dismaying speed. 'I think it not reasonable for me to let such an ornament to his family, and example of virtue, be wholly forgot and lost, or perhaps, *nomine tenus*[15] only, confined to a petit cycle in some musty genealogy,' he wrote of John North (*John* intro, section 2).

To write a biography can be a protest against death, a restoring to life, an antidote for loneliness. It can also be a cure for nostalgia. There had been strain, admittedly, during those years in London; nevertheless, now that he looked back over his life, he could see that the moments shared with his brothers had been among the happiest he had known. In writing of those times he could to some extent relive them, as we see from a letter that Roger wrote to Francis North's son announcing his intention of writing the Lord Keeper's life, 'wherein I shall gain an exquisite pleasure in reviving the ideas of my happy times when he lived.'[16]

Another spur to writing was the need for vindication. As the histories of the Restoration period began to appear, they seemed to him to distort the times generally, and when they bothered to mention the Norths at all, they were grossly unjust. He therefore wrote to set the record straight. White Kennet's contribution to *A Complete History of England* (1706) was the most infuriating of these histories and, indeed, resulted in a separate book of refutation, the *Examen*. But North was also disgusted by *State Tracts* (1689), Jean Leclerc's *Life and Character of Mr. J. Locke* (1706), the anonymous *Lives of all the Lords Chancellor, Lords Keeper, and Lords Commissioner* (1708), and Laurence Eachard's *History of England* (1708-18). As a historian Roger North was as incapable of objectivity as the most biased Whig writer, but his biographies are packed with detailed information that is still useful to students of the period.

The desire to preserve a memory, to relive past times, to put down one's side of the story will not alone produce worthwhile biography. Such motives make a good start, but some sort of artistic consciousness is also needed. North had such a consciousness. He always read biography avidly and thought long and deeply about it. As he planned the *Lives*, wrote and rewrote them, many questions came to him. What was the relation of biography to fiction? How could one separate history and biography? How did one solve the many practical difficulties confronting the biographer? What was the particular use of biography? He wrote down his conclusions in a long essay which he entitled *A General Preface* (also *General Preface*) and which was intended to precede the three *Lives*. When his son Montagu published the biographies in 1742 and 1744, however, he left out the *General Preface*, and it remained unpublished and virtually unnoticed until 1962 when James Clifford included excerpts from it in an anthology of essays on biography.[17]

In the history of the development of biography the *General Preface* is of considerable importance. Before North there is little critical writing on the subject. Dryden's brief discussion is the most substantial as it is the most significant, and what remains consists mainly of remarks found in introductions to biographies, such as Burnet's prefaces to his lives of the Dukes of Hamilton and Castle Herald (1677) and Sir Matthew Hale (1682) or Baxter's preface to his *Breviate of the Life of Margaret* (1681). However, North was not alone in paying biography the compliment of treating it at length and as a separate genre. A few years after the final version of the *General Preface*, Edward Calamy wrote an intelligent and broad survey of autobiography and biography which was to form an introduction to his *Historical Account of My Own*

Life (published 1829). But Calamy's impressive and much neglected discussion is nothing like so long and analytical as North's.

Before the full significance of North's theory can be appreciated, it is necessary to remind ourselves briefly of the prevailing attitudes towards biography at the time North was writing – the early eighteenth century, more than sixty years before Johnson's *Lives of the Poets*, and more than seventy before Boswell's great work.

The first thing to notice is that in North's day there was almost no 'pure biography' in the sense suggested by Harold Nicolson in *The Development of English Biography* (1927). That the record of a living being should be written for itself, for its own intrinsic interest, was a concept practically unknown. In almost every case the biography was written 'for some other special by-end or purpose,' to use Roger North's own words (*Gen. Pref.*, section 18). One of the most common forms of biography, the prefatory life, owed its existence merely to the need to give some sort of authority to the works it preceded. And in that age of bitter controversy it was inevitable that biography should be debased to serve the ends of propaganda, political or religious. William Winstanley, for instance, in the preface to *The Loyal Martyrology* (1665), a very popular book, can describe Cromwell as 'an English Monster, the Centre of Mischief ... a pattern for Tyranny, Murther and Hypocrisie,' while Charles I becomes 'the most Glorious Martyr of this late Age, the exact pattern of Piety, Patience and Prudence.' It is obvious that Winstanley's chief concern is not biography but politics, but in his almost hysterical partisanship he is typical of dozens of seventeenth-century biographers.

Although biography was an important tool in political propaganda, overwhelmingly it was used to serve one of two purposes: either to persuade to virtue, or to illustrate history. That biography's main purpose was to warn against evil and incite to good was taken for granted and was repeated with monotonous regularity in preface after preface. 'Good examples are for imitation, bad for evitation,' declared the ubiquitous Samuel Clarke,[18] whose fat volumes of lives must have been a familiar sight on booksellers' shelves, and to this simple formula the entire body of seventeenth-century biographers would have added an automatic 'amen.'

The identification of biography with history was also taken for granted. Since Anglo-Saxon times, after all, the history of the country had been told mainly in the chronicles of the kings, and it was a concept that died hard. When William Winstanley, therefore, decided to include the lives of lesser men in his *England's Worthies* (1660), he was aware that he was pursuing 'our English History in no ordinary method, but such a one as to my knowledge the like is not extant in our English tongue; the general way of writing being of the Chronicles of Kings ... the lives of particular persons being in them either obscured or too lightly toucht on' (sig A6 v). This was a tiny step forward, but a significant one: the lives of lesser men were now seen to be important.

Winstanley's example was eagerly followed, and the latter half of the seventeenth century saw an enormous number of lives of men prominent in public affairs. Almost without exception, the primary interest in the subject was a result of his role in history, but over and over again one finds the authors of these lives facing the inevitable problem: how can the biographer realistically separate the public life from the private? This struggle, evident for example in the works of Strype, Hacket, and the influential continental scholar Jean Leclerc, is an indication that, almost accidentally, historians were becoming biographers. But we are still a long way from 'pure biography.'

Given that the main concern of most biographers was either to provide a moral example or to illustrate history, then obviously their choice of subject was limited to those who were holy and those who were great, or, as often happened in an age of princely prelates and Christian statesmen, those who were both holy and great. That the subject had to be lofty was taken for granted so completely that it is difficult to find anyone bothering to write down an argument justifying it. This is not to say, of course, that no secular lowly person was ever taken as the subject of a biography. Donald Stauffer has described, for instance, the interesting group of biographies that, feeding on the pride of the London guilds, took as their subject a clothier, shoemaker, merchant, or some other member who had achieved eminence.[19] And in the case of the puritan biographies, it is the subject's holiness that qualifies him, not his rank. But as a glance at a representative list of seventeenth-century biographies would show, the most frequent subjects were persons of high estate. They were, most of them, relentlessly virtuous.

The manner had to suit the subject. Most seventeenth-century biographers observed a strict sense of decorum that led them to suppress not only the more dubious facts in their subject's moral life but also what they usually termed 'trivia.' 'Trivia' seems to mean those details of everyday life – a man's relations with his family, his eccentricities of habit, his clothes – that tend to detract from the heroic qualities of the subject and identify him with ordinary human beings. Unfortunately, they happen to be the details that give life and individuality to a subject. The most authoritative dictum on the matter came from Burnet in his preface to *The Life and Death of Sir Matthew Hale* (1682):

> others have fallen into another extream in writing Lives too jejunely, swelling them up with trifling accounts of the Childhood and Education, and the domestick or private affairs of those persons of whom they Write, in which the World is little concerned: by these they become so flat, that few care to read them, for certainly those Transactions are onely fit to be delivered to Posterity, that may carry with them some useful peece of knowledge to after-times.

So spoke the great bishop, and would-be biographers no doubt also remembered the words of another great cleric, Thomas Sprat, who had refused to publish Cowley's letters (full of the 'Native tenderness, and Innocent gayety of his Mind') for similar reasons of decorum.[20] No wonder that when a biographer did slip in some domestic detail, he usually felt constrained to apologize for it.

Biography at the beginning of the eighteenth century, then, as it was generally accepted, did not have quite enough status to stand alone but usually had to justify its existence by serving some other purpose – most frequently to illustrate history or to provide a moral example. Secondly, it tended to be limited in subject, although there were exceptions, to holy or great men. Such, very roughly, was the situation when Roger North in his retirement at Rougham began to work on the lives of his brothers and to think over the whole subject of biography. The result of North's cogitations was the *General Preface*: a long discussion of the theory of biography (and to a lesser extent of the theory of history). The *Preface* is, in effect, a plea for a new kind of biography that will entertain its readers while teaching them valuable lessons. Such lessons would be the usual moral ones, but (and here North makes a significant departure from most of his fellow-biographers) they would also be practical ones. Most important, this biography must deal with ordinary people in ordinary situations. The problem is how to arrive at a personal biography that has all the attractiveness of fictional romance and the immediacy of comedy, yet that will be more effective than either because it is true. By such a route North arrived at a concept of life-writing that was revolutionary in its implications and that anticipated the vivid, full, and personal biography that developed later in the century and culminated in our greatest work in that genre, Boswell's *Life of Johnson*. It is interesting to speculate whether North's essay would have speeded up the advent of such biography if he had published it in his own lifetime. As it was, it remained in manuscript, apparently unknown and unread.

The central theme of the *General Preface*, and essential to North's purpose, is that biography should concern itself with the ordinary man. The reason for doing so is that the lives of ordinary people, suitably moralized, would be more effective as an example to most people than the lives of the great which are so remote as to seem almost like fiction. The gauntlet is thrown down in the very first sentence of the *Preface*, and North elaborates on his theory at many points. This insistence on the importance of the private man is the most significant new element in North's discussion. One effect of the doctrine, if generally accepted, would be to widen enormously the horizons of biography. The subject would derive his importance, not from his high position in government or church, but from how he dealt with the personal problems that face most people at one time or another – his importance, in fact, derives from his very ordinariness. Biography would move out of the impersonal palace or cathedral into the more familiar and robust world outside. Something like this democratization of biography did in fact take place later in the century.

Another important effect of such a theory is the separation of the private life from the public life, and in the process the freeing of biography from its subservience to history. North is very critical of lives that are not focused directly on their subject but which are written to serve some auxiliary purpose, such as illustrating history. He is unhappy about the entanglement of biography and propaganda as well, and is scathing about lives that are written 'purely for favour to certain theses, opinions, or sects' (*Gen. Pref.*, section 20).

Not stated directly, but implied throughout the entire discussion in the *General Preface*, is a plea for an approach to biography which, if followed, would also help revolutionize the genre. It is a plea for greater realism. If the lives of ordinary men are to serve as examples to the average reader, the more realistic they are, North seems to be saying, the more convincing they will be. One reason why he dislikes biographies of men important in history is that they usually neglect the realistic details. For the clearest statement on the matter of realism we must go not to the *General Preface* but to the *Life of Francis North*, where he defends his practice of introducing minor details:

> Some may also allege that I bring forward circumstances too minute, the greater part of which might be dropped and the relation be more material, and being less incumbered, easier understood and retained. I grant much of that to be true; but I fancy myself a picture-drawer and aiming to give the same image to a spectator as I have of the thing itself which I desire should here be represented. As, for instance, a tree, in the picture whereof the leaves and minor branches are very small and confused, and give the artist more pain to describe than the solid trunk and greater branches. But if these small things were left out it would make but a sorry picture of a tree. (*Francis*, 1:327)

The importance of such a view can hardly be over-estimated. It is the little telling detail, the revealing anecdote, that makes a man live and makes him distinguishable from all others, and the texture of a character is formed by the careful multiplication of such details.

If the *General Preface* is unusual in its demands for biography dealing with ordinary people, independent of history or propaganda, and realistic in detail, it is just as unusual in the fact that it goes on to deal at some length with the practical problems of life-writing. The greatest difficulty in the way of the life-writer, as North is acutely aware, is to gain enough knowledge of his subject to write an accurate and complete life. Ideally, he points out, the biographer should be an intimate friend of his subject 'and so attached to the very persons, that little of importance in their whole lives could escape their notice' (*Gen. Pref.*, section 40). Even then, alas, the biographer has to trust to 'frail memory' because it does not usually occur to anyone to keep notes of his friend while alive. (Boswell, it must be remembered, was not yet born.) It would be a great help, North remarks, if the subject of a biography had the foresight to keep a journal. Another suggestion for the would-be biographer concerns the use of the subject's own works as a means of backing up the writer's claims about the subject. But most interesting for the modern student of biography is North's discussion of the place of imagination in biography. The accusation that the account of a private man's life will make dull reading is groundless, he claims, because 'after all, a dullness is never to be charged on a subject, but on the author, who should find spirit enough in himself to give relish to everything he writes' (*Gen. Pref.*, section 14). In his suggestion that biography should contain 'the same ingredients that are usually brought to adorn fiction' (*Gen. Pref.*, section 14), he is really addressing himself to one of the central questions about biography, one that has much occupied twentieth-century critics: is biography an art or a craft? It is true that North seems to think in rather superficial terms of stylistic devices; even so, his appeals for biography which is 'lively,' which is done with 'spirit and judgment,' which is 'depicted in the strongest colours' (*Gen. Pref.*, sections 17, 21), all suggest a daring artistic approach. The biographer is limited to facts, yes, but he still needs imagination.

The same important question is indirectly raised in a passage – somewhat unfocused but full of interest – in which North deals with the relationship between the kind of biography he had in mind and another literary genre: comedy. Comedy is immediately and universally popular, he points out, whether in the form of drama, romance, epic, or burlesque, and he goes on to explain why. There is more than one reason, but mainly it is because comedies deal with 'men in the ordinary state of life, and to represent the great variety of incidents that may appear and concern them in their commerce one with another' (*Gen. Pref.*, section 22). Why not, then, North goes on, write the lives of actual people, set forth with all the attractiveness of fiction, but which will be more effective than fiction because the reader will know that it actually happened? In other words, he wants realistic biography, entertainingly written.

In his groping through existing forms towards a new one it is inevitable that North will remind us of other innovators of the period, and particularly of Fielding, who reveals much the same process in the famous preface to *Joseph Andrews*. The differences between the two writers are too obvious to need mentioning, but the similarities are instructive. Like Fielding, North rejected heroic forms and seized on the comic which he would adapt for his didactic purposes. Like Fielding, North had read Fénelon's *Télémaque* (*Gen. Pref.*, section 23), knew his way around continental comic fiction (*Gen. Pref.*, sections 14, 23), and was particularly fascinated by *Don*

Quixote, as the numerous references to it throughout the *General Preface* prove. Both North and Fielding seemed to feel the urge towards a new realism, involving characters in situations recognizably like those of the average reader; Fielding approaches it through the novel, North through biography; Fielding wished to improve through ridicule, North by practical example. However, we should remember that North wrote his *General Preface* between 1718 and 1722, roughly twenty-one years before the writing of *Joseph Andrews*, and twenty years before another great novel that was considerably closer to the spirit of North in its realistic didacticism: *Pamela*.

I have singled out the main points of North's theory. Some of his remarks seem so far in advance of his time that we might be led into thinking of him as a pheno-menon standing isolated from his age. But truly innovative as he was, such a view would not be entirely correct. In his unswervingly didactic aim, for instance, he is thoroughly in accord with his own time, even though he is unusual in his insistence that biography is valuable not only for moral lessons, but for practical ones too, and a careful combing of prefaces to seventeenth-century biographies will reveal that many of his concerns had been touched on, albeit briefly, by biographers before him. Nevertheless, North speaks more loudly and clearly of new things than anyone else. The very fact that he was discussing biography objectively, as a separate genre, is significant. The points that other writers merely touched on in passing he examines thoroughly and at length. He anticipated by many years almost every point that Dr Johnson was to raise in his essays on the topic in *Rambler* (no. 60, October 1750) and *Idler* (no. 84, November 1759), and he suggested a formula for biography similar to that arrived at by Boswell towards the end of the century.

If we ask ourselves what it is about North's theory, and indeed about the lives he wrote, that most makes him seem distinct from the biographers who preceded him, we finally arrive at the conclusion that it is above all the sense of fact. The whole tendency of his theory and practice is away from the unspecific quality of most of the older biographies in which the form is stylized and the content generalized. The biographer must know his subject intimately so as to be able to record accurately and fully; his claims must be backed, whenever possible, by the subject's own writings – evidence that the reader can check. That a thing actually happened is, almost, sufficient reason for recording it. A journal becomes important.

This sense of actuality is typical of the age and had its effect, as Ian Watt has pointed out, on the novel as well, resulting in a new sense of 'realistic particularity.'[21] North is an illuminating example of the effect of the new pragmatism on life-writing. That he was an enthusiastic supporter of the empirical science which transformed thinking in the seventeenth century is obvious throughout his writings. In the 'Dissertation' originally included with the *Life of Dr John North*, for instance, he reveals himself as an admirer of Bacon, whom he regards as one of the founders of the New Philosophy, and as we have seen he was one of the host of gentleman amateurs who dabbled in science. Although he was never a member of the Royal Society, he haunted the fringes of it. Through his brother Francis he might have known both Evelyn and Aubrey (*Francis*, 1:374–5), and there is a delightful account in the *Life of Sir Dudley North* of the visits to St Paul's on Saturdays to chat with the great Sir Christopher Wren about his masterpiece, then well advanced in its construction (*Dudley*, 2:238). North accepted the Baconian doctrine that all nature, man included, was suitable for objective study, and, as the 'Dissertation' makes clear, he endorsed Bacon's view that the scientist should observe, record, and then make deductions. Something like this process takes place in the *Lives*. In the *Life of Dr John North*, especially, we see him forcing himself to record the doctor's eccentricities with almost clinical detachment, then drawing a general conclusion from them. It would not be difficult for a pathologist to arrive at a convincing diagnosis of John North's mental and physical ailments from Roger North's account. Roger North loved his brothers, and the *Lives* are full of warmth and sympathy, but to a certain extent he does seem to regard his subjects in rather the same way as, say, a zoologist regards the animals he is studying, noting their habits and peculiarities. There is a revealing passage in one of the manuscript versions of the *Life of Francis North*, a passage that did not survive through to the printed version. After relating an anecdote of Francis's dealing with his irritable old grandfather, Roger feels it necessary to excuse himself: 'these may seem trivial passages, not worth remembering, but being exactly true, are part of the natural history of mankind, which is everyone's interest to know.'[22] The phrase 'part of the natural history of mankind' is illuminating and goes a long way in explaining North's whole approach to life-writing. To some extent a biography really was, for him, a document in the natural history of man. Each life was like an experiment which, if written up properly, would yield certain results beneficial to everyone. The results could be practical, ranging from such small matters as which course of medicine had proved successful and which was to be avoided, to larger concerns such as which system of government was most beneficial to the individual. The most important result of the experiment, however, would be to prove the worth of moral values and to demonstrate the vital necessity for ethical behaviour in ordinary living.

Hence North's argument, already noted, that it is the record of the ordinary life that will be the most useful, since it will have relevance to the greatest number of readers. But there are other reasons for North's insistence on the value of the private life. The *General Preface* contains a memorable attack on political ambition together with a lament over the injustices that await every disinterested servant of the state. The plea for biography of ordinary people comes, to some extent, from North's own political experiences. The best life, he decided, is one lived in modest and useful contentment, safe from the duplicity and turmoil of public office. It was his political experiences, too, that were behind the interesting discussion of the ethical responsibilities of the historian which he embedded, somewhat digressively, in his essay.

Considering the direction of North's thinking, it is not surprising that he would question traditional concepts of authority. In a passage in the *General Preface* he criticized the habit of Grotius, in *De jure belli ac pacis*, of peppering his work with quotations from the ancients as if to rely on them for the truth of conclusions: 'and he has so much spared his own judgment ... that one can scarce find out the author amongst them, whose sense perhaps from himself might have passed as well as if it had come from Livy or Polybius' (*Gen. Pref.*, section 19). This challenge to the practice of using the ancients as authorities, and the insistence on arriving at conclusions for oneself, is in accord with the new scientific spirit, seen at its most obvious in the vehement rejection of Aristotle by such writers as Bacon and Sprat, and indeed by Roger North himself (in the omitted 'Dissertation'). It is an attitude that suffuses the whole of North's theory of biography.

No biographer of his time, not even Aubrey, displayed as clearly as North the influence of the new scientific outlook, but other influences were at work. There were interesting developments in biography on the continent, as Professor de Sola Pinto has pointed out.[23] An influential book, he explains, was Jerome Cardan's *De vita propria* (1643), a clear and accurate record of facts that was much admired in England. We know from the *General Preface* that North had also read it, although he was not impressed (*Gen. Pref.*, section 39). Another book from the continent (also mentioned by de Sola Pinto) seems to have influenced North much more. This was Gassendi's *Vita Peireskii*, first published in 1641 and translated into English by W. Rand in 1657. It is a delightful account of a nobleman, connoisseur, and scholar. It is obviously written by someone who knew his subject intimately, and the wealth of personal details gives an effect of vividness and reality. North singled out this biography for praise in the *General Preface* (section 20), and it has so many similarities to the *Life of Dr John North*, both in style and content, that it seems likely that Roger North read the book thoroughly and learned much from it. Like John North, for instance, Peiresk was of a frail constitution; he took the same morbid interest in the condition of his urine and was always ailing in one way or another. Like John North, too, Peiresk had an insatiable intellectual curiosity; he studied unremittingly and had a passion for books: 'As for the Room wherein his Library was kept, it was indeed too small, though the whole walls were filled, and nests were placed likewise on the floore, filled with Books. Also he had Books in the Porch of his Study, and likewise piled on heaps, in several Chambers.'[24] Unlike John North, Peiresk did not breed spiders in glass jars, but he did keep nightingales and songbirds in cages, whose singing he preferred to the voices of men. As he read the book, Roger

North must have been struck by such resemblances, particularly when he read the following passage: 'As for his Brother, his Affection to him was so great, and his Brothers love likewise, so great to him again, that it deserves to be recorded as an example to Posterity.'[25] John North's affection for his brother Francis, as expressed in letters to him, was intense: 'I have seen some of those letters, which as I remember were in a fervent or rather flaming style, upon the subjects of his friendship, esteem, value, and his own wretched unworthiness' (*John*, section 106).

Whether Roger North consciously followed Gassendi or not, the fact remains that in *Vita Peireskii* he had a captivating example of a biography written with the same 'simplicity and plainness,' with the same awareness of the value of 'petty businesses,'[26] and with the same pleasant strain of humour that we see in North's own biographies.

There is another factor that may have led to the new objectivity and sense of fact which are apparent in North's *Lives*. The seventeenth century saw some of the bitterest political and religious clashes that England had ever known; so much was at stake, both of principle and of property, that it is not surprising that all sides resorted to language that was at best highly coloured, and at worst downright dishonest. One has only to think of the partisan histories, the virulent pamphlet wars, or the extended perjuries of Titus Oates to realise the depths to which language could sink. From the general abuse of truth decent men would naturally recoil, as this sad and angry passage from one of the century's best men testifies:

> Only that Posterity may not be deluded by Credulity, I shall truly tell them, that Lying most Impudently in Print, against the most notorious Evidence of Truth, in the vending of cruel Malice against Men of Conscience, and the fear of God, is become so ordinary a Trade, as that its like, with Men of Experience, ere long to pass for a good Conclusion.[27]

There was bound to be a reaction against the excesses of propaganda, and when that reaction came it apparently caused a healthy change in the attitude to history and to biography. Readers were now suspicious of writers who simply made assertions about their subjects. Gilbert Burnet remarks on the change in the preface to one of his biographies. People now tend to discredit the older historians, he points out:

> for they reckon that men in all Ages were pretty near the same temper they find them to be of at this day, and there is such foul dealing in the Histories of our own Time, and things that are so eminently false are positively asserted, that from thence many conclude all other Writings of that nature are likewise to be suspected ... These common failings of Historians have in this last Age made people desire to see Papers, Records, and Letters published at their full length ... the world desires nothing so much as to see

the Truth of things as they were really designed and acted, rather from some Original Papers, than from the Collections or Extracts of persons of whose Fidelity or Judgment they are not well assured.[28]

To a large extent it was this desire to let the reader judge for himself that was behind North's suggestion that the subject's 'remains' should be produced in a biography to back up the biographer's claims: 'Friends may, but things will not, prevaricate or falsify' (*Gen. Pref.*, section 41).[29]

North as Biographer

Roger North's biographies of his three brothers, familiarly known as *Lives of the Norths*, are among the most lively and engaging in the language. It is as if John Aubrey had worked out a consistent theory of what biography should be and then sat down and actually completed some examples. The *Life of Francis North* is Roger's longest and most ambitious work. It tells of the lawyer's meteoric rise to favour in the service of Charles II until his unexpected death while still occupying the post of Lord Keeper of the Great Seal. The *Life of Francis North* is weighed down with large amounts of information about the multitudinous legal and political concerns that Francis found himself enmeshed in, but still he emerges as a living figure, desperately careful not to leave the smallest opening for his enemies, too uneasy to enjoy the rewards of his efforts. Sir Dudley North, the subject of Roger's second biography, was a bluff, energetic man, with a fierce love of truth and a first-class financial mind. With great enthusiasm Roger describes Dudley's crafty adventures with the Turks, his equally skilful dealings, back in England, with the customs office, and his addiction to physical pursuits. The third life, the *Life of Dr John North*, is the shortest and most compact of the works. It is a memorable portrait of a solitary, stubborn, hypochondriac scholar, who lived for his Greek studies, kept spiders in glass jars, looked like a *madame en travestie*, and was at continual war with his students and fellows.

The tone varies somewhat from life to life, depending on Roger's differing attitudes to the three brothers. It was Francis who evoked the most powerful response – love mixed with esteem, even hero-worship, yet tinged occasionally with irritation. Roger felt he owed everything to his 'best brother.' Francis took charge of the young lawyer as soon as he arrived in London, shepherded him through the thorny pathways of the legal profession, and almost certainly played an important part in the promotions that soon came to him. Francis was not only an elder brother, a senior in their common profession, but also, in Roger's eyes, vastly more intelligent. It is no wonder that Roger looked up to him. It is also not surprising that there were tensions, and it is typical of

Roger's objectivity that these are duly reported. Occasionally, for instance, Roger chafed under his dependency and resented the 'many mortifications by little contempts' that Francis placed upon him. 'He had somewhat of humour that way,' Roger says testily, 'of raising his own by depressing others' characters.' After putting up with it for ten years Roger confronted the surprised lord chancellor, who from then on was careful not to offend his touchy brother (*Auto*, 3:89–90). But such frictions were rare, and for the most part the life shines with Roger's regard for his brother. Roger travelled the western circuit with Francis, lived in his house in London (he was allowed to use Francis's horses for his own carriage), watched over his health, and worried with him through various legal and personal crises. Above all, they shared endless, blissful conversation on a multitude of subjects: music, smoke, the barometer, perpetual motion, law, mathematics, and on and on.

Roger's attitude to Dudley was different. They were nearer in age, there was no sense of obligation, less feeling of inferiority, particularly since Dudley's profession was far removed from Roger's interests. Dudley himself was an exhilaratingly vigorous and cheerful man, and Roger enjoyed his company immensely. Dudley was much less intimidated by the dangerous manoeuvres of their political enemies than was Francis; he was full of self-confidence and seemed not to have a nerve in his body. Roger must have found his company something of a relief. He responded eagerly to Dudley's warm family life, and to the affection that this extremely able financier felt towards his brothers. The two appear in *Dudley* as happy companions, relaxed and ready for fun, visiting the construction site at St Paul's together to examine progress, or building a laboratory at Wroxton where they delighted in the dirt and sweat, and each other's company.

It is clear that John North was less dear to Roger; he esteemed him but found it difficult to love him warmly. Imprisoned in his strange neuroses, John North was not an easy man to get to know. In any case, he lived at Cambridge for most of the year, so that Roger could not spend extended periods of time in his company. These circumstances gave Roger the distance necessary to make *John* the most objective and in some ways the most shrewdly analytical of the three lives.

The three accounts of his brothers, incidentally, especially when read with Roger's own *Notes of Me*, not only are remarkable as individual achievements, but also can be seen as combining to present a many-sided portrait of a family relationship, surprisingly 'modern' in its complexity and psychological realism.

However, it has to be admitted that as a biographer Roger North does have his faults. One of them is an unmovable political bias that made it impossible for him to view his subjects as objectively as one could wish, and certainly not as objectively as he thought he could. He was born and bred a royalist, he made his fortune as a servant of the court, and it did not occur to him for one moment that there was anything good to be said for any other political point of view than the monarchist one. The effect of his prejudice is seen at its most damaging in the *Life of Francis North*, where he is led to defend several dubious transactions, such as his brother's part in the suppression of coffee-houses, and in the trial of Stephen College. Indeed, Roger's political bias, joined with his ardent love for Francis, accounts for a curious discrepancy between his view of the Lord Keeper and the one that the reader finds himself receiving. Roger saw his brother as a long-suffering servant of the state, utterly in the right, receiving malicious injustice from his enemies and only lukewarm support from his friends. From the pages of the biography, however, Francis emerges as a not very likeable person. He is too careful, too much concerned with appearing in the right. And throughout the latter part of his career there is the unpleasant suspicion that he was being used by the court and that he knew it. He appears ill at ease with the king and with those close to him. He claims to be a friend only to the law, but in a case involving the king's interest there is seldom any doubt as to who will win. Roger seems to sense tragedy in his brother's life, but it never occurred to him that it might be the tragedy of a good man who had sold himself for a price.

Another of Roger North's faults, at least in the case of the *Life of Francis North* and the *Life of Sir Dudley North*, is prolixity. When Montagu North came to edit *Francis*, he had to deal with ten volumes of manuscript material, four containing largely undigested biographical accounts, the other six given up to the Lord Keeper's own writings.[30] Roger had put it all together as the total record of a man and his work, as if to omit were to diminish. It is an example of an interesting theory not properly realized. In an essay dealing with biography's influence on the novel Clarence Tracy has drawn attention to what he calls the open quality in the form of certain novels and biographies of the later eighteenth century. It is part of that period's preoccupation with 'literature as process' to use Northrop Frye's phrase. Tracy declares that for 'Sterne and Boswell, time is an unending continuum, and the whole story of any man's life is coterminus only with it.' And therefore, long as Boswell's biography of Johnson is, 'it is only the beginning of an ideal one that might have gone on for ever, there being no logical limits in the form itself.'[31] This process is already to be seen in North's lives of Dudley and Francis, many years before Sterne or Boswell: 'My design is to leave behind me all that I can remember or warrantably collect concerning the life of the Lord Keeper North' (*Francis*, 1:10).

But if North's form is open, it has to be admitted that it is not quite controlled. Certainly in the case of the original version of *Francis*, and to a lesser extent in the case of *Dudley*, Roger failed to bring his material within satisfactory bounds. The result is an uncomely assemblage which, while interesting as an experiment in *biographie verité*, will not do. Montagu North did what he could to reduce the mass to a readable size, but even in his greatly pruned version Francis frequently disappears from sight while Roger North pursues some point of no great significance to the Lord Keeper's character, such as the industry in a region he happens to be passing through, or the intricacies of some long-forgotten piece of litigation. Dudley North, too, is occasionally overwhelmed by extraneous matter, such as a digression on trade, or an explanation of some eastern custom. To some extent the fault is in Roger North's personality and mental processes. 'I have observed in myself somewhat of confusion and disorder of thought,' Roger confesses disarmingly in his autobiography (*Auto*, 3:21), and while it is just as dangerous (not to say ungracious) to take him at his own assessment as it is to take Boswell at his, it is true that his thought seldom moves in a single line forward. At times North seems not so much Sterne, brilliantly manipulating the open form, as Tristram Shandy himself. In a world bewilderingly full of interesting things how on earth does one decide what to leave out? And in the data of human experience, where cause and effect are so intricately intertwined, where everything, in a sense, is of equal importance, how on earth does one simplify? North tends to pile it all in, with a muttered excuse or a half-hearted attempt to justify it on historical grounds. North's biography is certainly not the kind that became fashionable earlier this century under the influence of such writers as Lytton Strachey and André Maurois. He did not preserve 'a becoming brevity – a brevity that excludes everything that is redundant and nothing that is significant.'[32]

No doubt *Francis* and *Dudley* could be improved by some excisions. Yet having conceded so much, a word of warning is in order. The pruner would need to be very careful, for something might easily be lost. The present fullness of information at least makes it possible for the reader to glean an interpretation of the subject other than the author's, which is more than can be said for Strachey's system of ruthless selection. And, oddly enough, North's prolixity convinces in a way that modern selectivity often does not. 'It is all there,' North seems to be saying, 'all the quarrels and speeches and activity around them; that is what it was like.'

In any case, Roger North's 'confusion and disorder of thought,' his failure in these two biographies to realize fully the revolutionary theory behind them, need not surprise us. He was breaking new ground, and complete clarity is not to be expected. The disjunction between concept and performance which they show is typical of much of Roger North's writing, and illustrates a characteristic that helps make him such an interesting figure: again and again in the *General Preface* and in the unpublished essays one sees him grope towards a thought of considerable significance, perhaps decades ahead of its time, and then move away from it without developing it to its clearest form. In an age in which major intellectual and social changes took place Roger North becomes a sort of weathervane, picking up the shifting currents and pointing, sometimes a little unsteadily, to the new directions and occasionally veering back to the old.

In any case, whatever faults Roger North might have as biographer are triumphantly outweighed by his virtues. He may be occasionally overwhelmed by extraneous material, but he never loses his sense of the general flow and shape of his subject's life. The form of the *Life of Francis North*, for instance, is quite clear. It is the story of a man who sinks lower into a troubled mind as he rises higher in public office, until finally he is released by death. The *Life of Sir Dudley North*, on the other hand, reveals the sure forward movement of a man who is basically at peace with himself, who knows what he wants and knows how to get it. In both cases the impression of the total personality of the subject agrees pretty well with the brief sketches of Francis and Dudley North inserted in the course of the narrative in North's historical work, the *Examen*, and completed before the *Lives*. There, in miniature, we have the men who appear full length in the biographies – further proof that North started out with a complete concept of his subject in his mind.[33]

North's characters are clear in outline; they are also vivid in detail. He shares with John Aubrey the all-important gift of being able to add just those touches that bring the portrait startlingly to life and that make the subject clear in our minds, distinct from all others. Above all, North loved anecdotes, and seemed to understand their power in biography. He knew that one small incident can reveal more about a personality than pages of careful analysis. Anyone who studies the various manuscript versions of the *Lives* will be struck by the care that North took over his little stories, rewording them in revision after revision until they had achieved the greatest possible dramatic effect.[34] The results justify the effort. Take, as an example, the incident in the *Life of Sir Dudley North* where Sir Dudley is being called to account by a hostile House of Commons for his part in various acts of an earlier administration. Roger North describes the packed house and the growing excitement as Sir Dudley, a star witness, is called. The notorious Titus Oates is there, eager for the sport. Sir Dudley fields the questions well and manages to keep his temper until his interrogator begins to implicate the Lord Keeper. At this, he

> began to warm and his blood to mend its pace: and, had that been perceived, any one that knew him would have expected something extraordinary to follow. Then Mr. Colt went on, and, 'I ask him,' said he, 'if Secretary Jenkins did not come down to the city and persuade him to take the office of sheriff upon him?' 'You hear the question,' said the chairman. After which there was a profound silence, expecting the answer. All which time Sir Dudley North was gathering as much breath as he could muster, and then out came a long 'N-o-o-o-o!' so loud as might have been heard up to the House of Lords. This was so violent and unexpected that I could see a start of every one in the house, all at the same instant, as if each had had a dash of cold water in his face: and immediately all called out, 'Withdraw'; and my neighbour Titus Oates, being, as I suppose, frustrated of his expectations, cried out, 'Aw Laard, aw Laard, aw, aw!' and went his way. (*Dudley*, 2:228-9)

The suspense, the surprise, the clash of individual personalities representing the clash of larger ideas, make this incident a good example of what might be thought of as the dramatic element in North's biographies. North's discussion of the various comic genres has already been referred to. Among these genres was drama, which he singled out for special consideration: 'the best of dramatics,' he declared, 'is but an history (feigned) of the lives of each character combined ... And one might call out for the history of this or that actor apart, which given, is a branch of the history of that person's life, in a private state' (*Gen. Pref.*, section 22). The process, he went on to suggest, may be reversed: 'and as from comedy the concern of any one character may be extracted historically, so any history, whatever it is, may be represented by way of drama, or put into comedy' (*Gen. Pref.*, section 22).

North's awareness of the similarities between drama and biography is yet one more characteristic he has in common with Boswell. However, the influence of drama in North's biography is not so direct as in Boswell's *Life of Johnson*. We find, in North, no dialogue set out as in a play with the speech headings and stage directions so familiar in Boswell, and there are no scenes so theatrically 'set' as the Dillys' dinner party where Johnson met Wilkes, or the famous quarrel between Johnson and Dr Percy. Yet dramatic elements are present in North, and not only in his beautifully constructed anecdotes. He was fascinated, for instance, by people's accents and mannerisms of speech, and often tried to record them exactly. There are two examples in the *Life of Dr John North*. He is careful to capture the Honourable Henry Grey's aristocratic slovenliness in almost phonetic exactness: 'By G-d's iff, 'ware a breed' (*John*, section 4). Later, he is fascinated by the accents of John North's enthusiastic Welsh parishioners who declared themselves to be the pastor's 'sheeeep.' The most amusing example of North's interest in idiosyncratic speech mannerisms, however, is found, not in the biographies, but in his history, *Examen*. With great relish, and a certain amount of contempt, he describes the arrogant drawl of Lord Sunderland 'in his Court Tune (for which he was very particular, and, in speaking, had made it almost a Fashion to distend the vocal Letters) *Whaat*, said he, *if his Maajesty taarn out faarty of us, may not he have faarty athors to saarve him as well? and whaat maatters who saarves his Maajesty, so lang as his Maajesty is saarved?'* (p 77).

Not only this fascination with speech, but also the delight in idiosyncratic characters, the pleasure in unmasking villains, the rough and tumble of an often raw struggle for domination, all remind us of some of the aspects of Restoration comedy. But if North's drama is comedy with touches of farce, there is at the same time an undertone of tragedy.

Certainly the *Lives* have all the zest of Restoration comedy. Nothing can dampen the energy that runs through each one of them, an energy that comes from a love of life and an endless curiosity about it. There is an engaging sense of fun, too, that ripples through each book and which sees that, while life can be horrifying, it is also ridiculous. All this in a fresh, crunchy prose style that is curiously bracing.

That prose style was no accident. Several passages in North's writings reveal that he had thought consciously about language, or the appropriate mode of expression for various purposes. In the prefatory matter attached to the *Life of Dr John North*, for instance, he describes the strains placed upon language by the needs of the new and abstruse scientific discussion (*John*, intro, section 5). In the life itself he takes time to mention John North's efforts to refine his English style, and records the scholar's admiration for Thomas Sprat's clear English in the *History of the Royal Society* (*John*, section 67). At the beginning of the *Life of Dr John North* Roger describes what he intends for himself. The style, he claims, will be that 'of familiar conversation ... I intend it not polite ... but I can make sure it shall be English and that of the most vulgar usage, unless a touch of some other language, in a proverbial way, may be made use of' (*John*, intro, section 3). That is a good description of North's style in the biographies, although he might have added that he peppers his basically colloquial English with pleasantly esoteric Latinisms and with obsolescent images. His colloquialisms are vigorous: 'scoundrels and hang-bys,' 'carry guts to a bear,' 'the rest of 'em Greeks and Latins.' He can construct memorable phrases: 'a strange din at midnight,' 'a goer-about-to-complain-of-the-times,' 'mere froth whipped up to serve a turn,' 'cast an eye glancing.' There is a strong Elizabethan breeze blowing through his prose, and against the native sturdiness the touches 'of some other language' stand out like foreign visitors at an English country fair.

North is frequently innovative in his vocabulary, as a glance through the *Life of Dr John North* will show. He uses 'gallimaufry,' for instance, as an adjective when *OED* gives it only as a substantive. 'Redivival' appears in *OED* with North as the sole source, and judging by the same authority, he is also unique in his figurative use of 'laquering.' He delights in Latinisms. They can be ironic-professional, as in 'mutations of the dogmata,' 'tonsil glandules tumefied,' 'obstetricated forth an edition of Plato,' or they can simply amplify the resources of English: 'patroclus,' 'enervous,' 'enossated,' 'derelicted,' 'patrocinate.' North's printed works are already a frequent source of citations in *OED*; he would have provided many more if his early editors had not removed the more unfamiliar usages which they found in the manuscripts.

Style is certainly the man in the case of Roger North. But it is also true that, like many of his contemporaries in an age of rapid scientific and political change, North was casting around for a language suitable to his new purpose. He came up with an interesting and somewhat odd mixture, but it suits very well his avowed aim of writing intimate biography that would entertain and instruct a wide audience.

It is appropriate to end this discussion of North as biographer with a more particular examination of the *Life of Dr John North*.

In structure the *Life of Dr John North* is much the same as the other two biographies. North tells the story of the subject's life chronologically from birth to death, but will break the sequence to group information around certain themes – a process much the same as that followed by Boswell in the *Life of Johnson*. For instance, at the point where John North is made a fellow of Jesus College, we learn that he is at last in a position to 'lay the foundation of a competent library' (*John*, section 17). This leads North into a discussion of the doctor's love of books in general, his method of collecting them, his lifelong preference for books printed in italic characters, his addiction to bookshops, his method of studying the books, and we are even given, for good measure, a digression on the London book trade in the late seventeenth century. At another point North groups together most of the material he had collected about John North's friendships, describing his preference for conversation with the more intelligent of the students from noble families, his extreme distaste for the company of his fellow dons at Jesus, his circle of acquaintance in London, and so on. Later, we learn everything that North can remember about the doctor's preaching. Such a method is particularly appropriate for the life of a sedentary scholar, where the main interest is in the development of his mind and in revealing his interior personality.

The book is better focused than North's other two biographies. It demonstrates the truth, known apparently to few biographers, that if one concentrates attention fully on the subject, other matters take care of themselves, and that the mind has the capacity to supply a great deal at only a hint. North does not spend time painting in elaborate backgrounds or drawing complicated portraits of secondary characters, but keeps the attention on the strange little man he has chosen to write about. He does, however, give just enough information to fix John North in the places in which his life was mainly spent. There are brief and pleasant descriptions of the Cambridge routine with chapel, hall, debates, and college meetings filled with rancour and the skilled sniping so familiar within the two great universities. There is a fascinating glimpse of the new Cambridge coffee-houses that, according to Roger North, had a disastrous effect on the dons: 'For who can apply close to a subject with his head full of the din of a coffee-house?' (John, section 38). We are also given a brief introduction to the doctor's distinguished circle of friends in London, including the Godolphin family and the Capels, and we accompany the doctor on his memorable journey into North Wales, a territory that seems only a little less surreal than when Sir Gawain made his journey centuries earlier. But it is always Dr John North's world, and it is that incurably lonely figure that dominates our interest from start to finish.

The *Life of Dr John North* is rather more anecdotal than the other two lives. This is probably due to the fact that North had far less material at his disposal in the case of John North and consequently had to rely on his memory more – it is the little stories that stick in the mind. The importance of the anecdotes in the biographies has already been discussed, and their effectiveness is seen particularly clearly in this life. Some of them, it is true, seem fatuous, but most of them are telling. Seldom are they presented for their own sake; North's usual procedure is to make a general point about the doctor's personality and then illustrate it with an anecdote. Thus the story of the 'moon-shine night,' when John North forced himself to confront what he thought was a spectre, serves to demonstrate both his extreme nervousness and his courage. In the incident of the doctor's delirium, when he insists on his mother listening to his 'two notions,' we find concentrated the effect of the entire biography. This perfectly constructed little story is pathetic and absurd, but, after all that has gone before, not exactly funny.

The paucity of material was in some ways a blessing. North's helplessness in the face of huge amounts of information is revealed by his actions in the case of the *Life of Francis North*.[35] In the case of the *Life of Dr John North*, however, he had no thick bundles of notes in the scholar's own hand, no voluminous memoranda of transactions in which he took part, no sheaves of letters. In fact, it was as if the doctor knew that a biographer would want to write his life and deliberately set out to thwart him by ordering all his papers burnt and by obliterating almost every trace of his existence. All Roger had to go on, therefore, was a little notebook that had miraculously escaped the flames, a few entries in the Cambridge records, and probably some references in family correspondence. The rest he had to supply from memory. As a result, the biography presents more purely than the others the character as it had impressed itself upon Roger's mind, uncluttered by masses of material. Such facts as North had at his command are solidly present in *John*, but their relative paucity allowed more scope to the elusive, immaterial, shaping force of imagination; in this biography the granite and the rainbow unite more successfully than in the other works. There emerges from the *Life of Dr John North* a vision of the subject that is true to the facts yet transcends them, that gives unity to the life, and that infuses it with poignancy. This vision is best perceived through an examination of North's imagery.

Most of North's images are, like the rest of his prose style, vigorous, earthy, and often proverbial – part of the rich vernacular of his day even if a little old-fashioned. Usually they are employed in a somewhat *ad hoc* way, with no particular sense of their poetic possibilities. Every now and then, however, North strikes an image, or group of images, that go further. Two such clusters, one minor and the other major, stay in the mind.

The first, oddly enough, concerns birds, and while this group is small, the images are memorable. When John North was a student at Cambridge, he had a voracious appetite for knowledge, 'and the scholar soon fell to shift for himself, as a bird that had learned to pick alone, and having tasted the fruit of knowledge, pursued it with an uninterrupted perseverance' (*John*, section 23). Although North may not consciously have intended anything by this comparison beyond illustrating his brother's habitual solitariness, it does seem that unconsciously he was aware of something birdlike in John North. We have already learned of his fluttery nervousness: 'A natural timidity, owing to a feeble constitution of body, inclining to the effeminate' (*John*, section 11); and later we learn of his curiously ungainly movement, 'his going weak and shuffling, often crossing his legs as if he were tipsy,' rather like a longlegged bird on land. After his stroke John North suffered a temporary reversal of personality during which he delighted in smutty stories and 'paltry rhymes and fables' (*John*, section 101). To his mortified relatives he 'seemed as an high-flying fowl with one wing cut. The creature offers to fly and knows no cause why it should not, but always comes with a side-turn down to the ground. The doctor had some remembrances of his former forces when he could mount up and fly; now his instruments on one side failing him, he was forced to deal in low concerns and reptile conceits that scarce rose from the ground' (*John*, section 101). The tragedy of John North's life was that he never really learned to fly at all. At one point, when Roger was discussing his brother's notes, he claimed that his jottings 'show that his reaches were not short nor his flights low' (*John*, section 70). Yet those ideas were contained in a little notebook that ought to have been burnt with the rest of John North's writings in accordance with his strict instructions. He was terrified of exposure, of the launching into air that publication entails. He was never free.

Far more pervasive than the bird imagery is an imagistic theme that may claim to be the controlling metaphor of the biography. It has to do with the concept of a pent-up force breaking out in an explosion that destroys whatever was containing it. As John North was a man who had the power of flight but was too scared to use it, so he held back energies that were bound to build up within him until they found violent, and ruinous, release. The metaphor is developed slowly throughout the biography and comes to a moving climax in the description of John North's collapse.

Roger North was aware that in the life of this reclusive scholar 'there will not fall out much of action to be historically related' (*John*, section 57), so that what action there was would be emotional and intellectual. Yet the character of John North seems anything but sedentary, because we are made to observe in him the dynamic tensions of a man under great pressure. Early in the biography North makes it clear that we are dealing with 'a vigorous and active spirit ... quartered in a slight and feeble machine of flesh,' to whom ideas are life itself (*John*, section 12). John North's intellectual activities are invariably described in violent terms: mathematics should have 'fired' him (*John*, section 61); he 'threw out' hints (*John*, section 64); he was prepared to 'batter' the atheists and 'attack them with their own arms' (*John*, section 71). A debate was a boxing match: 'he loved to spar questions and foment disputes, and then whip into the chair as moderator ... And they must look well to their hits ... and they must make good their arguments, or let go their hold' (*John*, section 63). Such exercises were dangerous, because 'heats will kindle and exasperate' (*John*, section 63).

Yet, despite all the intensity of his thought, John North never found release for it. 'His mind was full and wanted a discharge,' explained Roger, 'and that drew a weight upon his spirits ... a learned man that gathers for writing may be so full charged that, until he hath unloaded his thoughts upon paper, and to his satisfaction, finds little ease' (*John*, section 68). John North never found that satisfaction. He fussed and worried over his works in search of the perfection he never achieved. In the end he ordered everything to be burned.

The problem was not confined to John North's intellectual endeavours; it was the same in his dealings with the fellows and students under his authority. He was never able to relax with them, there was always a stiffness and formality. When they crossed his wishes, which was often, the result was intense anger and bitterness. If only, Roger North laments, his brother had been freer with his inferiors and, for example, had indulged them with some wine for 'the nerve is cut with the glass and humour hath a free play' (*John*, section 85). But it was not to be; the Master of Trinity kept everything pent up within himself.

If North's imagery is any indication, he saw a connection between John North's dangerously pent-up energies and emotions and his fatal sickness – the metaphor remains the same in both cases. During the illness which preceded the actual stroke, for instance, North claims that the doctors erred in trying to stop the 'venting of rheum at his mouth' (*John*, section 93). Such a venting was nature's way of relieving the distemper, and the doctors' desperate and grotesque methods of stopping it hastened John North's death: 'the humour having no vent at his mouth as it naturally tended ... broke out in his brain, and threw him down all at once' (*John*, section 97). In such a way are we prepared for North's description of the stroke in a final, dramatic image that forms the climax of the book: 'Now the mine was fired, and all the fracas it could make upon a mortal bulwark of animated earth determined, and what remained was only ruin and confusion as the blast had left it, never to be recovered into its former order and strength again' (*John*, section 99).

It is only at this point, late in the book, that we realise why North had earlier included an account of the sensational explosion at the governor's castle in Guernsey. The perilous situation of the castle on the cliff above a stormy sea, the desperate danger to the governor as the lightning reveals the drop before him in the very midst of his home, all must have appealed to North, perhaps unconsciously, as a symbol of the forces at work to tear down what had been so laboriously built up. It was a symbol, too, for the vulnerability of all good men in authority who, like John North, were likely to receive nothing but grief for their pains – a theme that appears more than once in North's writing. The story of the castle's destruction, we now see, is not a gratuitous digression but a part of North's vision.

That vision goes beyond John North. As Roger builds up to the climax of his brother's collapse, there is a glimpse of a wider dissolution. In the description of the stroke itself he creates an extraordinary sense of a large structure crashing down, and one cannot help feeling that this is not just one man gone, but human endeavour and struggle ending in ruin. The struggle is against oneself, but it is also against forces outside. Around the dying Master of Trinity are the mocking, predatory fellows.

Beyond them is a whole shoal of unscrupulous people – politicians, self-seeking clergy, office-seekers waiting for his death – and, beyond that, a raging mob: 'Brute beast indeed ... but it hath horns and houghs, therefore stand clear' (*John*, section 84). John North is vulnerable and alone in what he has managed to gain; he is alone, too, in his integrity and in his position as a governor. Order and authority are always in peril. Such a vision is born of Roger North's own sense of isolation as the survivor of a once large family, as a man of strict principles that were no longer fashionable, and as a member of a class and political party that had been left high and dry by the shifts in power of the late seventeenth and early eighteenth centuries. Behind the vision, too, is the memory of a whole century of political turmoil and uncertainty.[36]

There is a rather bleak, Lockeian tinge, also, about the view of John North's ruin. Roger North was no admirer of Locke, whom he regarded with much the same suspicion and disapproval that he directed against Hobbes. Yet Locke's influence must have been all-pervasive in the early eighteenth century, and an informed man of those times could no more escape it than we can escape the influence of, say, Freud. Certainly, when North describes the effects of the stroke on his brother's mind, the terms he uses are Lockeian: with the erasing of John North's memory, North explains, a large part of his 'collections' also disappeared, which caused the doctor to 'relapse into a sort of puerility' (*John*, section 100). And then, 'The seat of his memory was ruffled by the disease falling upon his brain and nerves, which had made such havoc that he had no firm notion of himself or of anything, but had his experience to gather and his understanding to frame over again' (*John*, section 100). In other words, John North was a grown man, full of learning, whose memory had been wiped out by his stroke, so that he was reduced to the situation of a child at the beginning of his experience, his mind a *tabula rasa*.

However, in the midst of this Lockeian description, North defiantly asserts earlier, traditional values: 'during the extremity of his mental weakness, his religious principles, resolution in justice, and good will to the world, which I may call universal charity, continued as integral and intemerated as they were in the strongest moments of his life' (*John*, section 103). This leads to the observation that 'strength of parts or understanding, which in itself is not free, doth not control the will, which is free' (*John*, section 104). Morality and will, therefore, are independent, inalienable parts of a man. In his attitude to Locke, as in so many other things, Roger North is an interesting transitional figure.

The *Life of Dr John North* had the bad luck to be noticed by Lytton Strachey who, apparently in need of a few eye-catching pages, used it as the basis for a sketch which he included in *Portraits in Miniature* (1931). It is Strachey at his worst. By the simple method of exaggerating what was ridiculous in the doctor's life and excluding everything else, he creates a silly caricature in which John North is grotesque and

Roger North stupid. In this case Strachey is not merely unjust but also imperceptive – or else he is being deliberately mischievous. Roger North knew perfectly well that much about his brother would seem ridiculous and it cannot have been easy for him, fiercely loyal as he was, to relate the painful details of the doctor's neurosis. He forced himself to do so because that was what his concept of biography required – the relation of all the facts, decorous and admirable or not. North relates many of these facts with apparent detachment. Strachey interprets this detachment as naïveté and ignores an emotion which is present throughout *John* and which gives it a quality entirely lacking in his account: that emotion is compassion. Reading only slightly between the lines, one can see that at times North must have been exasperated by his brother's finicky, obsessive behaviour (notably by his hypochondria), but North seems always aware that John was the victim rather than the perpetrator, and that sympathy was a more appropriate response than mockery. He also recognized qualities in his brother that presumably did not interest Strachey. Stubborn as John North undoubtedly was, so wrongheadedly wasteful of his own life, he was nevertheless a courageous man, and he possessed an unassailable integrity. Of course, we cannot accept Roger North's evaluation of his brother in all respects. We cannot help feeling a certain amount of sympathy, for instance, with the students and fellows of Trinity College in their dealings with their stubborn and uncommunicative master, and there are other points where charity has made Roger a little blind. But basically, Roger North's view of his brother is a true one – he was a good man who, for psychological reasons no one understands, seemed determined to pursue unhappiness.

The Text

In his biographies North has not been well served by editors. The problems began
with his son Montagu (1712-79), who brought out the *Life of Francis North* in 1742,
and then in 1744 published together the *Life of Sir Dudley North* and the *Life of Dr
John North*. In the case of the *Life of Francis North* Montagu faced difficulties. The
book as Roger North finally left it comprises more than three thousand pages in ten
volumes.[37] The first volume contains what might be called an overview of Francis's
life; in it Roger traces the main events of his life from birth to death. Three more
volumes contain all the material concerning Francis's life that he could not conve-
niently put in the first; it is divided under headings, such as 'Benefactions,' 'His
Match.' To these he added six final volumes containing the Lord Keeper's 'Remains,'
including law reports and essays. Clearly Roger North left a formidable editorial
problem, and the solution Montagu apparently chose was, roughly, to follow the life
as given in the first volume but supplement it with material drawn from the next
three volumes. At the same time he omitted much from Roger's original one-
volume life, and it is also possible that he incorporated passages from earlier
versions. However, any remarks on Montagu's editing of the *Life of Francis North*
must be taken as tentative until a full study of the manuscripts is made. Such a study
might also throw light on whether or not Roger agreed to the changes.

Montagu's editing of the *Life of Francis North* was especially drastic, but he was
also cavalier in his treatment of the *Life of Sir Dudley North*.[38] He omitted some of
the 'divers relations, tracts, censures' referred to in a manuscript version of the life in
the British Library and presumably intended by Roger as appendices to the book. He
also omitted several passages of a personal nature, such as a delightful account of Sir
Dudley making toys for his children, as well as some revealing anecdotes.

Some of Montagu's excisions from the three lives were due to the sensitive
political climate of the day. Roger could be scathing in his opinions of personalities
or political issues that were still controversial and no doubt Montagu decided to play

it safe. The more personal passages, however, were probably removed to satisfy some concept of decorum which dictated that certain passages were too trivial or undignified to appear in a biography. If so, Montagu either did not read his father's *General Preface* very carefully where it deals with such matters, or else disagreed with him.

The *Life of Dr John North* received the same sort of treatment at the hands of Montagu North. He put his pen through the same kind of personal passages and anecdotes that had troubled him before, and he decided to leave out the long digression on the New Philosophy. We can sympathise with Montagu about this latter excision. It has to be admitted that 125 pages of close discussion on Newtonian and Cartesian physics in the middle of John North's life do not exactly aid the flow of the narrative, and indeed the present edition also excludes the digression. The omission of the personal passages and anecdotes, however, is another matter, for it is precisely these touches that give the character life and individuality. For instance, Montagu suppresses the fact that John North, an advanced hypochondriac, was convinced that he would become blind and used to read the passage on blindness in *Paradise Lost* as a sort of advance comfort. Neither are we told of the indiscreet remarks made by his mother when he was a child that produced in him a morbid horror of being laid out after death. Much of the psychological subtlety of Roger North's portrait is lost in this way.

Montagu North, possibly with some help from the printers, also altered the texts of the biographies by modernizing. Roger's old-fashioned and erratic punctuation with its heavy dependence on the semicolon was replaced by a system much nearer present-day practice. The spelling was also modernized, foreign tags often trans-lated, and 'hard' or Latinate words replaced by more familiar ones. This last practice, in particular, resulted in a considerable dilution of the strong flavour of Roger North's prose. A comparison between the author's final manuscript version and the printed text of the *Life of Dr John North* reveals over three hundred substantive alterations, minor and major.

Montagu North's versions of the *Lives*, therefore, are quite different in form and flavour from what we can assume Roger North intended. They are blander, less racy, less intimate. When Henry Roscoe brought out a new edition of the *Lives* in 1826 he followed Montagu's text, as did Augustus Jessop in 1890 for his edition in Bohn's Standard Library. The present edition is the first to be based closely on the text as left by Roger North.

TEXT OF THE GENERAL PREFACE

The present edition of the *General Preface* is based on a manuscript in St John's College, Cambridge, part of MS James 613. It is a fair copy by a scribe, complete, and contains minor emendations in Roger North's hand. It is entitled throughout *A General Preface*, or *General Preface*, but a note identifies it as 'Second Preface'; it comprises forty-four pages. MS James 613 also includes another draft of the preface on which the scribal copy is based. It is in Roger North's hand and is marked 'First Preface.' This version lacks a few final pages which are to be found in the British Library as part of Add. MSS 32,526 (ff 130-2). The British Library has yet another version of the preface, in Roger North's hand (Add. MSS 32,525, ff 43-63 v). It is a very rough draft, incomplete, and is the earliest of the versions. Finally, also in the British Library is an incomplete version of the preface in Montagu North's hand (Add MSS 32,525, ff 1-32 v).[39] Although Montagu's copy was written after the scribal copy, and is therefore the latest in time of all the versions, it does not incorporate the emendations that Roger North made to that copy. It seems safe to assume, therefore, that the scribal copy in MS James 613 represents Roger North's latest wishes.

It is now possible to identify the scribe. A letter at Rougham Hall, Norfolk, in the same distinctive handwriting as the preface, proves that Ambrose Pimlowe was North's amanuensis. Pimlowe (d 1750) was vicar of Rougham 1710-23, and judging from the letter at Rougham he was on terms of warm personal friendship with North.[40] This final version of the *General Preface* may be placed, with some certainty, between 1718 and 1722. A reference to the *Life of John Kettlewell* and to Laurence Eachard's *History of England*, both published in 1718, establish the *terminus post quem*. The *terminus ante quem* is provided by a reference to Edward Chute as alive and occupying the Vyne in Hampshire; Chute died in 1722.[41] Such an assignation fits well with Pimlowe's term as vicar at Rougham.

TEXT OF THE LIFE OF DR JOHN NORTH

There are four manuscript versions of the *Life of Dr John North* extant. They are all in the British Library and all are in Roger North's hand (Add. MSS 32,514-32,517). Comparison of the versions reveals that they were written in the following order: 32,517, 32,515, 32,516, 32,514. Internal and external evidence reveals that they were in hand over a long period of time, probably from the last decade of the seventeenth century until 1728.

The four versions represent a good example of North's method of writing and rewriting in order to make his ideas clear and his form more polished. The version in 32,517 occupies only thirty-five pages and is mainly taken up with a transcription of the notes that Roger North found scattered throughout the little notebook which had belonged to his brother. It gives only the barest facts of John North's life and supplies no dates. It represents the first uncertain jottings in preparation for what had probably originally been intended as a brief life to accompany the publication of John North's notes. The Horn-type watermark suggests a date of 1690 for the paper, and it is almost certain that this version dates from the 1690s. MS 32,515 is a much fuller version of John North's life, but still in a rough, undigested form, covered with excisions, emendations, crossings-out, and marginal additions. At one point it lists all seven of Roger North's children, and therefore it must have been written after 1712, the year the last of the children was born. That it was finished before 1716 is suggested by the fact that information supplied in a letter from Hilkiah Bedford dated that year has been added interlined, that is, after completion of the version. The next version, 32,516, incorporates most of the alterations indicated in 32,515, but itself bears all the underlinings, crossings-out, and marginal additions that show it to be a work definitely still in progress; the details contained in Bedford's letter of 1716 are now incorporated into the body of the text and it must, therefore, have been written after that date. Version 32,514 is a fair copy, with only a few minor emendations. It has adopted alterations indicated in the earlier versions and is considerably more polished; the first page bears the date 1728. Its neatness, its relative freedom from error or emendation, and, above all, its late date, all strongly suggest that it is the last version of *John* to leave the pen of Roger North. Consequently, it is the basis for the present edition.

The present edition of the *Life of Dr John North* restores all the passages dropped by Montagu North from his printed version, with one important exception. The largest of Montagu's omissions, as already mentioned, is the digression on scientific matters in the middle of the *Life*, occupying 125 manuscript pages out of a total 330. It is entitled 'A dissertation of the new and modern (new) philosophy.' North himself was uneasy about including it, as the 'Apology' at the beginning of the *Life* admits. It really has no place in the biography, he conceded, but he was the victim of an *impulsus philosoficus*[42] when he wrote and simply could not help himself. Whatever interest the digression might have for the historian of science, it bears absolutely no relation to the *Life* and has therefore been dropped. It is appropriate, however, to give some account of it here.

Like much of North's writing, the digression tends to be rambling and repetitive, but its main concern is to compare the cosmological systems of Descartes and Newton, to criticize both, and to prove that, of the two, Descartes's theory is the more acceptable. Newton, far from making progress, has pushed science back several centuries – Aristotle and his followers had created a mist of words, Descartes had dispelled it, and now Newton with his talk of 'attraction' and 'powers' was re-creating the mist. North demonstrates, to his own satisfaction at least, how reasonable was Descartes's theory of vortices in a plenum and how specious, if ingenious, was Newton's theory of masses of matter attracting other masses through empty space. North also has much to say about scientific method. He voices the obligatory suspicions of a priori reasoning, asserting that the correct way to proceed is to gather accurate data by means of experiments and then to infer 'principles' from the process – a procedure, incidentally, which he by no means always followed himself.

North's inability to accept Newton's system ought not to surprise us. It is easy enough now, after two and a half centuries of Newton triumphant, to recognize his supreme achievement, but it was not so easy for his contemporaries. Descartes's theory, with its practical illustrations drawn from everyday experience, was easily grasped, while Newton's complex mathematics were comprehensible only to a few.[43] But even if North had been able fully to understand Newton's mathematics, he was still not prepared to admit a necessary relationship between them and the nature they purported to describe, so that however brilliant Newton's mathematical exercises might be, they had to remain mere hypothesis until it could be demonstrated by practical experiment that the universe operated in the way he claimed.

There was an even more powerful objection to Newton. His findings inevitably touched on the question of how an immaterial Omnipotence cohered with the material, and therefore the controversy became, as scientific questions often do, a religious one. Like many of his contemporaries, North was alarmed by the mechanistic nature of Newton's system. It seemed coldly self-supporting, and detracted from the power of God, thereby tending towards atheism. North's indignation is memorably expressed during the course of the digression when, after briefly describing Newton's cosmic system, he declares: 'Now is not this a spruce contrivance of which an engineer or clockmaker would have been proud? But to charge such a whim piece of machinery as here is paumed upon the almighty creator of all things, whose works are incomplex and direct, is *plusquam*[44] unreasonable.'[45]

Unsatisfactory as the digression might be as science, it is not without interest to students of the period, for it reveals clearly enough the kind of intellectual turbulence caused by the great scientific and philosophical discoveries of the seventeenth century at what might be called the intellectual grass-roots level. However, it has no place in the biography of John North.

PRESENTATION OF THE TEXT

The editor's aim in this edition is to preserve Roger North's prose as accurately as possible in all its distinctive form, flavour, and rhythm, while at the same time saving the reader from the more distracting features of his antiquated usage. Consequently, the text has been modernized, but conservatively. Quotations from printed sources, however, have not been altered.

Annotations are of two kinds: those required for direct textual elucidation (e.g., glosses, translations, correction of errors in the manuscript, cross references) and those offering information for a fuller understanding of the text (e.g., identification of people referred to, clarification of references). The first kind are signalled by superscript numbers and appear at the foot of the page; the second are signalled by asterisks and appear at the back of the book.

Photographs of specimen pages of the manuscript are provided so that the reader may see the effect of the editorial method (see pp 58, 140).

Punctuation

North's punctuation frequently brings the reader to a halt. Semicolons and commas are scattered throughout his writing in distracting plenty, but not always where they help. For instance, he will use a comma or semicolon in a position that cries out for a period, or he will use one of them where nothing is really needed – yet a little later he might neglect to provide any punctuation mark at all. He will encumber the plural with an apostrophe and ignore it in the possessive – but not always. It is quite arbitrary. The editor has removed those features that would cause the reader to trip, but has tried to avoid imposing too drastic a modernization or insisting on too great a consistency. North wrote roughly two and a half centuries ago in a style for which modern punctuation was not designed. His prose tends to be a series of loose-running clauses, not always under control, the sense drifting through them often a little carelessly. Syntactical ambiguities are part of the nature of his thought. The editor has tried to respect this special quality of North's prose and has avoided using punctuation to resolve an ambiguity where a resolution might be intrusive, or where the reader should decide for himself.

Capitalization, also completely inconsistent in North, has been brought into line with present-day conventions.

Spelling

Caution has also been observed in the modernization of North's spelling which, like his punctuation, is bewilderingly inconsistent. Where forms are clearly obsolete, the spelling has been changed; for example: *flourished, public, do*, instead of *flourish't, publick, doe*. Where there is any possibility that 'modernization' would in fact be a change in the meaning of the word, the old form is retained; for example: *petit, pratique*, rather than *petty, practice*. Another example of editorial conservatism: the form *enow* has been retained because of the possibility that North thought of it as the plural of *enough*, which is a form recognized by Dr Johnson (see *OED*).

Contractions

North's frequent contractions have been altered to accord with modern usage. His abbreviation *Dr* has been expanded when it is used, as it frequently is, not as a title but as a substantive for John North (e.g., *our doctor*). In those cases where North gives an initial followed by a surname, the Christian name has been supplied in full. The expression of numbers, also, has been regularized and modernized.

Involuntary errors
Minor errors in the manuscript due to a slip of the pen, or inadvertent repetition, are silently emended. When an addition of some kind is required to rectify involuntary errors or to clarify the text, such additions are indicated by square brackets. When any further explanation is called for, a note is provided. One or two mistakes in the numbering of sections both in the *General Preface* and *John* are silently corrected. (In the case of *John* North supplied an index in which he listed the section headings. When he came to write the headings in the text, however, he frequently varied the wording. These variations have been preserved).

Emendations by Montagu North
The manuscripts of both the *General Preface* and *John* bear signs of emendation by Montagu North, Roger North's son and first editor. They are ignored in the text of the present edition. A typical example of Montagu's editorial interference is found in the *Preface*, where he underlined a sentence that seemed derisory of contemporary politics and in the margin opposite wrote the words 'left out.' His emendations suggest that at one time he thought of publishing the *General Preface* – an intention never realized.

The manuscript of the *Life of Dr John North* has eight emendations by Montagu; they correct slips of the pen, clarify the sense, substitute English for Latin, and in one case the word *smart* is put in the place of Roger's *piquant*. When Montagu came to publish *John* he no doubt produced his own copy-text since his printed version contains hundreds of emendations, far more than appear marked in North's manuscript.[46]

Additions from other MS Versions
While the basis for this edition of *John* is Roger North's final manuscript version, Add. MSS 32,514, the two preceding versions, 32,515 and 32,516 contain many interesting passages later dropped. Some of the more significant of these are preserved in the notes to this edition. They have been selected because they throw additional light on the character of John North, or because they reveal something about his contemporaries, or because they are of historical interest. The passages concerning Milton and Newton have been added not because they contain anything new but because any contemporary reference to two such men is worth recording.

Notes

1 From an autobiographical fragment, BL, Add. MSS 32,545, f 3v.
2 The titles of the biographies vary between editions. In the first edition they appear: *The Life of the Right Honourable Francis North, Baron of Guilford, Lord Keeper of the Great Seal, under King Charles II and King James II...* (1742); *The Life of the Honourable Sir Dudley North, Knt. Commissioner of the Customs, and afterwards of the Treasury to his Majesty King Charles the Second. And of the Honourable and Reverend Dr. John North, Master of Trinity College in Cambridge, and Greek Professor, Prebend of Westminster, and sometime Clerk of the Closet to the same King Charles the Second...* (1744). *Francis* was 'Printed for John Whiston, at Mr. Boyle's Head in Fleet Street'; the book containing *Dudley* and *John* was 'Printed for the Editor, and sold by John Whiston, at Mr. Boyle's Head in Fleet Street.' Henry Roscoe's edition was published in 1826 and Augustus Jessop's in 1890. An abridged version of *Francis*, edited by E.E. Reynolds, was included in the Nelson Classics series (Nelson [1938]).
3 An excellent, but brief, account of Roger North's life against its historical and intellectual background may be found in F.J.M. Korsten, *Roger North (1651–1734): Virtuoso and Essayist* (Amsterdam: Academic Publishers Associated 1981).
4 In his edition of the autobiography Jessop gives North's birthdate as 3 September 1653, but cites no authority (*Auto*, 3:286). John Wilson, in *Roger North on Music* (Novello 1959), pp xv–xvi, claims that 'the available evidence favours an earlier date,' but he does not explain what that evidence is. Perhaps Wilson has in mind such facts as North's matriculation at Cambridge in 1667 and his removal to the Middle Temple in 1669, when he would be a surprisingly young 14 and 16. But Jessop's specificity of date gives pause and raises the suspicion that he was able to consult parish records. (Existing parish records do not cover the period in question.)
5 See Korsten, *Roger North*, pp 9, 11. See also Roger North's 'Account of my being closeted about Michaelmas term' (Korsten, *Roger North*, pp 223–6).
6 Intrigues; factions.
7 See Wilson, ed, *Roger North on Music*.

8 Montagu North to Ann Foley, 28 November 1704, BL, Add. MSS 32,501, f 15; Dudley North (Roger North's nephew) to North Foley (Dudley's cousin), 13 August 1705, BL, Add. MSS 32,501, f 32; Montagu North to Ann Foley, 12 February 1706, BL, Add. MSS 32,501, f 45; Montagu North to North Foley(?), 16 March 1706, BL, Add. MSS 32,501, f 48.

9 See Peter Millard, 'The Chronology of Roger North's Main Works,' *The Review of English Studies*, NS 24 (August 1973), 283–94.

10 The treatise on architecture has been edited by H. Colvin and J. Newman, *Of Building: Roger North's Writings on Architecture* (Oxford: Clarendon Press 1981). Apart from the books on fishponds and accounting, the only works by Roger North known to have been published in his lifetime are two pamphlets and a translation:*Arguments and Materials for a Register of Estates* (1698) (see G.A. Starr, 'Roger North and the *Arguments and Materials for a Register of Estates,*' *The British Museum Quarterly*, 31, nos 1–2 [1966], 17–19); *Reflections upon Some Passages in Mr. Le Clerc's Life of Mr. John Locke* (1711); *Reflections on Our Common Failings* (1701), trans from Pierre de Villiers's *Réflexions sur les défauts d'autrui* (Paris 1690); this translation was identified by Korsten, *Roger North*, p 24. North also edited and published an economic treatise by Dudley North, *Discourses upon Trade* (1691).

11 Colvin and Newman, eds, *Of Building*, p xv.

12 George A. Aitken, ed, *The Tatler*, 3 (1899), 291.

13 For an account of North's part in the movement to defend orthodoxy see Larry Stewart, 'Samuel Clarke, Newtonianism, and the Factions of Post-Revolutionary England,' *Journal of the History of Ideas*, 42:1 (1981), 53–72.

14 Roger North to Robert Foley (his brother-in-law), 31 December 1691, BL, Add. MSS 32,500, ff 139–40.

15 In name.

16 BL, Add. MSS 32,500, ff 208–10v.

17 James L. Clifford, ed, *Biography as an Art: Selected Criticism 1560–1960* (New York: Oxford University Press 1962), pp 27–37.

18 Samuel Clarke, *A Collection of the Lives of Ten Eminent Divines* (1662), sig A2.

19 Donald A. Stauffer, *English Biography before 1700* (Cambridge: Harvard University Press 1930), pp 142–7, to which this outline is much indebted.

20 Thomas Sprat, *An Account of the Life and Writings of Mr. Abraham Cowley* (1668), prefixed to Cowley's *Works*. Sprat goes on to make a plea for the lives of ordinary men as opposed to the great.

21 Ian Watt, *The Rise of the Novel* (Berkeley: University of California Press 1957), pp 9–17.

22 BL, Add. MSS 32,509, f 9v.

23 Vivian de Sola Pinto, ed, *English Biography in the Seventeenth Century: Selected Short Lives* (Harrap 1951), pp 27–9.

24 Pierre Gassendi, *The Mirrour of True Nobility and Gentility. Being the Life of ... Nicholaus Claudius Fabricius Lord of Peiresk, Englished by W. Rand* (1657), bk VI, p 196.

25 Ibid, p 181.

26 Ibid, sig (a)2r.

27 Richard Baxter, *Reliquiae Baxterianae: or, Mr. Richard Baxter's Narrative of ... his Life and Times* (1677), pt III, p 187.

28 Gilbert Burnet, *The Memoirs of the Lives and Actions of James and William Dukes of Hamilton and Castle Herald* (1677), sigs a r–a v.

29 North's comments on historical method in the *General Preface* may be supplemented by a reading of the preface to *Examen*, where he considers such matters as moral censure, the value of contemporary evidence, the devices of propaganda.

30 See p 38.

31 Clarence Tracy, 'As Many Chapters as Steps,' in *The Winged Skull: Papers from the Laurence Sterne Bicentenary Conference*, ed Arthur H. Cash and John M. Stedmond (Methuen 1971), pp 109, 108; Northrop Frye, 'Towards Defining an Age of Sensibility,' *ELH*, 23:2 (1956), 144–52.

32 Lytton Strachey, *Eminent Victorians* (Chatto and Windus 1918), 'Preface.'

33 *Examen*, pp 512–14, 602–3.

34 For a discussion of North's handling of anecdotes see James L. Clifford, 'Roger North and the Art of Biography,' *Restoration and Eighteenth-Century Literature* (Chicago: University of Chicago Press 1963), pp 277–9.

35 See p 38.

36 For a sensitive discussion of Roger North's relationship to his times see T.A. Birrell, 'Roger North and Political Morality in the Later Stuart Period,' *Scrutiny*, 17:4 (1950–1), 282–98.

37 St John's College, Cambridge, MS James 613. For further information about the MSS of *Francis* see Clifford, 'Roger North and the Art of Biography,' p 277; Millard, 'The Chronology of Roger North's Main Works,' pp 288–9.

38 There are two manuscript versions of the *Life of Sir Dudley North*, both incomplete: BL, Add. MSS 32,512 and 32,513.

39 A sample of Montagu North's handwriting is found in a letter from him to the Earl of Guilford, Bodleian Library, MS North d 23, f 180.

40 According to Augustus Jessop, Pimlowe also held the rectory of Dunham Magna, five or six miles from Rougham, and was 'a clergyman after Roger North's own heart ... a cultivated gentleman with scholarly tastes, and much looked up to in the neighbourhood' (*Auto*, 3:302–3). Pimlowe witnessed a codicil to North's will: P.C.C. 223 Norfolk, Oct. 1734.

41 Chaloner Chute, *A History of the Vyne in Hampshire* (Winchester 1888).

42 Philosophical impulse.

43 For an account of the debate see Florian Cajori, 'An Historical and Explanatory Appendix,' in *Sir Isaac Newton's 'Mathematical Principles of Natural Philosophy' and His 'System of the World'* (Berkeley and Los Angeles: University of California Press 1934), vol 2.

44 More than.

45 BL, Add. MSS 32,514 f 77v. North's view of the religious and political implications of Newtonianism are discussed elsewhere: see p 11 n.

46 See p 39.

General Preface

1 *History of private men's lives more profitable than state history*
The history of private lives adapted to the perusal of common men is more beneficial (generally) than the most solemn registers of ages and nations, or the acts and monuments of famed governors, statesmen, prelates, or generals of armies. The gross reason is because the latter contain little if anything comparate or applicable to instruct a private economy, or tending to make a man either wiser or more cautelous[1] in his own proper concerns. But on the contrary where strength of mind or judgment is wanting, it may happen that great actions and events superior to a man's own condition made familiar by reading shall induce a positive inconvenience, as was feigned of Quixote. For the amusements of state policy, and private economy, will not indifferently serve the public and private capacities, and happening to work cross in men's minds often makes horrible blunders in their reasoning. Ministers of state may argue low and private men high of themselves and both very improperly and prejudicial to their several interests. I shall a little more enlarge this subject afterwards, but at present (with salvo to what is already observed) declare that I do not intend to depreciate general histories, however lofty the subject may be, but join in recognizing all the great and good that in authority or commonplace is usually ascribed to them, but always referring to a proper application.

2 *Readers of general history distinguished: antiquaries, menders, corrupters*
And thereupon I must distinguish readers of histories, of whom two sorts are to be noted. (1) The curiosos, who are richer in time than employment, and hunting after amusements and pleasure only, often find enough in literature of most kinds to answer their ends, especially history. I may subjoin as the perfection of this kind such men as criticize and improve history and spend their time in perusing memorials of antiquity, collating authorities, discovering of omissions, contradictions, and partialities of authors; or, in a word, antiquaries who render the current of history more limpid and authoritative. These are to be honoured as public benefactors although without a peculiar pleasure they never could persevere as some do. There have been some who with no regard to truth, but with wonderful industry and application, and all for false and ambitious purposes, have corrupted the histories of ancient and modern times; these are the Jesuits,* and as the good antiquaries merit all the honours posterity can ascribe, so these deserve also to be remembered, but with extreme detestation and infamy.

3 *Politicians. Ambitious. Public spirit*
Then second, the politicians, of whom there are also two sorts. First the ambitious, who aspire to government, and study the learning of pulling down and setting up of

1:1 Cautious; wary

powers, of which the methods are copiously found in the registry of turmoils, and troubles, wars, and confusions, that in most ages of the world have been grassant[1] as a pestilence among men, and so by listing themselves to co-operate in evil, acquire a merit with the doers thereof, and hope to share in the spoil. Next come the good commonwealth men who, purely to serve their country, put themselves forward in affairs of the public. These have need of the utmost aid and instruction in events of state, as by means of history or otherwise can be acquired; for the evil-minded men are so much more numerous and prevalent, that one sincere amongst them is treated as a common enemy, and the advantage the worst sort of men have is derived of their betters, and comes by seeming or pretending to be (as some really are) good. The difference is, one may steal an horse, but the other not look over an hedge,* and none so fierce to mortify good men for harmless slips and peccadilloes, as the worst of men are; and all *sub specie boni*,[2] for as the right honourable poet (by title I mean) says: 'Knaves will all agree to call you knave.'* These are the several professions of life that make the study of general history recommendable to such as have a fancy to embark in them.

4 *Private men are extra to all these purposes*
But now returning to our first proposition, what are all these aims to that of a common man, who hath but a private fortune to manage, and beyond that no reason to dream of government or of being either a public minister, or property[1] to any such? And of this sort are, if not the major, I'm sure the *melior*[2] part of mankind, and whom one would choose to oblige and serve. A restless humour affecting power, or, which means the same, to be soon and exceeding rich, must come by nature, and not reason. It is a battered paradox, that by how much a private person in an easy state is wise and honest, by so much will he less affect power. It is a sad truth that honesty and sleep are almost strangers in that province; the adventure of power-hunting is not slight even to courtiers professed, who perchance through certain habitual versatilities, learned and practised as children learn to walk and run, may extricate themselves from difficulties that would engulf an honest man. There is scarce an example of a zealous and successful patriot, however in the throes of his agency cried up and idolized, who in the end was not unthankfully mortified, or rather persecuted and destroyed. I must therefore recant so far as to allow that the reading histories of courts and state employments may be very useful to some persons of a retired condition, if it be only to keep down a rising spirit, and confirm a good resolution to

3:1 Raging
3:2 Under the appearance of good
4:1 MS has propty.
4:2 Better

have nothing to do with powers, and as little as is possible with those that wear the titles of them.

5 *The pravity of mankind drive[s] all honest men from the public*
This consideration hath drawn me to reflect, what should be the true cause of so great a mischief to humankind in the world, as it is, that men honest and wise cannot serve their country in a public capacity, with tolerable peace and security? It must needs proceed from a baseness and degeneracy in the spirits of the popularity, as if the majority, take them as they rise, were a very knave in the concrete; and adding to these the ignorants, who though not so bad intrinsically, but being deluded, act with them as all of a piece cut out of the same cloth, and one may be tempted to say (what will appear clearer afterwards) that 'there is none that doeth good, no not one.'* And fools have always the worst, for all the ill consequences prove their own, and come round as a deluge irresistibly upon them. Why else should it happen that men[1] left to themselves and their own wills are undone of course? But upon the whole, the sum of my observation is that no villainy can be so gross, which behind a fair screen common men will not perpetrate. If it be demanded what screen? I answer, one that is proof against punishment and infamy; and of the two perhaps the latter will be less ventured, as if to be esteemed or called knave only were the moral evil, but the being really so, provided it be also impunely, a very innocent, if not a commendable, thing; this screen from infamy men frame to themselves, by a community of guilt. Numbers and noise sanctify everything; scarce one in an hundred, who would decline being pointed at as singular in evil, yet if sheltered under such protection, would scruple to commit any manner of injustice, murder, parricide, and infidelity, even to deny the Lord that bought them; and being well backed, in their discourses, printing, and preaching, maintain the grossest of lies, prevarications, and staring contradictions, such as in other times would have been accounted the resolves of bedlam, rather than the sentiments of reasonable people.

6 *Folly considered in conjunction with knavery, and its catastrophe*
Therefore, together with the wicked part, which is not enough to resolve our doubt, we must still join its ordinary concomitant, folly, which shines no less bright in the blazon[1] of the multitude than the iniquity itself. Nothing is so deceivable as the many, with whom passion and prejudice do all the offices of common sense; it is by turns tame and fierce in extremity (a peculiar crasis[2] not found in any other wild

---

5:1 Followed by illegible word or words, interlined on MS
6:1 Perhaps a conflation of three definitions given in *OED*: a heraldic shield; a description or record; a show or publication
6:2 Combination of elements, humours, or qualities; characteristic

species), but never so precipitous as when it is to purchase slavery, and after that it becomes as mild and mansuete[3] as a pedlar's ass. It is so prone to reach out for mischief upon itself that I can honour it with no better character than that of puerility, the incompassionate sport of which lies wholly in cruelty and perversities. I cannot afford it the condition of childhood, that is too innocent, and manhood (in singulars) too reasonable for the many, whom God in his infinite mercy hath subjected to governors, as the laws have subjected infancy to tutors. There cannot be a better parallel, for commonly if the pupil be not first milked, and then like a beast sold, it is not the tutor's fault;* and is it not fit that stupid and (as to themselves) unprofitable monsters should be made useful to their drivers?

7 The use that ill men make of fools
Now to return to the subject partly touched upon before observing the character of this leviathan, that turns so much upon fool and knave, whereof the composition ever was and will be ridiculous. Like acid and alkali they macerate one and other, and co-operate in nothing but what is worst, or rather enervates both, and never procure good in common, but by mere stupid and unforeseen accident. When the knave plays the fool, then the fool becomes knave, and all in order to be wise or (what in his sense is all one) to be thought so, the common cheats with a gigantic influence cleaving to the fools, who, being fearful of not seeming wise, become more obsequious and prostitute than the ladies of the cart,* and clamour for ruin fiercer than their more crafty leaders durst do. They are taught by detestable villainies active or passive to muster as saints, and by affected lying and treachery to recommend themselves to trusts and employments, and expect to reap the harvest more justly due to wisdom and fidelity. But what is the conclusion? The knaves, putting an end to all their lacquering[1] and refinements, fall to distinguish themselves into possession of the quarry, and breaking in all at once upon the fools, make havoc amongst them as wolves in a fold of sheep. So is the fable of those unthinking innocents who, being wheedled to deliver up their defences, became a prey, as men ever will be, who give up the forts of sacred honesty and truth, in exchange for tricks and undue advantages, and what is worst they become the derision of those who by such arts have surprised and held them enslaved; a comfortless condition if in return they had not the satisfaction of seeing their masters fall foul upon, and worry one and other, as all beasts do that gormandize a booty in common.

8 Fools set themselves right by applauding the knaves
But in this subject of ridicule, the merriest part is to observe how these silly sheep (so far the comparison holds), when by dint of nauseous sufferings and feelings are in

6:3 Tame
7:1 Disguising (literally, coating with varnish)

their own consciences attaint of stupidity and abject folly, to say no worse, straight apply to set all right by perseverances, and in order to cover their disgraces, they applaud their own sufferings, and bear the painful load with a stoical apathy. So children when they hurt themselves say they are glad, or at least that they care not. But we hear more, they are the happiest folks upon earth, they call ruin a glorious preservation, and notorious wretches (who are no better than homicides in the form of non-law saviours of the nation, common oppressors behind the vizor of authority) lords protectors, and heroes. Their groans are conscientious, as their purpose of sanctifying evils, by committing worse, and they account the essential ingredients of repentance and restitution to be a retrograde process.* They (I mean the populacy) are the most desperate of sinners, for true penitence, the only means of their redemption, seems denied them, and the retribution of political torments will ever be as public as they are sure.

9 *Hence reason against affecting power*
The moral of this no-fable (copied from '41,* when beasts did not speak like men but men like beasts) is obvious, viz., that it is the ordinary prudence of an honest man, if he would be happy, to live and die in peace, to decline the meanders of this monster, in the way of which he is like to get nothing but scratches. How great advantage is it then for a private man to persevere in that state and to frame his thoughts and studies upon models that suit his condition, and so make him properly and truly wiser, and, by the strength of his own reason and judgment, contented, or rather ambitious to continue as he is?

10 *Objection: low history contemptible*
All this to the understanding of a good man is best confirmed by histories. I mean such as are of the behaviour and successes of private persons in fortune and condition like himself, and not out of histories of states and empires, wherewith he hath no reason to concern himself. But some will say that low history is contemptible, it is of kings and mighty things that reading advances, and all the actors and events must be of the first magnitude, to rouse the attention and compensate the time, and to this tune most of our critics chime. They will scarce muster the relations of petit states and republics, and on this account divers of our lesser Italian histories such as Guazzo and Capriata* suffer. Nothing but invincible art and eloquence could have saved Thucydides, because the Peloponnesian war was but a strife of two cities for the mastery, and did not influence the revolution of vaster powers, and make such a clutter in the world, as the actions of Xerxes, Alexander, and Caesar did. What regard then, say they, is to be had to histories of private men, whose conduct never touched the public? Let their own descendants entertain themselves therewith as citizens with the stories of their own corporation; persons more refined will drop such impertinents, whatever pretended useful surprising incidents may be found in them.

11 *Answered: low history hath like virtues as lofty history*
Those who say all this and more against low history shall yet declaim in the praise of history in general, and in Ciceronian scraps declare it the mistress of life, etc. What, only lives of state would-bes, traders in politic cabals, wars, and butcherly sieges, which show us little but immane[1] ruin, destruction, or misery, such as the giants of courts and camps bring over their own, as well as other nations? Such as are ever plotting to keep blood abroach, to the mortal affliction of not only the innocent, but the most deserving of mankind? Like to, or rather more pernicious (*si parva cum magnis*)[2] than thieves or padders, supposing them to be in perpetual brigue[3] and strife for the monopoly of the road. As if this kind of political life, and no other, though in example infinitely more beneficial to the public, were not to be indulged any literate assistance at all;[4] but the understandings of common men, in the circle of their own affairs, must needs lie uncultifiable and neglected under the same contempt, not to say oppression, as sometimes befalls their persons and estates. It is ordinary to mistake great for good, and glory itself is for the most part but a varnish upon transcendent evil.

12 *Low history hath the virtue of counsel and experience*
What is more proper for any economist to know than the examples of his own economy, with the events and reasons of them? He may thereby calculate advantages and hazards with probability, and applying the circumstances to his own concerns, regulate the course of his life, and make his retirement satisfactory and beneficial; to which the stories of caballing, and fighting, will but little conduce. This kind of history is really the perfection of counsel, and proceeds from a multitude of counsellors, and (in the wise man's sense)* ought to be valued accordingly. Do we not continually declaim in favour of business and conversation, by which only the manners of men are formable, and their judgments maturable with regard to good breeding, and conduct of life? And what is that but a tradition or private history of a man's own gathering? And can the same be unprofitable when gathered and historically preserved by others? The difference is only in more and less, because no historical relation hath that force and efficacy as a man's own observation hath, but

---

11:1 Monstrous; inhumanly cruel
11:2 If small things with large things [may be compared]; perhaps derived from Virgil, *Georgics*, 4.176
11:3 Intrigue; faction
11:4 North has lost the sense. He seems to mean: As if only this kind of political life, and no other, though in example infinitely more beneficial to the public, were to be indulged any literate assistance.

yet *in genere*[1] it is the same. Where the observation is not to be had, the reading is a proper succedaneum[2] to supply the defect, and I must needs say that in many respects it hath the advantage, as first, a man by reading can come at examples in kind and number more than he could ever have come at by usual observation, and secondly, it is true a good genius may find out the virtue of an example presented before his eyes, but it is not the lot of every man to have that genius. But in history the example may and ought to aid the natural faculty by the application expressly attending it, which none that reads can well let slip. Thirdly, the reading, being solitary and deliberate, helps very much towards an apprehension of incidents, which in conversation might be let slip oscitanter[3] as not remarkable or of any consequence, and thereby serve as eyes to the blind.

13 *Such history is preferable to travel, and the reasons*

What is more of course than to send young people abroad, either to capacitate them for services and employments, or for civil education, and (nearer home) into promiscuous company? In which method all the good that is gathered is historical, but attended with a more lively impression than books can insinuate, especially with youth, for that hates attention of mind, and leans to the representation of sense. But if in the description of a private life the ideas most agreeable and touching to young people were held forth, and there were extant much of that sort of writing of a good spirit, lively style, and sound discretion as might engage youth to read, there would be less need of travel. And it is no bad reason that in most men's opinion travel and conversation is preferred to books, because the latter doth not condescend to such minute information as the former doth. It is certain historical learning of men and manners is in effect much superior to all kinds of ethic discourses be the reasoning never so strong, and for enforcing it, even those discourses must appeal to history, whence all the authority sustaining them is derived; and this is further to be alleged, that histories show evil actions as well as good, but yet are not such snares as vicious company, for that, on pretence of showing, enticeth to all the evil in the world; which makes many think that more of evil than good comes to gentlemen by travel. And I should think so too, but for one reason, which is that evil company at home stick like a burr, and prove often tenants for life; but in travel every remove shakes off the scoundrels and hang-bys that are leaguer[1] in every place, like spiders watching to seize upon raw gentlemen who come near their web. Books are always friendly, because they are not calculated to anyone's particular humour, to meet with his foible,

12:1 In kind: sort
12:2 A substitute
12:3 While gaping from drowsiness
13:1 In siege (*O.E.D.*, however, does not record so direct an adjectival use.)

General Preface

not continually declaim in favour of business, and conversation, by
wch onely ye manners of men are formable, and their judgments
maturable with regard to good breeding, and conduct of life. And
what is ye but a Tradition or private history of a mans own gathering?
and can ye same be unprofitable when gathered, and historically per=
formed by others: the difference is only in more and less; but no his=
torical relation hath therefore ye force and efficacy, as a mans
own observation hath but yet in general it is ye same, where ye
observation is not to be had, ye reading is a proper succedaneum
to supply ye defect, and I must needs say in many respects it has
ye advantage, as first a man by reading can come at Examples
in kind and number more, than he could ever have come at
by usual observation, and as it is true, a good genius may find
out ye virtue of an example presented before his Eyes, but it is
not ye lot of every man to have ye genius; but in history ye &c
ample may and ought to aid, ye natural faculty by ye applicatio
expressly attending it, wch none ye needs can well let slip. 3dly ye
reading being solitary and deliberate helps very much towards
an apprehension of incidents, wch in conversation, might be
let slip oscitanter, as not remarkable, or of any consequence
and thereby serve as Eyes to the blind.

Such history is pre=   What is more of course than to send young people abroad with
ferable to travell and   to capacitate them for services, and employments, or for civil education
the Reasons.   and (nearer home) into promiscuous company? in wch method all
                         ye good ye is gathered is historical, but attended with a more lively im=
                         pression than books can insinuate, especially with youth. for ye
                         takes attention of mind and leans to ye representation of sense.
And if I do find rea=   But if in ye description of a private life, ye ideas most agreeable
son that in most   and touching were held forth, and there were extant much of
were a opinion true;   to young people
well a conversation   that sort of writing of a good spirit, lively stile and sound discretion
becase the Labour did   if penned to books as might engage youth by read, there would be less need of Tra
not tend ye cause to such
minute instruments   vell. It is certain learning of men and manners, is in effect
of ye former date   much superior to all kinds of Ethick discourses, ye ye reasoning
                         never so strong, and for enforcing it, even those discourses must

A page from the copytext of the *General Preface* in the hand of Ambrose Pimlowe, with later additions in Roger North's hand. St John's College, Cambridge, MS James 613, p 8 as rascally company, with their flatteries and treacherous insinuations. They are friends and enemies to all alike, and no one more than another is bribed to part with, or to trust them. There are very few, if any, that in the characters of men, or descriptions of their actions, do not drop or rather suppress what is scandalous and unfit for common practice, and consequently as against common manners unfit to be related; nor do they express the ordinary froth and levities of society, or vain babble of fools, which with some that inherit more wealth than good sense passeth for wit and good humour. In a word, the kind of history that I am here recommending hath most of the advantages, but none of the inconveniences, that conversation affords.

14 *Objection: dullness. [That]*[1] *is the author's fault*
But now to resume an objection touched before, and to consider it more fully, some will say what pleasure can there be in reading the account of a private man's economy, how he was educated, matched, governed his family, conducted his affairs, or passed his time? However pertinent and lively the descriptions may be, yet there wants a spur to engage one to go through with them. And admitting them pregnant of good counsel and example, yet the entertainment, compared with the haut-goût[2] of state, will be jejune. For as men are apt to court greatness itself, so the relation of great things pleaseth and consequently engageth. To all which I answer that pleasing is not so much contended for as profit, for the sake of which the other is courted, and with good reason too, for (if I may so use the word) temptation may be unto good as well as evil purposes, and then it is pity it should be wanted on the right side. But as to pleasing, the best histories to airy people are dull, and the more so as the subject is great and solemn. A young man had rather read the life of a tinker than a Caesar or Pompey. Apollo was in the right to punish a tautologist with reading of Guicciardini,* which, saving the use and authority of it, is to a reasonable creature but a leaden diversion. After all, a dullness is never to be charged on a subject, but on the author, who should find spirit enough in himself to give relish to everything he writes, whether of low or of lofty matters. An Italian found means to raise up an heroic poem upon a village quarrel about a waterbucket, and a Frenchman upon the lazy friars' contest about the reading desk, not forgetting Rabelais' bloody war about a plum cake.* It is objected that the beauties of those species are owing to the fiction, which no history allows of. I answer that the same ingredients that are usually brought to adorn fiction may come forward, and be as well applied to the setting

14:1 Deleted in MS
14:2 High or piquant flavour

forth of truths; that is, choice of words, charming periods, invention of figures, interspersion of sentences, and facetious expressions. We see in many ordinary instances the power of words and composition, as of the most filthy obscenity, which may be so couched in figurate terms as not to be fulsome or so much as indecent, but rather acceptable; for words are like dressing, that covers the indecorums of nature which all persons know, but none will endure to observe in the very nudity.

15 *Plain truth without impertinence never properly dull*
The parallel is here taken in the extremes, but holds in all mediocrities, of which Thucydides may be an instance, who (as was said) by dint of language and judgment hath turned the paltry squabbles of the Greek towns into a stately history of human affairs. But it seems that fiction, however deliciously dressed, hath not those advantages to improve as history hath, for that it is not true is a cooling reflection. And what force can any moral arguments or sentences have that are derived upon feigned events? Nothing can invigorate eloquence like truth. It may sometimes happen that the subject-matter is not apt to receive the ornaments of language and composition, which occasioned the great P. Paolo, in his history of the Council of Trent, to apologize for a want of vivacity in his work,* which consisted much of theologic controversy that runs on in strain of uniform matter, and so might seem dull; and to those who look no further than *passar-tiempo*[1] it is verily so. But those who would know the differences of things which men have disputed and do yet fiercely contend about, and how much knavery lies couched in the shell of pretended honesty and truth, will be extremely well pleased when in any subjects those sound discoveries are made. There cannot well be an excess of truth, and when it seems tedious, it is because there is intermixed too much chaff, such as discourses are often overcharged with, things neither true nor false but impertinent, of which kind little is found in P. Paolo, whose history, being full charged with facts perfectly well understood and judiciously exposed, is reputed among the capitals now extant. And one must want taste that at the first reading will not be well pleased with it; perhaps a second may not be so agreeable, because the curiosity part, and the dogma, or moral of the history, viz., that the whole was a cheat of the popes to stop the clamour for reformation, and to impose upon the world, [is fulfilled].[2] And the further use chiefly lies in knowing the state of the several subjects in controversy and referring to them. I knew a reverend divine who upon discoursing of Titus Livy seemed in a great concern and passion. 'Well,' said he, 'I wish I had never read the book.' 'Why?' said one, expecting some notable objection. 'Why?' replied he, 'because I would have the pleasure of reading it over again.' There is great art, as well as felicity, in making a good descrip-

15:1 To pass the time
15:2 Deleted in MS

tion of plain facts, and it is not affected amusements, but justice and integrity of sense, and significancy of language, that sets it off.

16 *State history to private men is a species of romance*

When I consider the delight many pretend to take in reading histories, whereof the subjects are lofty, as of sovereign kings, queens, favourites, councillors, and intrigues of state, far above their condition, although such books are not romance, yet as to consequences I must be of opinion that they are nearly the same, and may be accounted little if at all better; for both are but amusement of time, without profit; it may be worse. Youths are wonderfully delighted with the common romances of the old style, with the feats of knights-errant and giantry, which about the time of *Carolus Magnus* and some ages since were the reading of quality;* but now the goût is turned to that of courts, councils, and intrigues, and so abroad to armies, encampments, sieges, and ambuscades; but most of all with stratagems, and routs, governments falling and rising, and the like great turns of chance, or rather dispositions of providence. And are not common men placed as widely distant from the state of kings, generals, or any species of demagogues, and as unfit to conform their actions to any of them, as young men are from the chimeric exploits of knights and giants, or to act and fight as they are represented to do?

17 *Romances preferred to pompous histories, and the reasons*

To pass time in a course of reading errantry is as reasonable as it is in reading state history itself, when it is of things unequal, unfit for imitation; the fancy is gratified alike, and the readers may be as gentle one way as the other. We know that all persons who hear or read of heroic actions fall straight into party, and, marking some characters for their own, interest themselves in their proceedings, and so are gratified by letting loose their passions of joy, and sorrow, at their friends' good and evil fortune; and this favour falls commonly upon the hero, who by his good intentions and hard labours deserves it; and persons indifferent, and even those who have nothing good or virtuous in themselves, yet shall take in on that side, so much is unbiased nature a friend to the *exarchia*.[1] All this takes place as well in the gravest of histories as in the most frivolous of romances, and so far maintains the level betwixt them. History shows often the prosperity of ill men, which is a sort of commendation of them, but romance never, and as to that point, without great discretion in the historian, the romance carries it. At the bottom of this philo-historical humour there is really found little but self-conceit and pride, as if men were engaged to act with the party they espouse. And there is a rejoicing in the conceit, how much better and wiser kings and councillors they should have made than some of those they read of. And at

17:1 Chief; leader (probably a form of Latin *exarchus*)

this rate state histories might inspire a Quixote, as romances are fabled to have done. I shall find a place to show that if histories of nations are not duly poised, they will tend more to disturb than to compose republics.[2] Hobbes declares the Greek and Latin history the pest of modern times.* At present, I only confirm what I insisted on at first, viz., that histories of men, and things of common condition, nearly parallel to the state of most men's circumstances, and in which no handles are held out for uplifting vain humours, and whereof the whole subject falls within ordinary understanding, done with spirit and judgment, would be incomparably more profitable to the community of men than the pompous histories of governments, and great changes happening in the world.

18 *Private life history rare, for they commonly are wrote to serve turns*
And as this sort of history is most. diffusively useful, so is it rare, for in all our bibliothecs we scarce find a book writ of lives, but what is done chiefly to introduce the history of the time, or for some other special by-end or purpose. And if any pages are spent upon the person, or his ordinary behaviour, it is perfunctory, as beside the grand design, and introduced only to make the relation more formal. And for this reason it is that biographers have selected certain lives of the first magnitude, and having saluted the place of their nativity, and noted the time, hurry into intrigues of state, and lofty ministrations. Among the ancients, Diogenes Laertius is famed for his *Lives of the Philosophers*,* but is in truth a work of philosophy more than of philosophers, yet that little which is now known of their characters and course of life is chiefly taken from thence, so useful a book is it. Plutarch's *Lives* fall more professedly into the history of the times, and under the dress of life-writing may be allowed among the best of the ancient Greek histories, and if they had given us more of the retired manners of the heroes, it had been as well, but compilers have not means to come at a just account of men's lives, for which I shall give reasons afterwards.[1] The *Life of Apollonius* by Philostratus* is wrote to a false purpose, and so fastidious in it, that since the Pythagorean sect declined, the common fables of wizards and witches are more tolerable than that.

19 *Antique histories are unfit for imitation, with a note on Grotius' 'De jure belli et pacis'*[1]
But now to say truth, all the antique histories have lost much of their virtue as histories, and are become a learning rather philological, and as to all example, not much better than romances, so little do the images of persons and things in them quadrate with anything practicable among us. If anyone should form his course of life

17:2 See sections 31-4.
18:1 In sections 36-7
19:1 *Of the Law of War and Peace*

after a pattern found there, he must retreat to bedlam, or perish. To give one instance, public spirit was the glory of the ancient grandees or heroes; now that is the character of a fool. Then a man that did a bold action was safe, even among enemies, but now, the more valiant and great a genius is, so much more dangerous, and on that account, right or wrong, ought to be suppressed. It is a wonder that when the manners of men are so changed, authors of justice and policy should stuff their works only with antique maxims and precedents. As for instance the book of Grotius, *De jure belli et pacis*, is made up of little else but quotations at large of Herodotus and the rest of 'em Greeks and Latins.* What is it to us what Themistocles, or Demetrius, did? Are times and circumstances the same? But when Grotius wrote such was the fashion, that is to fill up books with long and numerous citations, and he has so much spared his own judgment and by filling up so many opinions and examples of others, that one can scarce find out the author amongst them, whose sense perhaps from himself might have passed as well as if it had come from Livy or Polybius. The book was wrote to patrocinate[2] a revolt, and a new set up pretended republic,* for which design the Greek and Roman writers gave the best umbrages, and consequently the book hath been cried up by a sort of people who had such views, and so gave it a credit as if it had been the sum and substance of all human literature.

20 *Some errors in life-writing, with instances of some good*
But as to the rarity of private life-writing, it may be opposed that authors of that kind have not wholly slighted the characters and economy of their subjects, but have touched men as well as their public behaviour; and instances are given from Plutarch. I grant there is somewhat, and if we are so pleased we may think it all, because we know not what is wanting; if we did, I guess it would appear little enough. Nor doth the manner of the writing promise much; and how should Plutarch or anyone gather the privacies of so many men remote in time and place from him but from loose fame, which is but a poor instruction? How and where we may expect it to be tolerably done I shall touch afterwards.[1] As for the many sketches or profiles of great men's lives, pretended to be synoptical, or *multum in parvo*,[2] we are sure there is nothing we look for in them. One may walk in a gallery, and extract as fair an account from the air of their countenances or the cut of their whiskers. What signfies it to us how many battles Alexander fought? It were more to the purpose to say how often he was drunk, and then we might from the ill consequences to him incline to be sober. Some have wrote lives purely for favour to certain theses, opinions, or sects; and then all is in an hurry to come at them. We have many of this sort, but none more

19:2 Defend; champion
20:1 In sections 37, 38, 40
20:2 Much in little

infamous (not excepting the popish legends) than the late piece called *Baxter's Life,* which is no better than an harangue for presbytery and nonconformity.* I do not quarrel with all, but allow many to be very well wrote, as those of the German reformers by Melchior Adam, of Peiresc by Gassendus, of Morinus by _____,³ and of four eminent divines by Walton,* in all which we find the man at home, as well as abroad. But there is a pair left to conclude with, one is that of Dr Bull by Mr Nelson, and the other of Mr Kettlewell by [Francis Lee],⁴* either of which may stand for a specimen what a written life should be, although the latter enters deep into the history of the time and is an aurora of truth such as we may hope will rise with more lustre in future times. And according to that pattern where the person wrote of hath been concerned with the state or public, so much must necessarily be comprised else his story is not true, and not the worse because great; but yet the private state, even of a great man, is what I demand in his history and by no means is to be omitted.

21 *How few have given just account of private examples of good and evil, and the use of such as do*
I do not pretend to catalogue or censure more of these authors, although I have many at the pen's point. But I must own that amongst them all I have scarce found a person taken up and set down again in a private capacity. I should gladly meet with an author that in the course of a written life delineates to us in lively examples the precipitous steps and dangerous meanders of youth, the difficulties of riper years, and the fondnesses of old age, and where one may see distinctly the early application of some persons to proper employments, with the eventual prosperities attending them, as by what small beginnings they advanced to great estates, with the methods and true causes of it stated. And on the other side the devious courses and errors of persons vicious and idle, who from plentiful fortunes and fair reputations fell to want, and more than balanced the account of their luxury and folly by substantial misery and infamy. These cases appearing in a strong historical light must needs touch the very vitals of a person who reads, and inspire a satisfaction in the consciences of those who find they have done well, and a sensible reflection in others who may there see the precipice before them; and thereby many persons undetermined may be engaged to choose for the best. But besides these moralities, with the proper effects as to good and evil, most fit to be depicted in the strongest colours, there is also a copious harvest of discretion and wisdom in common dealing, and disposing the affairs of a family, and making fit provisions for it, and also for the education and settlement of children, and other emergent concerns of human life, to be gathered from the patterns of private men, who have at their great risk proved divers ways of living, and it may be have found out the best at last, and possibly suffered by their mistakes.

20:3 Gap in MS
20:4 Gap in MS

Therefore nothing can be more profitably instructive to private men than relations of other men's proceedings in like condition.

22   *All this confessed by an universal love of comic poems and descriptions, though fictitious*

I know that the prudent world is (insensibly) agreed to what I advance, though few or none otherwise than by their behaviour own it; as to instance particularly by an universal fondness of comedy, of which the profession is to show men in the ordinary state of life, and to represent the great variety of incidents that may appear and concern them in their commerce one with another. Even children when they play Ladies (as they term it) or School Masters are both comic poets and actors, so much is it in human nature to busk for lively representations of things that do or may concern them, and the best of dramatics is but an history (feigned) of the lives of each character combined, so far as the drama carries it. And one might call out for the history of this or that actor apart, which given, is a branch of the history of that person's life, in a private state. It is the narrowness of human capacity that restricts comedy to rules, whereby a very small time and single action is allowed, though it have diverse movements, and intrigues. But in nature, the representation may dilate to infinity, and show the whole life of a man, or of a political state or government; and as from comedy the concern of any one character may be extracted historically, so any history, whatever it is, may be represented by way of drama, or put into comedy. And I cannot but smile to think what a good play the last thirty years' occurrences in Europe would make. And all other books that fall under the chief rule of comedy, that is probability, of what kind soever they are, whether romances, epics, or burlesques, are most diverting to common readers, because they show, though feignedly, the manners of men in mean states and conditions, and the rather because they find themselves so much flattered in their proper and peculiar pride by the low and ridiculous characters often set forth. And why may not the real truths of men's lives exhibited more indifferently in exquisite histories of them, which by the sincerity presumed should be more touching than all the probables of mere invention that can be, operate to invite and consequently to profit men by reading? If fiction is contrived to touch the passion, why may not truth effectually touch the understanding? Let us note a distinction as of child and man in the same adult person, we may then imagine that history belongs to the man, and fiction to the child; which shows how unjust it is to indulge low poem, and reject low history, and at the same time argue from common topics how much the one abstractedly, that is history, is more excellent and useful than the other.

23   *The meanest history useful to the greatest men, even in their heroic intents*

It was a good note of the great Joseph Scaliger: *omnis historia bona est*, which means that all truth, which the word history ever supposes, is useful to be known,* for it is not as fiction contrived to seduce, but if men are seduced by truth, it is the fault of their understandings, and not of the subject-matter. There is no subdivision of humankind, be it so low as soldiers, pedlars, gypsies, and tinkers, but their actions and behaviour, well related, would be a capital learning to men of the same condition and not amiss to those of a better, nay of the best, education, and highest employment. The diversion or curiosity of it is somewhat, and for that reason the Spaniards (who are the most affected moralists in the world) turn their wit that way, and bring forward images of extreme wickedness, penury, and hunger, and the shifts of the vilest rogues (seasoned with moral but tedious reflections) help to furnish out an useful idea of humankind at large, which must contain the states and conditions, as well below as above us. But there is more in it yet; for the greatest and best administrators of the public, in pure compassion, and designing to make timely provision for men in low estates, have used all the means they could contrive to know them. Some have gone about eavesdropping in the dark, others put themselves in the disguise of poverty in order to know the wants and injuries which poor men suffer, and to redress them: a practice more heroical than all other exploits of greatness and power. And in a sphere somewhat lower, where charity doth, or should, constantly reside, I mean the order of gentry, or common rich men, what can be more moving to excite their commiseration than a direct view of poor men's cases, and comparison of them with their own? And if in particular and sensible instances under immediate view this passion strikes so hard upon men's natures to provoke them to compassion and charity, the like represented historically, in variety of instances of mean men's lives well related, must make a considerable impression tending towards the like tendernesses in the minds of them that peruse them, however high in the world their place is. And of this let the case of Mr Stow, the chronicler, bear example (as his life is wrote by Mr Strype), who had a royal brief to encourage charity towards him.*

As far as history itself is superior to romance, so much is that of men's lives, sincerely and truly wrote, more valuable than some works under that title and pretence, which are made up and sewed together of diverse pieces and patches of what hath perhaps happened to some men, not without fiction commixed and interspersed as sauce or seasoning to make the mess of medley[1] relish. Of this sort are the Spanish *Guzman*, the French *Histoire de[s] Larrons*, and the *English Rogue*.* These pretend to be the lives of mean men, but where the characters are such, nothing but strict truth can compensate the meanness of them, and that is (in worth) lofty wherever it is found. Some rise higher, and are adapted to the state of kings and emperors, as the Greek *Cyrus* and French *Telemachus*;* at least they call upon the state of manhood, and not of puerility, to be the readers, as many romances do. But I must needs say that fine-wrote moralities grounded on fable will weigh but

23:1 Dish of mixed foods

little with men seasoned in affairs, and those of fortune enter into the world sooner or earlier in age than their inferiors. If anything toucheth them, it must not be dull prescriptions, or feigned events, but solid truths, which having really fallen out so as they are represented, demand no less than a plain reflection that what hath really happened will in like circumstances happen again, and then induce the like consequences, whether it be for good or for evil, which everyone may apply to his own case.

24 *Of the old romances, and the use of them to youth in some respects preferable to the common school-books*

I must confess the world is very much altered, and the fashion as to the entertainment of books changed; and if it be for the better, I wish the manners of men were so too. We are by all relations informed that from the time of Charles the Great downwards for divers ages, there reigned a spirit of fighting entirely gothic which they called honour, and that had its foundation upon the noble virtues of relentless courage, rigorous fidelity, truth, and justice. And if any man then styled of honour, professing arms, was impeached in any of these articles, mortal battle ensued, which was their way of proving or disproving matters of fact, and of convicting crimes or purging innocence. And as in all ages books are wrote according to the genius of the time, so then came forth the poetical proses, called romances, which Miguel de Cervantes feigned to have intoxicated his Quixote. And it is most certain that however gallimaufry[1] the figures in them are, honour, truth, and justice were elevated to the highest pitch of praise and commendation; which being then the lecture for entertainment of the *beau monde*, male and female (for the moral virtues of the latter were no less extolled and made heroical), it is reasonable to think that from hence the humour of honour was exaggerated, whereby most people would suffer anything rather than be impeached in that point. And it is thought that the Spanish people, since their rodomontade profession of scrupulous honour hath been so ridiculed (as in Cervantes), hath bated much of their rigours that way. But now this class of authors is devolved upon the good nation of schoolboys, who, meeting with such elegancies, are wonderfully affected, that is, with the hideous exploits of knights, giants, and enchanters, and exhaust their petit revenues sometimes to purchase history books, as they call them. But I find the vulgar schoolmasters much concerned to have their disciples entirely addicted to Homer, Hesiod, Virgil, Horace, etc., and not to meddle with any other than classic, or what they call school-books, at least not such extravagant compositions as the old romances are. To this protesting that it is allowed the chief labour lies among the classics, which I would not be thought to exclude absolutely, but at times only, and consistent with other reading. Therefore, in favour of low romance, I would ask the learned, first, if they desire boys

24:1 Mixed; jumbled (normally used as a noun)

should love to read? That is a general proposition to which they will answer yea. Then reading must be made easy and familiar to them, for if they puzzle, and stick by the way, all books are fastidious. It is easiness in reading that makes it pleasant, and as other pleasing habits, so that is gained by exercitation. Then supposing there are books, though none of the best, which youth will greedily read over, and others better, which they will not with a good will read at all, which party is most likely to make reading easy and agreeable to them? Certainly the former; therefore never let youth be debarred from books, however trifling, if the subjects are not immoral, supposing of their own accord they will read them, and then probably they may spend their vacant times in the most profitable of all play, and that is in idle books, and soon come to affect what are better, *legendo disces legere*, as well *scribendo*,[2] etc.

25 *They give a right turn on the side of virtue and the consequent morality of young persons*
But there is somewhat more weighty in the case, which is the determining the manners of young men towards that which is virtuous and honourable. Boys for want of ordinary knowledge of things by proper experience have no ideas in the[ir][1] minds that may create in them a value for truth, which makes all grave history as well as morality dull to them, nor do they know probabilities, but it is the admirable and extravagant only that strikes them. And it is their propension always (as I have said) to side with the hero of the fable. Now when that hero is set off with all the ornaments of virtue, true value, and honour, will it not create in them a favour for his qualities as well as his person, and consequently impress in their minds a prejudice in favour of those good qualities, and not unlikely determine the whole course of their lives accordingly, when perhaps, without such an early start on the right side, the equilibrio may determine the other way? For sometimes there happens such indifferency that a small advantage turns the scale of a wavering disposition either to good or evil. I conclude, therefore, that such sort of lecture should be recommended to young people, rather than discouraged or deprived.

26 *The common school-books and infamous morals are a pernicious discipline to youth*
Especially when it is considered what gear it is their masters afford or rather enjoin them for their private diversion: the *Pantheon*,* and such collections of the absurd heathen theology, a mass of all manner of debauchery, theft, rapine, rebellion, and adultery, and what not of wicked and beastly living, matters fitter for utter suppression than to be applied for the institution of youth. They must needs have an indifferency (at the least) if not a penchant towards vice, finding it the laudable

24:2 By reading you will learn to read [as well as] by writing.
25:1 Conjectured completion of word obscured by close binding

practice of the (celebrated) almighty powers. And will the alleging it to be all a fiction disarm the prejudice with those that are caught by images of pleasures as they are expressed, and little regard whether true or false? The masters have pretended to geld the obscene books, and so hand them clean to the scholars, the effect of which is only to make them procure the whole authors on purpose to compare them. Then they say that otherwise they could never make them understand Homer, or Hesiod. If it be so, an antidote should be procured by giving them to read somewhat more moralized, and which they will like better, or else defer Homer to riper years. And after all, it were better perhaps such books as Homer, Hesiod, and their followers had never been heard of or known. What can be showed worse to a youth than that the triumphant Jupiter was a rebel to his own father, and rose into dominion by crushing of him? And if one surveys the whole Cretan family, there is not a worthy character amongst them, or better than a race of rogues and whores, unless we may borrow that of Diana for variety. And what a figure is the furious congress of Jupiter with Juno, whereof the ecstasy put all the favour promised to the poor Trojans out of his memory, and so they paid for it? And this to disguise a perfidy of the hero Jupiter, and that his character might not flag by his double dealing. There is history and morality enough to entertain the schools and perhaps instruct the languages, without such ribaldry to deprave the minds of young gentlemen, which should not be suffered, much less made the legitimate discipline of youth in a Christian country; but, instead of that, the paltry translators of them into English are encouraged, if not Homerified. And whereas it may be pretended that wits are not so well ripened without these – that is, lovers cannot so well deify their mistresses without the help of Venus and Cupid – I think such may be spared, and a little knowledge and morality in the room would do full as well.

27 *Passages in the lives of extraordinary persons extracted are rather romance than history*
There is one sort of authors more to be touched upon, and those are the florilegists, or gatherers of remarkables; they single out all extremes, whether of courage, perseverance, chastity, or piety, the more monstrous the better, and these are planted under heads, and sent forth as recommendatories of virtue. Of these, one of their Latin school-books, Valerius Maximus,* is a celebrated instance, who to every passage adds a fine-turned conceit of his own, as if the story was but a trap for the close, or as of an epigram, the whole poem contrived for the sake of the last verse. But whether the passages are true or not (for a great deal is to be allowed to authors, who for popularity follow common fame), they are in themselves so very extravagant that none can propose them for models of behaviour; one might as well contrive a moral pandect[1] out of knight-errantry. Romance is the counterfeit of

27:1 System of law

nature, and labours after probability by pursuing common circumstances; but when nothing is produced but the extravagance of truth, and the circumstances that would make it appear probable (as I believe many are in histories) suppressed, then as to all use, but wonder, such truths are no better than romance. Be things true or false, to be out of all practice is in effect the same and, as I said, produceth no good, unless wonderment be a virtue? And pieces or scraps of truth are not in strictness truth, but rather enigmas. Therefore as falsity should not steal feathers from truth, so truth should not part with any ingredients that may enliven it, by making the native probability appear; for perhaps a few actions single or uncomplex, when all the real inducements are disclosed, will be very much admired (as few wonders related prove such to eyewitnesses), and then the whole unites in one natural idea that speaks for itself. For this reason, if in private biography one would not mislead folks into extravagancies, it is required that the truth be unfolded just as in a legal testimony, whole, sole, and nothing else. And then the prospect will be clear, and a man may plainly discern whether anything is to be gathered there fit for his use or not. And without this point of sincerity the writing as to all profit is but a will-in-the-wisp.

28 *The style should be adequate, and promise justice rather than partiality*
The rigour held over all historical undertakings requires not only strict truth, and the whole, but all the tokens of veracity, and none of partiality, or suppression. So far is it from being reasonable to affect, as many do, to tell strange stories. Some people's style runs all in superlatives, as most wonderful, prodigious, excessive, and the like, and what is worse, often on both sides alike, for good one way and sinister the other. It is a very difficult task to adjust terms to things, so as they may not seem greater or less, better or worse, than the truth of them warrants; but the endeavour ought to be for it, the rather because if in any one instance there appears a sidling disposition, it casts a disparagement upon the whole. And this rigour of truth doth extend not solely to facts and existencies, but to characters and moralities, and some are so squeamish that to avoid seeming partial they do justice to nothing; and there lies the greatest difficulty, for truths may be so touchy that a plain telling them, with a proper and due reflection, will be termed partiality, of which afterwards.[1] But it ought always to appear that the writer is in his own mind and intent rigidly sincere.

29 *History should indicate and sentence, but covertly, human actions and their properties: (1) wisdom or folly*[1]
I affirm first that an historical writer (if he be free and secure which all ages do not fairly indulge) ought in most instances to interpose his own sentiment and censure,

28:1 Presumably sections 33, 34, 39
29:1 Close binding obscures some letters in this heading; they are supplied by the sense and by comparison with 'First Preface,' MS James 613.

(1) of wisdom and folly, and (2) of virtue and vice, or good and evil in all, as well religious as other respects. For the first, that is, wisdom and folly, it may be observed that the best of our antique historians have used the series of facts as perpetual texts, whence they have taken rise to instil their admirable remarks of human nature and its unaccountable propensities, showing at the same time their own as well as others' sagacity, all which a small knowledge of the Latins will demonstrate. They used the story, as Mr Bayes did his plots, to bring in fine things.* If any man in a plain discourse should deliver the result of his experience of human affairs, nothing would be more stiff and dull, and he could not do it tolerably well, or to his own content at least; for after all his pumping he would find that many of the chief items would scarce be at his command. And also what he did muster, without a world of circumlocution, he could not give a due force to his sentiment. But then in the course of any historical writing, the incidents would give a spring to the imagination, and thoughts turn up, which in the plain way of invention, would not have risen at all. Therefore it is not only allowed, but expected, that such a writer should intersperse sentences, bright and indicative of true wisdom and folly, to serve in quality of a soul to animate the work, which otherwise would be as a dead letter. The want of these hath made Guicciardini (the best relater of punctual transactions) intolerably tedious, even to a proverb, and for that cause he was ridiculed at Parnassus;[2] and on the other side Davila, a relater far inferior to him, yet grammercy[3] to the abundance of his politic remarks (although by the critics thought to be more his own surmises than the truth of the matter), is more esteemed and courted.* But this ornament of history fits best when artificially interwoven with the relation, so as the judgment keeps pace, and the matter is made, as it were, to speak, rather than the author. This is an excellence in Thucydides. But when the sparkling with sentences is too affected, they start forth, and are distinguished from the text, which is to their disadvantage. If the riches of observation lie concealed or couched in the style, they follow (as they say) naturally, or as if the reader and not the author supplied them. This perfection is not given to all, and indeed but to very few writers of history, and is much easier showed than executed; but all do, or should, aim at it – *audendum tamen.*[4]

30 (2) *Good and evil, the other with deference, this with authority*

(2) The other latitude of censure I mentioned is of religious or moral, of good and evil, tending to recommend the one and to dissuade the other; and it ariseth from hence (allowing my distinction), matters of human policy are often dark and problematic, admitting contrariety of opinion; what some may think wise, others will condemn as foolish, and much is ascribed to event. Wherefore the author's

29:2 See *Gen. Pref.*, section 14, n.
29:3 Thanks to
29:4 However, one must dare.

sentiment, being *sub judice*, should be modest; and without the plainest consequences he should not give out his political maxims, as if he were a legislator but with a sort of deference, as becomes well-bred conversation, to be decently and with respect carried on betwixt him and his reader. But as to good and evil, which are founded upon principles superior to all men's opinions or actions, and fall not in the district or arbitrament of either writer or reader, no author should be mealymouthed, but as they say call a spade a spade. Event often decides in cases of wisdom and folly but hath nothing to do with good and evil; nor any pretences of decency [ought to be permitted][1] to qualify the just censures of moral actions that one way or other may egregiously merit them, although the consequences terminate in the honour or dishonour of any people, families, or persons, for the reader hath a title in such cases not to be misled by any flatteries or urbanities. For this reason, good and virtuous actions ought never to be let pass without some lustre of honour reflected upon them, nor wickedness or impiety without some blur of disgrace. Let event say[2] its pleasure, a reader ought to be detained till his dispatch of prejudice in favour of virtue, and of detestation with regard to vice, is made and signed; and this done with fit and pregnant terms, fulfilling in his mind just images of moral duty, with a lively force, spirit, and efficacy, is so far from being in truth accounted partiality that it is the very gauge of good history, and without which it were better we had none at all.

31 *The story of Caesar divested of the proper moralities, and the bad use may be made of it*
I shall venture upon one instance of history, which I think may fully explain my meaning in this matter, and it shall be the story of Julius Caesar, shortly related, to show how the morality of history may be varied, *ex diametro*,[1] by the manner of it. As first for Caesar's honour: He obtained many and great victories over the fierce Gauls, which gave him reputation, and established his interest in the soldiery, and that drew to his side a potent party in the city, and of divers in the Senate of Rome. Thus armed he determined to execute his premeditated design of setting himself at the head of the republic. And with that view, pretending injustices done him by the Senate, he passed the Rubicon with his army. Little opposition was made on the part of the republic, so he entered the city, and was master of it. The other party had left the city, designing to come back upon him with an irresistible force, enrolled under Pompey their general. But Caesar followed, and with incomparable courage and perseverance, strove against the united forces of the republic commanded by Pompey. And not without having had the worst of it in divers actions of war, he came to a

30:1 Conjectured interpolation to clarify the sense
30:2 A slip for stay?
31:1 In the opposite way

general battle in the fields of Pharsalia, and obtained a complete victory. Pompey fled, and Caesar, through immense difficulties and hazards, followed, and in Asia procured his final destruction. Then he cleared Africa and Spain, where musters were so strong against him that he had no advantage but in his conduct. And in these wars he moved with incredible expedition and intrepidity, and at length, not without fortune's favour smiling upon his measures, he settled himself in the dictatorship, and governed Rome and its territories as an absolute monarch, till a confederacy of certain senators, divers of whom he had signally favoured, was formed against him, and executed by stabbing him in the Senate-house. A barbarous action detested by the citizens, who drove the assassins out of the city, and burnt their houses; and no one of them ever returned in peace, but one after another were all destroyed; but the commonwealth was never restored.

This is history, but in the moral part very faulty; for this rebellion of Caesar's, in itself treacherous and undutiful, is represented in such a passive way that, without better thoughts intervening, would rather invite than discourage a man to attempt the like. And really in our common histories, this most perfidious action, being successful, is delivered down to posterity with advantage of honour to Caesar, as much as if he had rescued his country from utter ruin; all which is largely harangued by Mr Edmundes, his commentator in English.* Would not any other general say: 'If Caesar passed the Rubicon, why not I? If I succeed I am an hero, and as for falling in the Senate-house, I can be more cautelous² than he was.' Now to show how this ill use of history may be obviated, I propose to make the same relation true as the other, but in this manner:

32 *The same story told a little better moralized*
Caesar was learned and eloquent, but withal a vicious spendthrift, and one of those ambitious spirits whom nothing would content but the absolute dominion of Rome. By factious arts he obtained and held on the province of Gaul for five years. In that time he made great conquests, and augmented as well as modelled his army; after which he thought nothing too hard for him. He despaired of obtaining fairly a longer continuation of his province and, losing that, lost his army. He had also a considerable party of his side in the city and Senate, for corruption had taken the very head of the republic. Being thus prepared, he served himself of a pretence that he had not justice done him by the Senate, and, contrary to his duty as a commander of the forces of the republic, he marched as an enemy against the city itself, and passed the Rubicon, with this vile sentence in his mouth: *Jacta est alea*.¹ The government in the city was not prepared to resist him, or else their great Pompey chose to command an

31:2 Cautious; wary
32:1 The die is cast: Suetonius, *Divus Julius*, 32.

army to be raised in the provinces, as fitter for his designs (no whit better than Caesar's), than to gather it in the city, or the Italian towns. Therefore, together with the party for the republic, he retired from the city, and left it open fairly for Caesar to enter, as he did, and then disposed all things without contradiction, as he thought fit. After this he pursued Pompey, and met with divers sharp rebukes, but at length the citizens in the camp pressing for an end of the war, their general, full against his will, and relucting as one dispirited (for all that work was besides his model, who had rather have been in Caesar's place), came to a general battle at Pharsalia, where he commanded in a manner as if his good genius had forsaken him, or was subdued by Caesar's. In a word, Caesar prevailed, and the republic, though much superior in numbers, lost their army. Pompey fled, Caesar pursued, and through desperate hazards and difficulties, at length in Asia overtook him, and procured his destruction. As to Pompey, the infidelity of his heart made him be pitied by few, for he that could say *Scylla poterat, et ego non potero*[2] deserved no better end. Then Caesar, having cleared Africa and Spain, came triumphant to Rome, where, as dictator, he governed all affairs despotically. How seldom is it that men persevere with so much courage and contempt of danger, in virtuous designs, or for the common good? But these successes scarce paid Caesar an equivalent for his sufferings in the procuring. For instead of enjoying the fruits in a long-lived government, as might have been expected, he found soon the reward of his treachery. For a knot of senators joined, and stabbed him in the Senate-house. The citizens resented this graceless action, and having drove all these percussors[3] out of the city, burnt their houses, and afterwards in a sort of exile, and unhappy warfare abroad, they all perished, and deservedly, for no law made them arbiters of lives in time of peace and mutual trust, though recently established. And the wicked citizens fared little better, for they utterly lost their republic, and being fattened with the spoils of nations whom they had unjustly oppressed, their own luxury and faction brought civil war over them. And after breathing a little in Augustus his time, their quondam tyranny was amply repaid them by a series of monsters called emperors. And now all stand almost indifferently upon record, to posterity, for precedents of evil-doers of all sides confounded.

33 *The nature and application of this sort of morality*
This is the same history as the former, but more commendable, as the moralities interspersed may be esteemed useful. Had the wickedness lay all on one side, as in public turmoils it sometimes happens, in such cases, to give the iniquity its due must not be accounted partiality, but a rectitude of historical justice, which ought not to be

---

32:2 Scylla was able and I will not be able.
32:3 Those who strike

spared. Such was the state between King Charles I and his parliament, that main-tained most illegally a wicked war against him, of which the whole proceeding was on their parts abominable, and ended in the mock trial and detestable parricide of his royal majesty. Are our histories partial in branding that scelerate[1] conduct and conclusion with infamy? But in this Roman story the whole detail on all sides is a series of iniquity; and besides the proper censures, there start from it divers useful maxims: as that all irregular change of settled governments tends to absolute power; when iniquity lies at the bottom, even prosperity itself is a curse; or take the vulgarly accepted, but rarely observed maxim, 'honesty is the best policy'; and if that will not please, go to the wise man, who says of the wicked, that the prosperity of fools shall destroy them.*

34 *The same matters pursued, and the torment of ill-got greatness*
I shall hazard the being tedious by prosecuting this point a little further, for which I hope reason and utility, if any is found, may make the excuse. I am sensible it is commonly expected that history should be charged only with pure facts, without any reflections, moral or political, at all. Those matters, as some may say, are of the reader's jurisdiction, which the writer ought not to usurp, either to anticipate or prejudice the freedom of judging, which may be done by the readers with as good justice and morality, as by the author. To all which I answer, [1] true, if all readers were right reasoners; but it is ordinarily their infirmity only to think themselves such, for which reason they are so touchy at the appearance of being led or instructed. But in truth very few have sagacity enough to discern moral consequences, and so lazy in thinking, as well as reading, that it is needful to afford them some help as children (pardon the simile) are showed with a festuca[1] to point out the letters. (2) Many persons are so undetermined of good and evil, and (as upon a vertical point) to turn any way, in case a vain conceit of self-interest invites, that their blundering upon a mistaken consequence, or fond construction of facts, may taint their judgment by creating prejudices in favour of evil. And as true judgment excites useful maxims, so error raiseth pernicious ones. As from the Roman story just told, an ill-disposed person may set up such a maxim as this, viz., attempts to usurp governments, however lawfully established, boldly pushed on, upon opportunities fairly offered or contrived, seldom fail of success. Against this it is obvious to oppose: when such attempts are made, although the success, that is, change of the government, follows, yet those that first engage in them perish, and others reap the fruit. So on one side: that the pleasures of government are so great, above the enjoyments of any private state, that it is reasonable to adventure against odds of the chance to obtain it. On the

33:1 Atrociously wicked
34:1 Pointer used to indicate letters; the more usual form is 'fescue.'

other side it is opposed: that of the argument the major is a cheat, for no state of life is more miserable than that of a person possessed of ill-got government. For it is well known, that besides perpetual suspicions, and fears, which fail not to evacuate even the common repose of sleep, but the real hazards of being deposed, and losing life to boot (if we look no further), make all those pleasures, though undisturbed, a bad bargain, and such was the case of Caesar, Cromwell, and some others.

35 *A good historian is both orator, and philosopher, for the advantage of good against evil*
Here it is seen how necessary it is for a writer, by his moralities, to obviate the worse sort of inferences, and for that purpose he ought to play the orator, and use all reasonable arts of insinuation in order to prefer good in the world, against evil. And for the same reason, as all the famed authors of rhetoric affirm, that no person can be a good orator without being a good man, I am bold to affirm that an historian cannot write well unless he be an honest man. It is remarkable that the most gallimaufry[1] nonsense in fable, as when beasts, birds, stocks, and stones are made to speak, is well accepted, purely for the sake of the moral. There the moral is prior, and the fable doth but declare it, but it is posterior in history, which is like premises from whence the moral is inferred. But either of them without a proper application to human life is but as timber to an house, until it is applied a capacity only, and in all other respects insignificant, and for that purpose useless. In sum, history is or should be the best philosophy, or ethics in perfection; for it hath the advantages of a congenial union of example and precept; the former alone is a body without a soul, and the latter all soul, and no body, and so both uncapable of performing well the instructive part, unless combined in just and well-penned relations of fact, sublimed with prudent and moral insinuations. And as for some histories that have appeared in our times, of a character directly contrariant to the virtues here recommended, I may find time and place to speak with them,[2] but decline fouling my pen with their nastiness at present.

36 *Life-writing harder to do well than state history, with the reasons*
To proceed, therefore, I must remember that, although I am here induced to say much of history in general, I am not out of my way towards that kind which I mentioned at first, and am now about more directly to profess, viz., private biography. For all fitting qualifications belong to every species of history, and as that of private men's lives is more rarely found good than that of nations (as hath been already noted), so is it much more difficult to compose, as it ought to be done, than the other kind is. For state history hath the assistance of public registers, records,

35:1 Mixed; jumbled (normally used as a noun)
35:2 Section 42

pamphlets, gazettes, and often the memoirs of private persons, which are the most serviceable to truth of any. Men that are capable, and usually apply to write histories, are commonly such as have lived in or near to courts, been of a broad acquaintance and conversation, as well as of themselves curious and inquisitive; whereby of their own gathering, a general notion of the history of their own time hath formed itself in their minds, which with the other assistances enabled them to write well. But where should we go to be informed of the course of any one man's life? How many excellent men, as well as vile debauchees, go off, and no person left behind capable or willing to represent their characters and successes in a just history? I question whether there is now in the world extant the history of any one man's life so full as it ought to be, and since we have nothing to judge by but what is left us, such as it is, who can say whether any one account is full and just or no? That which is remembered may be of the slightest kind, and the most momentous passages not touched, and the design may be apparently invective, or panegyric, such as Burnet's lives of the Lord Rochester, and Judge Hale, the persons of whom none ever knew, but must also know that those written lives of them are mere froth, whipped up to serve a turn.* I must grant that not only accounts of lives, but histories of nations, owe much to the ignorance of such as they are made to inform; for they, knowing no better, must take what they find. Therefore historical controversy is the most useful thing in the world; for that lets the readers into a capacity of setting themselves right, without being carried away with prejudice of good or ill opinions of men and things, contrary to justice and truth. For such controversies interpret enigmas, correct partial insinuations, supply defects, fill up blanks and omissions, and what is most of all, expose the knavery of writers, which is a disease that in the folio volumes of our time calls for a cure. But a life may be ill wrote, and none of these checks come forward to correct it, and of that kind people are very prone to take for truth all that is well writ. In short, all history of one sort or other is like painting, never exactly true; that which comes nearest is best, and however discrepant, there may be some use or other that makes it reasonable not to slight, but to preserve it.

37 *The many defects and imperfections in the way of good life-history*
No man at large, who is not expressly qualified, can fairly take upon him to write the life of any other man. They may make gatherings and excerpts out of letters, books, or reports concerning him, but those are memorials, or rather bundles of uncemented materials, but not the life, and it is obnoxious to this shrewd failing that all these gatherings, and the conjectures built upon them, are of course taken for positive truths, of which much or the greatest part most commonly are utter mistakes, and without a due check make a strange history. Therefore a life-writer in education, friendship, conversation, and all commerce of life ought to be the nearest of any allied to his subject, and not a contingent gatherer or compiler only, as I said

before; for such are but sewers-up of errors, either to the prejudice or for undue favour of the person wrote of. And what further qualifications are requisite I intend to touch afterwards.[1] But it is no wonder so few lives are tolerably wrote, when it is considered that men often change their residence, company, and manner of living; and there is seldom or never any one person that can answer for the whole life and actions of any man, but however friendly and intimate they were, there is removing, absence, employment, or somewhat that hinders a continual notice of his actions, determinations, and occurrences. But supposing a Pylades and Orestes,* never asunder, do such use to keep pocket-books to use for journal memorandums of each other? Or amongst all the friendships in the world, how many think, or dream, of giving an account of a friend's life before he is dead and gone? And then for want of notes, as to all that may be recollected, there is nothing but frail memory to trust to, which must needs be very imperfect both as to times and matters transacted. But admit a good memory, how few have a felicity of style and method, in their own opinion at least, proper for such an undertaking? And men that do not very much exercise the pen will soon find the want of those requisites, such as should invite them to do justice to a friend, or the public, in that manner. Nay, most people are so averse to that exercise they will not do right to themselves whom they may best account for.

38 *The very great use of a life-journal by a man of himself*
Whoever hath a mind either his family or the public should profit by his example, and would be known to posterity truly as he was, ought to keep a journal of all the incidents that may afford useful remarks upon the course of his life; for the aid and encouragement of such a journal would engage a good pen to work fairly upon it, and draw his picture well, which otherwise could not be reasonably attempted. This practice would be useful to a man in many respects; he might retrospect his actions, and seeing his errors and failings, endeavour to mend them; it would also be a check upon all his exorbitancies, and considering that being set down they would stain his reputation. Nay, the very pleasure of looking back upon past occurrences would amply compensate the pains, and I may well say that would be done by the very exercitation of daily penning and writing, the profit of which those may consider who want it, as many do, who had rather carry guts to the bears,* than write a letter.

39 *Divers examples of such journalists, and a caution against partiality towards self or friends*
There are many examples of this kind of idiography.* The famous, or rather infamous, Cardan wrote *De vita propria,** and doth himself more right than all the

friends or enemies he had in the world could have done; for he owns himself a very knave and a cheat, and proves it by divers immane[1] cruelties and impostures. Bassompier wrote the journal of his own life,* which (besides his first design) is printed, and there his true character appears, a very soldier and a rake, imprisoned by Richelieu because he was afraid of his merits – there's his vanity, though in some sort true. The petit journal of Edward VI,* even a youth, may be a pattern for the greatest men. But above all the great and good Archbishop Laud's journal had a sublime effect, by vindicating his integrity against the foul aspersions of his adversaries, which without that record had stuck more of calumny upon his fame than since that appeared by all their wicked means they have been able to do.* These registers are of greatest use in biography, but allowance must be made for self, which cannot but be partial. Some will say that all life-writing is obnoxious to the like infirmity, because ordinarily it is done by relations or intimate friends, whose very design is praise. And it is easy to panegyrize when there are no means either to prove or disprove the facts, and invention can bestow characters *ad libitum*,[2] and there are instances of criminals to the laws, who, on account of pure party, have been dubbed heroes, or martyrs; writers for faction will illuminate the sepulchres of their departed friends, to cast a lustre upon their living partisans. All that may be answered to this is that it is too often so, and there is reason for more jealousy of a life-writer than of any author whatsoever. But yet there may be a veracity, even in praises, and certain symptoms will discover a writer's partiality (I mean such partiality as betrays him to falsify); and on the other side, vouchers of his integrity may be produced, in some degree at least, by which, and the ordinary critical processes against authors, his proceeding whether just or unjust will be accordingly approved or condemned, as I may in course demonstrate.[3]

40 *The writer of a life must be qualified, and first by a confirmed character of honesty*
These considerations have made me recollect, as well as I may, what kind of authority or warrant a life-writer may hope for to credit his history of the life and behaviour of any private person, and more especially the moral character he gives him. And all that I can think of to that purpose is reducible to two heads: (1) the character and circumstances of the writer; (2) the remains of the person to be described, whether by the real monuments of his egregious actions or by his writings.

(1) The writer ought to be of good fame, and, as to truth and honesty, untainted; and so far the case is often notorious, for about the moral characters of men common

39:1 Monstrous; inhumanly cruel
39:2 At pleasure
39:3 Sections 40, 41

fame is seldom or never a liar, though as to particular facts seldom true. And secondly, he must be out of all roads towards preferment or gain, for those lead to all the abuses of history; the present age groans under such, heavier and more mortifying than ever was known in any age or country. What is to be expected from an history that comes with a flattering preface, and there's 300 guineas for that, or articled with a bookseller to contain —— sheets for £100, besides dignities in the sequel, to encourage the family of corrupters? * Nay, the very lucre of selling a copy is a corrupt interest that taints an historical work, for the sale of the book must not be spoiled by the dampness of overmuch truth, but rather be made vivacious and complete by overmuch lying. But of all authors, these I am treating of chiefly require a clear character, because less confutable directly than others are, for the most of the facts lean on the author's peculiar authority. But thirdly, besides all this, it must appear their course of life was such as rendered them capable of the undertaking, and that is by having been in almost continual conversation or converse with the subjects, and so attached to the very persons, that little of importance in their whole lives could escape their notice. Such friendships often happen between persons who live almost at bed and board together, and communicate to each other their most recondite thoughts and designs, and profit each other by mutual counsel. Such as these are so far qualified to be authors of lives. But where this intimacy is not found, men (as I said) may gather and compile what is called a life, but is in truth anything else rather than that of which it bears the name.

41 *The remains of the subject, as all monumental actions or writings*
(2) All these advantages granted, a man's character is not, and scarce can be, justly represented by mere words in the way of history without some specimens derived from himself, either of his writing, or some speaking testimony of things remaining, and referred to. Friends may, but things will not prevaricate or falsify, and no description can come up to the force and expression of them. These two criteria, (1) the qualifications of the writer, and (2) the monuments of the subject, joined together, promise a good life-history, but either apart are defective, and want the reciprocal interpretation that the one gives the other. If an author commends a man for being a good poet, and produceth none but silly verses; if for a good orator, and makes him speak obscurely or nonsense; if for a good soldier, and yet tells that for the most part he is beaten and the like, I doubt both author and subject will suffer contempt alike. As on the one side all the eulogies in the world will not sustain a character against the real testimony of fact, so the fact may be flagrant, and get the better of all the prejudice and malice of times, abetted by powers, and then a written character will less suffer by the imbecility of the pen, in case a weak brother undertakes the vindication of it.

42 *An account of the undertaking of the lives of the Lord Keeper North,*
Sir Dudley North, and Dr John North

But now it is more than time to check this course of essaying about historiography (a
subject of infinite *copia*,[1] as well as commonplace in authors), and advance to a
declaration of what is here hoped for by it, and that is chiefly some apology for an
officious, I might say unqualified, undertaking to be a life-writer, and as such to dress
up my remembrances of three honourable brothers and friends: the late Lord
Keeper North, Sir Dudley North, and Dr John North. They were all persons of
celebrated worth and ability in their several professions, and whose behaviour upon
the public stage, as well as in their retirements, was virtuous, wise, and exemplary.
But now if they are not quite forgot, that little that is whispered of them inclines to
the sinister, and is wider from truth than distant from the time when they flourished
(pardon the disparata), and if we look out for their names in history, all is the same.
There is a two-handed one in folio whose excellency is the coming after a worse.*
The author, among his eulogies, could not find room to drop a good word of any of
these, though he hath condescended to adorn the characters of departed quacks,
poets, fanatics, and almanac-makers. When *nil nisi bonum*[2] was the case, it was
prudent malice to say nothing; better forgo the very marrow of history, than do right
to any of these. But for my part, if the consideration of common good, which always
flows from the bright examples of good men, were not inducement enough, yet the
usage of these poor-spirited writers, who hunt counter to that good, is a sufficient
call to this undertaking. Whereby I hope to rescue the memories of these distinguished persons from a malevolent intent to oppress them; and for that end bring
their names and characters above board, that all people may judge of them as they
shall appear to deserve. I have reason to be concerned lest my tenuity of style and
language, not meeting with candid interpretation, may in some sort diminish the
worth that belongs to them. But I have no means to meliorate that affair, and must
lay aside that scruple, for it is an office devolved upon me, which I cannot decline;
there is no person now living who can, or at least will, undertake what I am about, or
do anything towards it. Therefore hoping for the *tale quale*[3] indulgence, I march on,
and endeavour to rectify want of art by *copia* of matter, and that upon honour
punctually true. But I am not at all concerned lest frequent eulogies (which by way of
avant propos[4] I must here declare will advance themseves) should make me appear
as partial to my subject. For who is partial that says what he knows and sincerely

42:1 Abundance
42:2 Nothing unless good
42:3 Appropriate(?) (perhaps a legal phrase)
42:4 Advance notice (normally, preamble)

thinks? I would not as some, to seem impartial, do no right to any; when actions are honourable, the honour is as much the history as the fact, and so for infamy. It is justice as well historical as civil *reddere suum cuique*,[5] and whoever engages in such designs as these, and governs himself by other measures, may be a chronographer, but a very imperfect or rather insipid historian.

43 *These lives, although of persons concerned in the public, yet wrote as private*

One thing remains for me to clear, and that is the reason why, after so much as hath been said of private biography, I produce here three lives of persons who had all considerable posts of preferment, and two of them concerned deep in affairs of the public. I grant this to be so, and yet I stand to my point, that the lives I write are private; for I shall not go out of my way to fall upon foreign affairs or national concerns, at least not so much as may be expected, and indeed no more than in the lives of those persons is absolutely necessary to account for their passing their time, and what they immediately transacted, and no further. And if I am asked why not, since ears itch after that sort of news, I answer that it is not my talent. I neither concerned myself to note nor to remember strictly the items of government. I mingled not with the intrigues of the times , but pursued the employment of a profession. And most of the conversation we had was familiar and easy, rather about arts and sciences than court brigues,[1] and at times when we were retired, and cared not for repetitions of such uneasy matters, oh! how pleasant and agreeable were those days, when in the midst of storms we lay safe and fearless in retired harbour, and never so well pleased as when we were escaped from the billows, if I may term crowds such.

44 *Incidents common to all the three to be remembered*

But to conclude this tedious preface, I must remember some things which concern all these three brothers in common, and that is their parentele[1] and family relation;* and then proceed to the lives, beginning with the youngest, Dr John North, then the second, Sir Dudley North, and come at last to the Lord Guilford, Lord Keeper of the Great Seal of England; and so as I rise in the eldership, I shall also advance in the dignity of the subject.

42:5 To give everyone his due.
43:1 Intrigues; factions
44:1 Parentage

45 *The parentele, relations, and first descendants of his aunt*[1] *the Lady Dacres*
Sir Dudley North, Knight of the Bath and Lord North, Baron of Kirtling (*vulgo*[2]
Catlidge) in Cambridgeshire, was their father.[3] His father was Dudley also,* and had
three other children, one a son named John, who had three wives, of whom the first
best deserves to be remembered, for she left him an estate in St John's Court, by
Smithfield, upon the ground where the chief house and garden were placed, and now
a set of fair houses are built, making three sides of a square, and is called North's
Court. He survived all his wives and died without issue. The old lord had also two
daughters, of whom one died single; the other, Dorothy, married the Lord Dacres of
the South, and by that match had a son and a daughter. The son married the Irish
Lord Loftus' daughter, and had divers children; he had an estate given him upon
condition to change his name from Leonard (that of the Dacres family) to Barret.
His eldest son is also matched, and hath children. His seat is at Bell House Park near
Purfleet in Essex, and they write their name Barret-alias-Leonard. The Lord Dacres
had issue by a former wife, of whom the now Earl of Sussex is descended. After the
death of the Lord Dacres, his widow, the Lord North's daughter, married Chaloner
Chute, who was once speaker to the pseudo House of Commons. She had no issue by
him, but his son Chaloner (by a former wife), marrying his wife's daughter (by the
Lord Dacres), had issue three sons and a daughter: Chaloner, the eldest, died single;
Edward, the second, married the widow of Mr Tracy, a daughter of Sir Anthony
Keck, and having divers children, lives at the Vyne in Hampshire;* the youngest,
Thomas, was once clerk of the Crown in Chancery, and married [Elizabeth], the
daughter and heir of [Nicholas] Rivett of [Brandeston] in Suffolk, and left children,
of whom Thomas Leonard Chute, the eldest son, now lives at Pickenham in Norfolk.
And here concludes all the descents from the old Lord North by his only married
daughter, the Lady Dacres.

46 *An account of the grandfather, father, his mother, and relation*
That nobleman[1] was a person full of spirit and flame, yet after he had consumed the
greatest part of his estate in the gallantries of King James his court, or rather his son,
Prince Henry's, retired, and lived more honourably in the country upon what was
left, than ever he had done before. He was a great wit, and published a folio-book
tituled *A Forest*, etc.,* and there may be found the idea as well of his gaieties as of his
moroseness. He bred his eldest son, Dudley, the father of these three brothers, after

---

45:1 That is, *their* aunt: Roger North and his brothers
45:2 Commonly; popularly
45:3 See *John*, section 1, n.
46:1 That is, Dudley, 3rd Lord North, Roger North's grandfather

the best manner, for besides the court, and choicest company at home, he was entered amongst the Knights of the Bath, and sent to travel, and then into the army, and served as captain under Sir Francis Vere.* At length he married with Anne,[2] one of the daughters and coheirs of Sir Charles Montagu. He served his country in divers parliaments, and was misled to sit in that of '40,* till he was secluded; after which he lived private in the country, and towards the latter end of his life entertained himself with justice, business, books, and (as a very numerous issue required) economy. He put out a little tract of that subject, with a preface lightly touching the chief crises of his life.[3] Afterwards he published a small piece tituled *Passages Relating to the Long Parliament*, with an apologetic, or rather recantation, preface. He wrote also the history of the life of the Lord Edward North, the first baron of the family, from whose daughter the Dukes of Beaufort are descended. He wrote also divers slight essays and some verses, which he tituled *Light in the Way to Paradise*. These two last his eldest son caused to be published with his name to it, viz., Dudley, the 2nd (misprinted for the 2nd Dudley) Lord North. These were at first designed to remain with his family in MS and not to be published, but there is no harm done, for he was a Christian speculatively orthodox and good, regularly charitable and pious in his family, rigidly just in his dealing, and exquisitely virtuous and sober in his person. All which will appear in his writings, although the style is not so poignant as his father's was. But to pursue the relation. His lady, by the mother's side, was descended of Sir George Whitmore, once lord mayor of London, which opens a large kindred towards Wales, of which it is said that above thirty came into coparcenary shares of the estate of Sir Charles Kemish. Her father was the before-mentioned Sir Charles Montagu, of five the youngest brother, of the Boughton family now honoured with a dukedom; from the other brothers as many noble families are also derived, as Manchester, Sandwich, and Halifax. Sir Charles had two other daughters; one married the Lord Hatton and had divers children, and amongst the rest the incomparable Captain Charles Hatton.[4] The other daughter married Sir Edward Baesh of Hertfordshire, who died without issue; then she married Mr John Cary of the Falkland family and Master of the Buck-hounds under King Charles II, and died also without issue.

47 *The sons of the second Dudley, Lord North, and their matches*
This last Dudley, Lord North, and his lady had six sons and four daughters who lived to appear in the world besides some who died in minority, viz., Frances, Edward, and Dorothy. The eldest son was Charles, who received the honour of knighthood, and married Catherine, the daughter of William, Lord Grey of Wark, and was in his

46:2 See *John*, section 1, n.
46:3 For details of this book, and the three works mentioned below, see p 170n.
46:4 See *John*, sections 41–3, nn.

father's lifetime called by writ to the House of Peers, by the title of Charles, Lord North and Grey of Rolleston.* They had two sons and two daughters who survived; the eldest son, William, is the present Lord North and Grey,* who is matched with Maria Margareta, one of the daughters of Mr Cornelius de Jonge van Ellemete, late receiver general of the United Netherlands. The second son, Charles, a major in the late wars in Flanders, died there of a calenture;[1] the eldest sister, Katherine, died at sea coming from the Barbadoes, and the youngest, named Dudleya, having emaciated herself with study, whereby she had made familiar to her, not only Greek and Latin, but the oriental languages, under the infliction of a sedentary distemper, died also, and both without issue.* Her library, consisting of a choice collection of oriental books, by the present Lord North and Grey, her only surviving brother, was given to the parochial library of Rougham in Norfolk, where it remains.* The Lord North's[2] second son, Francis, the third, Dudley, and the fourth, John, are the subject of the three life-treatises intended to follow, where will be remembered the state of their families. The fifth son was Montagu, a Levant merchant who died without issue. The youngest, Roger, married Mary, the daughter of Sir Robert Gayer of Stoke Poges near Windsor, and having had two sons, Roger and Montagu, and five daughters, Elizabeth, Anne, Mary, Catherine, Christian, lives (out of the way) at Rougham in Norfolk.

48 *The daughters of the same and their matches, noting also the benefit of an honourable relation*
Of the four daughters of Dudley, Lord North, the eldest, Mary, was married to Sir William Spring of Pakenham by Bury in Suffolk; she had issue a son, but lived not to have any more, and the son died in his infancy. The second daughter, Ann, married Mr Robert Foley, a younger branch of the (now) Lord Foley's family, and their eldest son, North Foley, having married a daughter of Sir Charles Holt of Warwickshire, lives now at Stourbridge in Worcestershire. The third daughter, Elizabeth, married Sir Robert Wiseman, a younger son of the Rivenhall family in Essex, Dean of the Arches, who dying without issue, she is since married to the Earl of Yarmouth. The fourth and youngest sister, Christian, married Sir George Wenyeve of Brettenham in Suffolk. And they have left divers children, of whom the eldest, (John), married a daughter of Sir Christopher Musgrave, and now resides in the place of his father at Brettenham. This is the family relation of these three brothers whose lives are upon the carpet before me. So much of particularity concerning them (although a just pedigree ought to have taken in much more) may perhaps be thought superfluous, as not being of any general concern; yet really the case is memorable, for the happy

47:1 Tropical fever; delirium
47:2 That is, Dudley, 4th Lord North, Roger North's father

circumstance of a flock so numerous and diffused as this of the last Dudley, Lord North's was, and no one scabby sheep in it, considering what temptations and snares have lain in their way, is not of every day's notice. It was their good fortune to be surrounded with kindred of the greatest estimation and value, which are a sort of obligation to a good behaviour. It is very unfortunate for anyone to stray from the paths of virtue who hath such precautions and sonorous mementoes on all sides of him; and it is almost enough to be educated in a family wherein was no instance of irreligion or immorality either practised or allowed; such virtue or efficacy hath an early example to affect the manners of good-natured youth. I would not have it thought that beyond this advantage I hold forth a family relation as matter of merit to anyone in particular, but say only that (allowing no peculiar instrinsic worth, in a particular person, derivable from the honour of his family, because his own value and not his ancestors' must set him off, although a *buena castra*[1] is not to be slighted) yet there is some good comes from it, which is that the descendants must know that the world expects more from them than from common men, and such a perpetual monitor is an useful companion. And if there be any persons of such upstart principles that with them antiquity of families is rather matter of ridicule than of honour, let them enjoy their epicurean prospect, and see their posterity run riot into destruction, before the earth covers the corruptible ingredients of their composition.

48:1 Good stock (literally, good pruning)

Life of Dr John North

Portrait of John North as a schoolboy, by Blemwell

Apology

The author of the following life desired me to say for him that he looks on himself as one pressed to the service, and then his failings, like invincible ignorance, demand excuse. And favour is asked only on account of a large dissertation intercaled[1] in the midst of the story, for which he can allege no constraint, and, with salvo to the subject, might have been as well, perhaps better, left out, for what hath history to do with academic disputes? And the little he hath to say for himself is that he was under an *impulsus philosophicus*,[2] and occasion being given by the subject, and the pen once entered, *besogna sfogare il capriccio*,[3] the rage, like fire, would not stop till the fuel was spent. But that no injury might happen to anyone, due warning is given, and whoever they are that fall among the thorns and the thickets may thank themselves. If he is accused for the matter, he pleads to the jurisdiction; there is nothing against morality, religion, nor government, and that granted he demands the privilege of thinking and debating. In a philosophical state, which is a pure democracy, every cobbler is a statesman; the cause is universal, and if the defence be weak, it may perhaps excite better and stouter advocates to undertake it.

---

1 Inserted as extraneous matter. The 'dissertation' is omitted in this edition (see pp 41–2).
2 Philosophical impulse
3 One must satisfy the whim.

Index

THE DISSERTATION

[The index lists seventy-seven sections comprising the 'dissertation' on the new philosophy.]

THE HISTORY RESUMED

Introduction

1 *The design and wherein recommendable*
My design in these papers is to frame a short history of the life of an honourable
person, not long since deceased, and to represent his character as near to truth as my
stock of materials will enable me. Works of this kind may be useful to such as had
rather profit by the example of others than apply any invention or industry of their
own towards a moral improvement, or it may be to wear away some heavy hours in
reading. As for the importance of the present subject, I shall hang out no bush, but
submit to the peruser the determination, *de bono et malo*,[1] whether there was need
of such a proverbial signal or not.* Some have affected to write the lives of persons
long since dead and gone, and their names preserved only by some formal remains
and (ever) dubious traditions. So painters copy from obscure draughts half obliter-
ated, whereof no member, much less the entire resemblance, is to be found. But
fiction, supported upon seeming probabilities, must fill up the blanks and supply all
defects. In this manner some lives have become redivival,[2] but with partial views
tending either to panegyric, the advance of some favourite opinions, or factious
intrigues, which are fiercely pursued, while the life-scraps come out very thin and
meagre. And after great length of time how should it come off better? My choice is of
what the present undertaking aims at, the life of a person known to some yet living,
and done by a close acquaintance and frequent companion, who· hath neither
inclination nor temptation to court the public or to flatter the private.

2 *To what end, and the reasons*
The moral intent here is to do justice to the person, and service to his family, both
which may result from the present endeavour to retrieve his character. And this is no

1:1 For good or ill
1:2 Of renewed vitality

slight task because he took express care that nothing real should remain whereby in after times he might be remembered, and my memory is now the repository of most that may be recovered of him. Therefore I think it not reasonable for me to let such an ornament to his family, and example of virtue, be wholly forgot and lost, or perhaps *nomine tenus*[1] only, confined to a petit cycle in some musty genealogy, and scarce that since the honour, nay the continuance, of families seem to be slighted and unregarded, and since titles and estates seldom distend a line of above three generations, which makes pedigrees good for little but to maintain titles to lands and tenements at law, and the remembrance of persons and families good for nothing at all. But yet it is hoped the defection is not so great but some families will remain who would not have anything valuable of their lineage forgot, and others unconcerned may be glad to know examples, whether of good or bad, one for choice and the other for aversion, I hope I need not say which. But these considerations have pinned me down to the work and I see no means I can have with decency to make an escape.

3 *Times wanted, the style familiar*

It hath not been in my power to gather up the precise times of all the passages of this life which I have mentioned, and for that reason I could not write it chronologically as I desired. But considering that here is little or nothing of the public or states matters which may ever require a nice retrospection, I chose to proceed in a style of familiar conversation, and as one engaged to answer such questions concerning our doctor as may be obviously demanded. I said our doctor, for to save often writing a few syllables, I shall treat him under that title, although usurped, until forms procure us a better warrant. And as to the style aimed at here, I intend it not polite, and if it be significant it is well, but I can make sure it shall be English and that of the most vulgar usage, unless a touch of some other language, in a proverbial way, may be made use of.

4 *Philosophic excursions excused*

There is one thing which may more violently demand an apology, and hath been touched upon a little earlier, and it is in wiredrawing the state of natural philosophy into a comparison of the earlier and later edition of it, and back into a disquisition of principles.[1] As for the latter, I know not how I shall come off, for the speculation requires such an absolute interdict of all manner of prejudice, and that so positive and universal, that I question whether humankind is capable to conform to it. I am sure Aristotle, Descartes, and Newton have failed. I have endeavoured upon their propositions to hold up as tightly as I might, but do not answer for myself as to what

2:1 In name
4:1 The digression is omitted in this edition (see pp 41–2).

most think invincible. I may fear what I have proffered may be mistaken for an hypothesis, but I mean only to state things so, as must be admitted to be true in all hypotheses. And I am forced to stand against the powerful negatives, as that this, that, and twenty things cannot otherwise be solved. But I let them rest in peace, and do not doubt but in the same method of thinking the chief secrets in nature, as motion in *pleno*[2], fire, explosions, continuity,[3] etc., in proper essays, may be explained so as not to seem, as now they do, almost miraculous. But as I hinted before, to prevent the fatigue of overmuch thinking, I have given fair warning of the danger, and how it may be avoided. And I have reason so to do, being conscious of augmenting the evil, by many obscure, and inadequate, expressions; and those almost unavoidable, because few (if any) persons in the world think by the same, and not in many respects different, ideas.

5 *The subject extreme difficult, and accepted by few*

The infelicity of the whole matter is that the life may be accepted by many, but such dissertations by very few, and those only who have tasted the Newtonian, to say nothing of other, philosophy – and it may be some academics, or singular vertuosi, who are for the most part devotees to their idol. And as for others, I cannot expect that such immane[1] abstractions as are here required should ever enter into their heads. Therefore, whoever deals in such matters should be qualified by a good Latin style, to address only to such as are (as I may say) of the profession. The stress will fall upon the meaning of words, and arts have those whereof the sense is agreed upon, and may not well be translated, because words must be used in translations that are not of import so nicely accorded. And it is no new notion that philosophers are deviously inclined to use words instead of things and can never give a good answer to the word 'what?' Therefore the application should be to things, which being once truly conceived, may be tolerably expressed in all vernacular languages, borrowing only some of the terms, the sense of which is general by artists agreed upon. But yet I am sensible the difficulty of expression is so great that my English will fall short of a due insinuation of ideas, therefore these papers shall lie *tinearum preda*,[2] to be perused only by candid friends, who will make allowances to one that, to pass his time, ploughs with a quill, and who will expect no better crop than the barren soil will afford.

4:2 Motion through space completely filled with matter
4:3 The principle that all change, sequence, or series in nature is continuous, and that nothing passes from one state to another by a 'leap'
5:1 Monstrous
5:2 Prey of worms

6 *The order of the 'Parrhasiana'*

It is hoped the want of a formal distribution and subdivision of matters, by *liber*, *capitulum*, and *sectio*,[1] will not be wanted here. The margin numbered may be equivalent to titles of chapters, and then the series may be continual, after the model of the Dutch Leclerc in his *Parrhasiana*,* whom (no more than the English Dr Clarke) I should not follow in anything but philology.*

6:1 Book, chapter, and section

The Life of Dr John North

1 *Parentele, and relation*

Dr John North, the fifth of seven sons of the Right Honourable Sir Dudley North, Knight of the Bath, Lord North, Baron of Kirtling,* and Anne, one of the daughters and coheirs of Sir Charles Montagu, a younger brother of the Boughton family.* He was born at London 4th September 1645, and had divers brothers and sisters elder and younger,* of whom, with the rest of his relation, which was widely extended among the chief of the nobility, a particular account is not here required.* And thus much is mentioned only to show, what in the following account of his life will be confirmed, *videlicet*, that the just value of an honourable descent received no diminution by his character.

2 *Temperature of body, and mind*

When he was very young and also as he grew up, he was of a nice and tender constitution, not so vigorous and athletic as most of his brothers were. His temper was always reserved and studious, for which reason his noble parents designed him early for the church, and the rather because they observed him not inclined to those puerile irregularities to which boys are ordinarily propense, but, with an unusual respect, resigned himself entirely to the order of his parents, and particularly in their professionary disposition of him; and even at school, as well as at home, he behaved himself accordingly. If anything so early seemed amiss in him, it was a non-natural gravity, which in youth is seldom a good sign, for it argues an imbecility of body or mind, or both; but his lay wholly in the former, for his mental capacity was vigorous, as none more.

3 *Passed Bury School under a loyal master in the worst times*

His scholastic education was altogether at St. Edmunds Bury in Suffolk, under Dr Stephens, then master of an eminent free school there.* It was a piece of good fortune to be no forwarder, for his residence there fell in the dregs of time, when after the martyrdom of King Charles I, a babel of misshapen powers tormented the people of England, until the happy restoration of King Charles II to the crown, and the nation to their laws; a fit time for a monastic retirement. The master was pedant enough, and noted for high flights in poetry and criticism, and (not a little derived from the last age) called jingling;[1] all which qualities were not amiss in his employment. The worst of him was, what his corpulence declared, the being a wet epicure,[2] the common vice of bookish professions. We pass by his partialities (which were indeed scandalous and pernicious to many of his scholars), because they happened to turn in favour of our doctor (for so I must, for brevity, thus early style him). For his master was exceedingly fond and proud of him. One happiness was that he was a noted cavalier, then the title of the king's friends, in opposition to the rebels, who from a precise cut they affected were styled Roundheads. In the worst of those times, the master in his family used the forms of loyalty and orthodoxy, but being reputed little better than a malignant, he was forced to use outwardly an occasional conformity, by observing the church duties and days of super-hypocritical fastings and seekings, wherewith the people in those days were tormented (though now almost worn out of all credibility), and walked to church after his brigade of boys, there to endure the infliction of divers holders-forth tiring themselves and everybody else;* and by these means he made a shift to hold his school. It happened that in the dawning of the Restoration the cancre of the times mitigated, and one Dr Boldero (formerly a captain in Scotland under Montrose, and between the ladder and the rope had narrowly escaped hanging),* now in episcopal orders, kept a liturgy conventicle in Bury, using the common prayer; and our master often went to his congregation, and ordinarily took some of his boarders with him, of whom our doctor was for the most part one.

4 *Parentele affects manners more than education; the doctor had both good*
There may be some doubt whether the genius of an education hath that mighty influence upon the conduct and morals of a future life as commonly is reputed, for we see daily young people coming up in a strain directly opposite to the opinions and usages of their families. But yet it is to be accounted a felicity to enter the world in a right way, especially in a political sense, for party runs *in traduce*[1] more than virtue, or manners; for strength of mind may get the better of all prejudice, and even of that which is the strongest, education. And I have reflected that if our doctor (as I yet presume to style him) had been bred in the horrid din of exclamation against prelacy,

3:1 To sound with alliteration, rhymes, or other repetitions
3:2 One who gives himself up to the pleasures of drink
4:1 Propagated (literally, in the vine branch)

Arminianism,[2] and popery, as the mode of those times rang, he had such a strength of reason and bias towards truth that in his riper years he could not have been a fanatic, whereof the composition was crossgrainedness, ambition, and malice. But herein I must distinguish parentele from education, for the latter affects chiefly those who are lazy in thinking, and coming to man's estate, are glad to be determined any way, rather than endure the fatigue of a serious deliberation. But from parentele are derived depraved will, inclination to evil, and manners every way corrupt, which made a venerable gentleman, the Honourable Mr Henry Grey,* use (in his particular phrase) to say often: 'By G-ds iff, 'ware a breed.'[3] Herein our doctor appears to have had a double felicity: a righteous education, and parents of just and honourable principles, if any such ever were.

5 *His picture in the Cavalier habit drawn by Mr Blemwell*
After the happy restoration, and while our doctor was yet at school, the master took occasion to publish his cavaliership by all the ways he could contrive, and one was putting all his boarders, who were of the chief families in the country, into red cloaks, because the cavaliers about the court usually wore such, and scarlet was commonly called the king's colour. Of these he had near thirty to parade afore him, through that observing town, to church, which made no vulgar appearance. It fell out that about that time one Mr Blemwell, a picture-drawer, resided in Bury. He was an early friend and acquaintance of Sir Peter Lely, who also spent some time at gentlemen's houses thereabouts. Mr Blemwell was allowed of by Lely to have had a very good judgment in the art of picture, but his performances were not equal to his skill. He was a civil and well-bred gentleman, very well accepted and employed in the town and neighbourhood, and among others he drew our doctor in his red cloak *alla naturalle*[1] just as he wore it. And I cannot but appeal to this portrait, now in my custody, for demonstration of what I have alleged concerning his grave disposition. The countenance is modest and composed, and copied from pure nature, wherein nothing is owing to the painter, for it was very like him.* This little picture is more to be esteemed because there is no other, for he could never afterwards be prevailed to admit any to be made of him, as will be afterwards observed.[2]

6 *An amiable gravity, and countenance always florid*
He was much observed for this amiable gravity, and after he grew up to man's estate, he retained a florid youthfulness in his countenance, of which more will be observed

---

4:2 MS has Armiasme (see *John*, section 71, n).
4:3 Presumably, 'By God's life, beware a breed.'
5:1 Natural; unaffected
5:2 In section 77
6:1 In section 78

posture and habit expressed in that picture. I may remember, for the credit of that scarlet troop and their scholastic education, that not above one or two of the whole company, after they came to act in their country ministrations, proved antimonarchic, or fanatic. The effect of which good inclination towards the person and government of King Charles the Second during the greatest disorders in his reign appeared in a celebrated union of the Suffolk gentry in opposition to the rage of an impetuous republican faction flagrant in that country. The state of which strivings may find a representation in another design, which may require this mystery to be unfolded, in order to resolve the famous law case between Soame and Barnadiston.*

7 *A perfect school-scholar, and of the discipline*

To return to our doctor, I need not stay to exaggerate his steps of proficiency in learning; it is enough to allege that he was an accomplished scholar, which the forwardness of his advancement afterwards demonstrated. It could scarce fall out otherwise with him, having good parts, and run through the whole course of a large school, always sedulously applied, and little diverted by play, as most of his age use to exceed in. And the methods of the school were no slight advantage, for the master required all his scholars to fill a quarter of a sheet of paper with their Latin themes and write the English in the opposite page, no matter which the original and which the translation. And at the presenting, a desk was set in the middle of the school, where the boy stood and rehearsed his theme in Latin, or English, as was required. And at this act, a form or two of boys from the lower end were called for up and placed by way of audience, and the master had opportunity to correct faults of any kind, pronunciation as well as composition. This discipline used generally in free schools might prevent an obloquy, as when it is said that in the grand assemblies for English affairs there are found many talkers, but very few speakers.*

8 *Before Cambridge, his noble father read logic and metaphysics to him*

After the doctor left Bury school, he passed some time at his father's house, before he went to the university, which time was not lost, for his father (according to his way used with some others of his sons) read and interpreted to him a common logic, Molineus* I think it was, with somewhat of metaphysics. This was some ease at his first entrance into the college, for many take such a distaste at what seems to them at first a mere rattle of words that they are very slowly, if ever, reconciled. As the scholar that could not conquer the sense of 'homogene' and 'heterogene' declared, if he were at home-again, he never would come hither-again. I ought not here to let pass the care and capacity of a nobleman who performed the office of an academic tutor to his sons, in order to ease their first undertakings at the university, of which there are not many examples.

9 *Sent to Cambridge as fellow commoner in Collegium Jesus, then nobleman*
At length, in the year 1661, our doctor was sent to Cambridge, and planted in Jesus
College under the tutorage of Dr Cook. At that time Dr Ferne was vice-chancellor,
and our liturgy non-con Dr Boldero, master of Jesus, with whom a previous
acquaintance at Bury (of Dr Stephens at least)* might be the inducement of his being
placed there. He was admitted a fellow commoner, but when his grandfather, the
first Dudley, Lord North, died, whereby the barony descended upon his father, he left
the post of a fellow commoner, and assumed that of a nobleman.* But notwithstanding that, he was diligent in his studies, kept chapel, and in person performed most of
his exercises, as were consistent with his station in the college. His quality assured to
him many advantages, especially in the way of preferment in the church. A master of
arts of his college used to say, he would give all he was worth to be a lord's son,
meaning that such a one, of ordinary learning and morality, could not escape being
early or late well preferred. This was no small encouragement to our doctor, who
thought it an instance of his good fortune that his father outlived his grandfather,
otherwise the advantage of precedence, etc., had come short of him.

10 *His studies directed, as the course is, for church preferment*
Here the doctor became settled in a severe course of study, which he pursued with all
the ardour of one that knew nothing but his learning could make him considerable,
or indeed capable to subsist as he desired, which the posture of his family, as will be
observed,[1] made him most sensible of. We read of primitive inducements to enter
into church orders, with open view of poverty, and persecution; but now the case is
altered for the only inducements are plenty and preferment. And since it is so that
the church is sought as a secular employment, we are not to expect, nor do we find,
more rigours of life and practice in ecclesiastics than in other common men who seek
their preferment in other professions. Therefore it is very unjust, under this change
of motives, that the cause of religion should in the least suffer or be scandalized by
the behaviour of particular clergymen. It is certain our doctor was embarked in that
vessel, and as for his behaviour in it, the rest of his life must show. At present we will
leave him to his studies, and retreat a while to consider his natural temper and propensities, such as of one kind or other all men living have, and which came into the
world with them, and are in their power to alter no more than complexion or stature.

11 *His natural infirmity was timidity*
The doctor's greatest or rather only infirmity was a natural timidity, owing to a feeble
constitution of body, inclining to the effeminate. This under some circumstances, and

10:1 In section 13

without a mind as vigorous and strong as his body was weak, might have oppressed him. He was always sensible of this weakness, and during the whole course of his life laboured to conquer it; and as to outward appearance prevailed, and what was insuperable, lay dormant within himself. One would have expected that a youth at the university, no freshman, nor mean scholar, should have got the better of being afraid in the dark; but it was not so with him, for when he was abed, if alone, he durst not trust his countenance above the clothes. For some time he lay with his tutor, who once coming home found the scholar abed, with only his crown visible. The tutor (indiscreetly enough) pulled him by the hair, whereupon the scholar sank down, and the tutor followed, and at last with a great outcry, the scholar sprang up, expecting to see an enorme spectre. This made a jest, but not much for the tutor's credit.

12 *Experiment of his conquering himself*

Another time, which was after he was fellow of the college, in a moonshine night, he saw one standing in a white sheet. He surveyed it with all his optics, and was confirmed it was a spirit (as they call it), and resolved with himself, if he could, to find out what it came for. He got out of his bed, and being still of the same opinion, went nearer and nearer, till he might touch it, and then reaching out his hand, he perceived it was only his towel hung against the wall, with the moon shining full upon it, and then he went to bed and slept well. I have heard him say that he was satisfied the devil could discover no man's thoughts, else he might shrewdly impose upon those who were inclined, like him, to be in that manner concerned. But it must be allowed that in this instance his strength of mind got the better of his bodily constitution, in forcing himself upon an experiment few would have cared to have made. I mention not these passages as of themselves worth remembering, but to show that, as in the case of our doctor, a vigorous and active spirit may be quartered in a slight and feeble machine of flesh. But this propense disposition to fear had a worse effect upon his spirits when applied to the consequences of his life, and not only sullied his character by making him seem avaricious, but even shortened his days, as by the following relation will be made [to] appear.

13 *His moral resolutions and strict conduct of his pittances*

He had in his nature a principle of justice and duty inexpugnable, and was fortified with a resolution not to run in debt, nor to help himself by any wicked compliances, whatever otherwise became of him. And while he was at the college he just shifted with a small exhibition from his family, and if it had been less (according to his strict economy), he had still shifted; and more he did not expect, knowing that the hereditary honour must devour the fat of the land.* And as to future preferments, nothing more uncertain, all his hopes hung upon mutable interests, and he found in himself but little inclination to courtship and flatteries for favours. His sheet-anchor was the life of his life, a dear brother and friend,* who might drop from him. He had an ambition to be master of a good library, but scarce hoped ever to obtain it, and when he became able to make a small purchase of books, he was so far happy and in himself pleased that his management succeeded so well, which created in him a sort of joy in a perseverance, even after the just cause, by his being better provided for, ceased.

14 *Successful care turns to pleasure habitual*
It is certain that studious and thoughtful men, having an honest principle, are apt over-critically to weigh the contingencies of life and possibilities of good or evil that may concern them, and as fears are always much stronger than hopes, commonly expect the worst, and that inclines them to act so as they may think may best secure them; and in that course please themselves so long that, after all cause of fear removed, they continue the same caution, which becomes an habitual pleasure to them, and towards old age, when wants are least, engenders a vice called covetousness. And the rather because that doth not contravene their principle of justice and honesty, according to the sentence of an old usurer* that used to say saving was the lawfullest way of becoming rich.

15 *The doctor's cares continued af[ter] the cause ceased*
This was literally the case of our doctor, who, by the ease he found in his mind out of a careful and saving course of life while it was most reasonable, could not forbear a penchant after the same way even when he was preferred to his heart's content, and thereby the former reason ceased, for so the mind is quasi-habitually gratified. But how well he conquered himself in that, as in all other instances of inclination contrary to right reason and the decorum of his estate, such as all men must have, more or less, the following account must determine. In the mean time, to demonstrate how obnoxious learned men are to these impotences, I may remember the famous Dr Cave and Dr Beaumont,* men of gigantic knowledge, yet having rose from small beginnings, fell under the same passion towards increase, and their fame not much impeached thereby.

16 *Made fellow of Jesus College, much to his content*
But now to recover our doctor, we find him at Jesus College settled in a fellowship, which he procured not long after he was capable. I find the entry thus: *Admissus est socius Collegii Jesu mandato et literis regiis, 28 Sept. 1666,** when he was about six years' standing in the college. That society is divided into north and south, and the order is to elect two into each vacancy, one of each side, to be presented to the Bishop of Ely, who makes which he pleaseth fellow. The doctor came in the place of a northern man, and the bishop (then Dr Wren) made an odd interpretation: 'For it's strange,' said he, 'that Mr North should be looked upon as a northern man, who had

nothing North about him but his name.'* Whether his lordship intended a compliment to the country, or to the scholar, is no profound question. This advancement was a great relief to the doctor's mind, for thereby he had a sort of home, with no small advantage in his economy, and all entirely consistent with his design of study, which he pursued with a full application.

17 *His desire of a good library and the advances*
Now he began to look after books, and to lay the foundation of a competent library. He dealt with Mr Robert Scott of Little Britain, whose sister was his grandmother's woman, and upon that acquaintance, he expected, and really had, from him useful information of books and the editions. This Mr Scott was in his time the greatest librarian in Europe, for besides his stock in England, he had warehouses at Frankfurt, Paris, and other places, and dealt by factors. After he was grown old, and much worn by a multiplicity of business, he began to think of his ease and to leave off. Whereupon he contracted with one Mill of Paul's Churchyard near 10,000 deep,[1] and articled not to open his shop any more. But Mill with his auctioning, atlases, and projects, failed, whereby poor Scott lost above half his means. But he held to his contract in not opening any shop, and when he was in London (for he had a country house), passed most of his time at his house among the rest of his books, and his reading (for he was no mean scholar) was the chief entertainment of his time. He was not only an expert bibliopole, but a very conscientious good man, and when he threw up his trade, Europe had no small loss of him.* Our doctor at one lift bought of him an whole set of the Greek classics in folio of the best editions. This sunk his stock at that time, but afterwards, for many years of his life, all that he could (as they say) rapp or run[2] went the same way. But the progress was small, for such a library as he desired, compared with what the pittance of his stock would purchase, allowing many years to the gathering, was of desperate expection.

18 *His opinion of books in general*
He was early sensible of a great disadvantage to him in his studies by the not having a good library in his reach, and used to say that a man could not be a scholar at the second hand, meaning that learning is to be had from the original authors, and not from any quotations, or accounts in other books. For men gather with divers views, and according to their several capacities, often perfunctorily, and almost always imperfectly, and through such slight reading a student may know somewhat, but not judge of either author, or subject. He used to say an old author could not be unprofitable, for although in their proper time they had little or no esteem, yet in

17:1 To the extent of almost £10,000
17:2 Seize or snatch for oneself

after times they served to interpret words, customs, and other matters found obscure in better books, of which Aulus Gellius* is an apt instance. He courted as a fond lover all best editions, fairest characters, best bound and preserved. If the subject was in his favour (as the classics), he cared not how many of them he had, even of the same edition, if he thought it among the best, either better bound, squarer cut, neater covers, or some such qualification caught him. He delighted in the octavo editions of the classics by Sebastian Gryphius,* and divers of his acquaintance meeting with any of them bought and brought them to him, which he accepted as choice presents, although perhaps he had one or two of them before. He said that the black italic character agreed with his eyesight (which he accounted but weak) better than any other print, the old Elzevir* not excepted, whereof the characters seemed to him more blind and confused than those of the other. Continual use gives men a judgment of things comparatively, and they come to fix on what is most proper and easy, which no man upon cursory view would determine.

19 *His industry in collecting*

His soul was never so staked down as in an old Latin-boo[k]seller's shop, for having (as the statutes of his college required) taken orders, he was restless till he had compassed a supellectile,[1] as he thought, necessary for his profession. He was for the most part his own factor, and seldom or never bought by commission, which made him lose some time in turning over vast numbers of books, and very hardly pleased at last. I have borne him company at shops for hours together, and minding him of the time, he hath made a dozen proffers before he would quit. By this care and industry at length he made himself master of a very considerable library, wherein the choicest collection was Greek, as may yet appear by what remains of them in the library of his nephew, the Right Honourable Lord Guilford.*

20 *Alterations for worse in the bookselling trade*

It may not be amiss to step a little aside, to reflect on the vast change in the trade of books between that time and ours.* Then Little Britain was a plentiful and perpetual emporium of learned authors, and men went there as to a market, which drew to the place a mighty trade, the rather because the shops were spacious, and the connoisseurs gladly resorted to them, where they seldom failed to meet with a conversation agreeable, and few or none departed without buying somewhat. And the bibliopoles themselves were knowing and conversible men, with whom, for the sake of bookish knowledge, the greatest wits were pleased to converse. And we may judge the time there as well spent as (in latter days) either in tavern or coffee-house, though the latter hath carried off the spare hours of most people. But now this emporium is

19:1 Furniture; equipment

vanished, and the trade contracted into the hands of two or three persons, who, to make good their monopoly, ransack not only their neighbours of the trade scattered about town, but all over England, aye and beyond sea too, and send abroad their circulators to visit, and inquire of deaths of clergymen and others, sweep their studies, and so get into their hands all that is valuable. And the rest of the trade are content to take their refuse, with which and the fresh scum of the press, they furnish one side of a shop, which serves for the sign of a bookseller rather than a real one; but instead of selling, deal as factors, and procure what the country divines and gentry send for, of whom each hath his book factor, and wanting anything, writes to his bookseller, and pays his bill. And it is wretched to consider what pickpocket-work, with help of the press, these demi-booksellers make. They crack their brains to find out selling subjects, and keep hirelings in garrets at hard meat to write and correct by the great,[1] and so puff up an octavo to a sufficient thickness, and there's six shillings current for one and a half hours' reading, and perhaps never to be read or looked on after. One that would go higher must take his fortune at blank walls and corners of streets, or repair to the sign of Bateman, Innys,* and one or two more, where are best choice and better penn'orths. I might touch other abuses, as bad paper, incorrect printing (no erratas, for those are out of fashion), and false advertising, all which, and worse, is to be expected, if a careful author is not at the heels of them. But I fear myself led by these too far out of my way.

21 *Read through, noted, but not commonplaced his authors*
I return therefore to our doctor, who in his studies was very regular, and took his authors one after another, and pursued effectually through them, not leaving behind any passage which he did not understand, or at least criticize, as far as he could reach. He noted as he went along, but not in the common way by commonplace, but every book severally, setting down whatever he found worthily to be observed in that book. And these he kept by themselves, as commentations upon his authors, till he had a considerable body of them. But they are all confounded by a deplorable sentence of which I shall give an account afterwards.[1]

22 *Applied to the tongues, and lost no time*
Greek became almost vernacular to him, and he took no small pains to make himself master of the Hebrew language, and seldom failed carrying an Hebrew bible (but pointed)[1] to church with him. He was a notable husband of his time, and contrived to

20:1 At a fixed price for the whole amount
21:1 In sections 69–70
22:1 With marks to indicate vowels, stress, accent, etc.

make his very scraps and intercalary[2] minutes profitable; and accordingly during those short intervals, between dressing and dinner and such like attendances, when he could not engage in the texture of his study, he used to get the best-penned English books and read them aloud, which he said he did to form or improve his English style and pronunciation. And on such occasions, he used to say, it was pity to lose any of his time. And for the advantage of his Latin, he used to keep his accounts in that language, and as near the classic dialect as he could.

23 *Made society instructive*

He had a very researching spirit that would not rest, even in ordinary company and conversation, for with such as studied, he never failed to ask or propose some points of literature, and then by throwing out his own sentiments fish for the reasons and opinions of the company, and thereby, perhaps, found occasion to correct himself as to some oversights or mistakes he had been guilty of. In short, there was not an opportunity that fell in his way whereby he might improve himself which he willingly let slip. And all this derived upon a native good sense; he had nobody at his heels to urge him forward. His tutor was passive, and the scholar soon fell to shift for himself, as a bird that had learned to pick alone, and having tasted the fruit of knowledge pursued it with an uninterrupted perseverance.

24 *Empty discourse and pastime not to his taste*

And somewhat less of that might have been better for him. He kept himself bent with perpetual thinking and study, which manifestly impaired his health. Even conversation, which used to relieve others, was to him an incentive of thought. He was sensible of this, but did not affect any expedients of relief to his mind. I have heard him say that he believed if Sir Isaac Newton had not wrought with his hands in making experiments, he had killed himself with study; a man may so engage his mind as almost to forget he hath a body, which must be waited upon and served.* The doctor could oversee in himself what in others plainly appeared to him. After dinners and in evenings he kept company with the fellows and fellow commoners in the garden, but not long, for he could not be pleased with such insipid pastime as bowls, or less material discourse such as town tales and punning, of which take this instance: one of the fellows had a fancy to cut upon the trees the first two letters of his name, T.P. The doctor asked the fellow what ailed him to make his mark so upon every tree, and he answered, 'The more there is T.P., the more's the P.T.,' as if the fellow had caught what he fished for, a pun.*

22:2 Interpolated; intervening

25 *Attempted music upon the organ, but failed*
The doctor had no favourite diversion or manual exercise to rest his mind a little, which he held bent with continual thinking. His parents, who were much addicted to music, recommended that to him for a diversion, and particularly the noble organ, as the fullest and not only a complete solitary consort, but most proper for an ecclesiastic. And indeed if study had not had the upper hand of all his intendments, he must of course have taken up in that way, being *quasi ex traduce*,¹ for after the care of prayers and meals, nothing was more constant and solemn than music was in that family.* He was sensible the advice was very good, and accordingly got a small organ into his chamber at Jesus College, and suffered himself to be taught a lesson or two, which he practised over when he had a mind to be unbent. But he made no manner of advance, and one accident put him out of all conceit of it. His under-neighbour was a morose and importune master of arts,* and one night the doctor could not sleep and thought to fit himself for it by playing on his organ. The bellows knocking on the floor and the hum of the pipes made a strange din at midnight, and the gentleman below, that never heard it so before, could not tell what to make of it, and at length found it out to be his neighbour's organ. And thereupon to retaliate this night work, got out of his bed and with his two couple of bowls, went to bowls by himself, which made a much louder noise than the organ, and the doctor was as much [at] a loss to know what that meant, but suspecting how the case stood, left off and scarce ever touched his organ after. The pleasure of music is like that of books, never true and good unless easily and familiarly read or performed, and then nothing is more medicinal to a crazy and fatigued mind than that – *musica mentis medecina moestae.*²

26 *Diverted himself with feeding spiders in great glasses*
The doctor had found out one petit entertainment in his study besides books, and that was keeping of great house spiders in wide-mouthed glasses, such as men keep tobacco in. When he had them safe in hold, he supplied them with crumbs of bread, which they eat rather than starve, but their regale was flies, which he sometimes caught and put to them. When their imprisonment appeared inevitable, they fell to their trade of webbing, and made large expansions and more private recesses. It pleased him to observe the animals manage their interest in the great work of taking their prey: if it was a small fly given them, no more ceremony but take and eat him; but if a great master flesh fly, then to work, twenty courses round, and perhaps not

25:1 As if propagated
25:2 Music is the medicine of the troubled mind, from Walter Haddon's 'De musica,' in *Poemata ... lucubrationes*, ed T. Thatcher (1567), p 69, misnumbered p 66.

come near him, for he had claws sharp as cats', and after divers starts to and fro, a web was with an hind leg dexterously clapped over two or three of his legs, and after all his claws were in that manner secured, then at a running pull a broad web was brought over him, which bound him hand and foot, and by an affixation to the spider's tail, the fly was carried off into one of his inmost recesses, there to be feasted upon at leisure.

27 *Their course of life, and casting their skin*

Spiders, like other creatures of prey, eat one and other, and for their continual design of eating are paid by a continual dread of being eaten. Two old spiders will not be kept in one glass, unless accidentally known to each other, or it may be male and female, but to work they go, coursing about, till the one hath got the better of the other, and then falls on, and heartily feeds upon him. They breed numerously, and the young ones, *patrizando*,[1] use the same trade. The danger, as well as fear, is common to all, there is little regard to relation or families, and for that reason, like pikes in a pond, none ever takes a prey but he turns suddenly round, lest another should take him. And when the young are hatched and can run about, they lie still, watching advantages over the rest, and care not rashly to expose themselves. If they are disturbed and some made to run, then the whole nation is alarmed, and many a life falls in the disorder before the wars cease, and then each that survives makes merry with his booty. Thus their numbers are reduced to a very few, who find means to retreat into castles of their own making. They cast their skins at certain periods, and the manner of doing it is remarkable. They hang themselves to the ceiling of their web, with their body downwards, and holding themselves fast up by all their legs brought together, remain striving and pulling each leg till it comes out of the hose, and their body is freed from its case, and then they turn about and run away, leaving the exuviae in their place, as we often see them hanging in cobwebs. The signal to them of this change coming on is a dry parting of the skin upon their backs, whereupon they fall to work as was described. The doctor used to divert us with describing the course of life which his poor prisoners led.

28 *Witty in company but rigidly sober*

When the doctor was abroad and absent from his studies, either by visits, friendly meetings, or attendances, his chief delight was in discourse, and would apply himself to all sorts of company, in a brisk and piquant manner. For he was very just and ready in his speech, facetious and fluent, and his wit was never at a nonplus. I have known him at act-keeping suppers* as merry as the best, and though he drank little or nothing, he sparkled and reparteed, not only saving himself harmless (for the sober

27:1 Taking after their fathers (*OED* records only the infinitive: patrizate.)

man is commonly the mark), but returned the bite. His sobriety was so extraordinary that, with entire assurance, I can affirm that never in all his life did he know what a cup too much (as they term it) was. And this continence was more singular in him, who was really a wit in conversation, and his company desired by all people that knew him; and it is well known how much such qualifications seduce men to come under the jurisdiction of the bottle. But this abstemiousness in extremity proved of ill consequence to his health, as will be showed in fit place.[1]

29 *Affected congresses with foreigners and virtuosi*
When any eminent or extraordinary persons came to the university, of whom some had considerable recommendations, and for the better knowledge of the university made some short residence there, and were by divers gentlemen civilly entertained, whether Swedish or Hungarian clergy, Oxonians, or other homebred virtuosi, the doctor very often, as he desired, made one in the conversation, whereby he thought to gather somewhat out of the common road. And being desired, he often wrote in the foreigner's albo (or travelling notebook) a sentence with his name, and that implies a small token, which I know well, being once induced by him to do the like. I remember one Mr Wagstaffe, a little gentleman,* had an express audience at a very good dinner, upon the subject of spectres, and much was said pro and con, but I carried away little but a good meal. The doctor often upon such occasions as these took me along with him, which was much for my advantage if I had been capable of making a true use of it. But as for the spectre affair, it was not long before the gentleman published his notions in a little book of witchcraft.*

30 *Left the common-room and passed evenings in private society*
At length the doctor declined the common parlour, and spent the (after supper) evenings in private society, sometimes at Dr Sherman's, the president's, and not seldom at his old master's, Dr Stephens',* who lived in the house over against the college. This agreed best with his humour, who did not love morosity and sour looks. He was always jocose, and free in his ordinary conversation, and that made him very popular with the airy folks, as young gentlemen, and even with the fair sex, for he was a person comely, and withal very decently behaved and respectful, which set off his piquant wit, and with that he always made them an agreeable diversion. Whatever his company was, he was always ready with proper discourse, and, as I said, no niggard of it. If he moved subjects that seemed slight, yet he had a design at the bottom, either to exercise some useful talent of his own, or to squeeze somewhat useful out of others, and for that reason he affected most the acquaintance and society of such as were in station or learning his superiors.

28:1 In section 85

31   *Affected the society of the young quality, and why*

Next to those, he affected to refresh himself with the society of the young noblemen and fellow commoners, and used to say that he found more of candour and sincerity in them than in the graver sort. And for like reason he inclined to those of the ancienter families, though he owned that the better parts were found with the latter. Sorting himself with these, he took great delight to oppose their raw wits with enigmatic questions, and often out of the classics. I have seen him as merry as a schoolboy, with a knot of them, like the younglings about old Silenus,* in deep consult about reconciling that passage in Ovid: *sine pondere habentia pondus*.[1]

32   *Among those, his choice was nice*

He was more attached to those who were noted for study and learning extraordinary, as Mr Walpole, Sir Edmund Bacon,* etc., which latter was a stout and early pretender to freethinking. The doctor used to pump him to fetch up his most reserved reasonings, and used to say that he found such conversation profitable, because it made him digest matters in his own mind more effectually than, not being opposed, he could have done. He was very intimate with Mr Hatton, a fellow commoner, afterwards Sir Christopher.* He was of a merry and free disposition, and suited the doctor's humour exactly, the rather because he found at the bottom of him a sound judgment and notable censure of most incidents, I might as well say persons. I have heard the doctor say that that gentleman had more good sense and understanding than many were able to discern.

33   *Advanced his acquaintance in London, and sharp upon the ladies*

These were his university society. But in and about London he fell into more considerable and important acquaintance. For when he gave himself the satisfaction to reside a little with his best brother in London, he was introduced, and a small inlet served to list him in a spacious catalogue of vertuosi: as the Capels* and Godolphins. First Mr Sydney Godolphin of the Middle Temple,* a very ingenious person and master of an exquisite library, which to rummage was to the doctor always a feast. After the death of that gentleman, his brother Mr Charles* succeeded him, as well in his chamber and library, as in the doctor's acquaintance, and continued in the same chamber, until by the fire, most unfortunately begun overhead, he was burnt out, and his choice collection of books consumed.* I shall venture to name one or two more. One was Sir John King, who was a Tully in Westminster Hall.* Mr William Longueville,* in polite knowledge as well as skill in the law inferior to none, and what exceeds all, of untainted integrity. And I might mention some ladies with whom he pretended to be innocently merry and free; and indeed more so (often)

31:1   Things having weight [strove against things] without weight (from the description of Chaos in Ovid, *Metamorphoses*, 1:20).

than welcome, as when he touched the pre-eminences of their sex, as for instance saying that of all the beasts of the field God Almighty thought woman the fittest companion for man. I have known him demand of the ladies at [the] upper end of the table, by right of their sitting there, to be carved,* 'Else,' said he, 'let 'em come down to their places at the lower end.' These passages and the like that he frequently uttered show somewhat of his humour and which made him very popular with the ladies and young company. For notwithstan[ding] all his seriousness and study, none ever was more agreeably talkative in fit company than he was.

34 *Meditated changing his college and why*
But whatever the cause was, he had no relish at all of the conversation of his fellow collegiates, and they, I presume, had as little of his. He might not conform in their measures or methods of living, or there being a seeming inequality betwixt them by his place in the university and advantages with respect to preferment, and his consorting rather with the younger gentlemen than the grave, and, as he thought, perhaps, empty seniors of the college, and affecting a select of the learneder sort in other colleges – all these ingredients turned sour, and jealousies, suspicions, and reflections, with morose countenances, bred out of them, so that he desired if possible without his great inconvenience to remove himself to some other college, where, as he proposed, he might pass his time more agreeably.

35 *Preferred by the Archbishop of Canterbury to a sinecure in Wales*
And in this he was gratified by the fortune of a preferment which fell to his share. It was a sinecure in Wales, being a moiety of the tithes of Llandinam.* He had the good fortune to be capable of preferment in the church, when Dr Sheldon* was Archbishop of Canterbury.* For that prelate was a friend to quality, but more to scholarship and good order, and could not overlook a scholar come forward in the university, so well recommended as the doctor was. And of his own motion, without any solicitation or so much as notice on the doctor's part, conferred this sinecure upon him, and at the same time declared that he chose to give him that rather than any other preferment, meaning such as in consequence might have removed him out of his station of learning and study in the university. And for the same reason it was most suitable to the doctor's own inclinations, for it set him free, with a power uncontrollable to settle himself in what way he pleased.

36 *His behaviour in concerns more public*
I have hitherto dealt enough with the slighter circumstances of our doctor's character, *sed paulo majora canamus.*[1] As to the public, and the orders of the university, about congregations and elections, which matters use to call the scholars from their

---

36:1 But let us celebrate bigger things: Virgil, *Eclogue* 4.1.

studies into faction and party-making, the doctor was always disposed to quiet, and little concerned himself with them. He held a due respect to superiors, especially in politicals.[2] And in all his behaviour and conversation in the university, he showed an innate hatred of popular faction, as well that which had been seminated all over England, and began to pullulate in the university against the court and government of King Charles II, as also all those perverse and contradictory doings in his time too much agitated, with intent to cross the heads, or some as irrational designs.[3] I have heard him say that he wondered men professing philosophy and learning should not judge, but follow one and other like a rabble blindly, as if they had not the use of thinking. And he used to say sharper things, but for the sake of our *Alma Mater*, I forbear them.

37 *Generally esteemed, observer of order and lectures, and his opinion of them*
Few persons ever had more propitious circumstances of recommendation to render him esteemed than the doctor had, for besides his person and countenance seeming always juvenile and flourishing, his relation to many noble families, being an excellent scholar, industrious, sober without interruption, and in his manners devoted to all good order, religion, and virtue, set him upon an eminence; and so many not common symptoms of speedy preferment made him be more than ordinarily observed, and (perhaps) envied. Nothing observed of him turned more to his credit than his due attendance at public exercises and lectures of most faculties in the schools, which was an unusual but very profitable diligence. I have been told this observation of him by some of our neighbour ministers that were his contemporaries, and also that great account was made of him for it amongst them, who knew little beside such remarkables of him. His opinion was that since books are so frequent as now they are, public lectures are not so necessary, or (perhaps) useful, as in elder times when first instituted, because the intent of them was to supply the want of books, and now books are plenty, lectures might better be spared, and the promiscuous use of books come in the place of them.*

38 *Kept chapel and followed no coffee-house*
The doctor conformed to all the orders of the college, seldom ate out of the hall, and then upon a fish day only, being told it was for his health. He was constantly at the chapel prayers, so much as one may say that being in town he never failed. This in the morning secured his time, for he went from thence directly to his study without any sizings[1] or breakfast at all. While he was at Jesus College, coffee was not of such

36:2 Political matters; politics
36:3 See section 90.
38:1 Food from buttery or kitchen

common use as afterwards, and coffee-houses but young. At that time and long after there was but one, kept by one Kirk.* The trade of news also was scarce set up, for they had only the public gazette, till Kirk got a written newsletter circulated by one Muddiman.* But now the case is much altered, for it is become a custom after chapel to repair to one or other of the coffee-houses (for there are divers), where hours are spent in talking, and less profitable reading of newspapers, of which swarms are continually supplied from London. And the scholars generally as so entête[2] after news (which is none of their business) that they neglect all for it. And it is become very rare for any of them to go directly to his chamber after prayers without first doing his suit[3] at the coffee-house, which is a vast loss of time grown out of a pure novelty. For who can apply close to a subject with his head full of the din of a coffee-house?* I cannot but think that since coffee with most is become a morning refreshment, the order which I knew once observed in Lambeth House, or somewhat like it, might be introduced in the colleges, which was for the chaplains and gentlemen officers to meet every morning in a sort of stillhouse, where a good woman provided them their liquors as they liked best, and this they called their coffee-house; but of this *viderit utilitas*.[4]

39 *Proved his forces in the pulpit, and preached before King Charles II*

His commonplacing, which is a sort of dissectation[1] upon some learned subject, in the chapel, was a sort of preface to his attempting to preach. But he used a precaution more positive, for before he went into orders, he procured a pulpit at one of the villages near Cambridge usually served by a fellow of the college, and there preached once or twice. This he did to prove his forces and acquire some assurance before he undertook to perform more publicly.* The first sermon that he preached in a solemn audience was before the king at Newmarket, upon a mission from the university. That was a severe trial of his spirits, and he went with a great reluctance of mind. But – *audendum tamen*.[2] Reason and resolution prevailed, and he was not abashed at so great a presence. He said that he made it a law to himself to confine his view above the people, to a certain space which he was not to exceed, and in speaking to a multitude it is a good rule to mind none of them. The sermon is in print by John Hays, 1671.* The text was the first verse of the first psalm, and the discourse moral, fit for an assembly not overzealous that way.* The king was pleased to signify his approval of it by saying as he came out of the church that the preacher would soon be

38:2 Infatuated
38:3 Attending, as at a court
38:4 Loosely, experience will show.
39:1 Critical analysis (perhaps a coinage of North's, an elaboration of dissection).
39:2 However, one must dare.

a bishop. And if his majesty had lived a little longer, he might have proved himself a prophet, but his as well as the doctor's untimely death fell in the way of that event. The ladies were pleased also to accept the doctor's discourse. One of them, being asked how she liked Mr North's sermon, said that he was an handsome man, and had pretty doctrine.

40 *Made his father's chaplain recant a vile heresy*
The doctor had an opportunity of exercising his divinity faculty upon one of his father's chaplains. His father, as had been sometimes used in that family, wrote formally to the University of Cambridge for a chaplain, and they sent him one Kitchenman,[1] a townsman's son. He was very illiterate, but thought to supply that defect by extraordinary giftedness,[2] and behaved himself so fanatically that he was not endured. After him came a brother of his, thought to be a little better scholar, and looked more like a minister of the English church. This latter, when the doctor was present, preached most damnable heresy, *videlicet*, that our blessed Saviour was the carnal son of Joseph. This nettled our young divine, and immediately after he had dined, took him to task in his chamber, and so tutored him that he thought fit next Sunday to preach a recantation sermon, begging God's pardon and the congregation's excuse for his vile error and heresy, unthinkingly preached there the Sunday before.

41 *Some of the doctor's journeys*
The doctor was no great traveller, but sometimes he affected to go abroad, and if he had his choice always on horseback, for he fancied that exercise good for his health, and particularly in the case of gravel, with which he was troubled. Between Cambridge and his father's house,* and to and from London, were the chief of his journeys. And if his post was in the coach, he chose to commute with an horseman. Once after riding a very long journey, he came into the room in the inn where the company was, and threw himself down upon the bed. 'Now,' said he, 'I have the pleasure of being very weary.' He often visited Sir Roger Burgoyne,* a virtuous and learned gentleman near Cambridge. And once at the instance of his mother he made a visit to the Lady Hatton, her sister,* at Kirby in Northamptonshire. He found his aunt there, derelicted by her husband, the old Lord Hatton.* He lived in Scotland Yard, and diverted himself with the company and discourse of players and such idle people that came to him, while his family lived in want at Kirby. He had committed the whole conduct there to a favourite daughter, who was not over-kind to her

40:1 MS has Kitch _____n (full name supplied from BL, Add. MSS 32,516, f 29).
40:2 Faculty or power from the Holy Ghost

mother. This noble lord had bright parts and professed also to be religious, for he published the book of psalms, with a prayer suitable to each, formed by himself, which book is called Hatton's *Psalms*,* and may be found in divers devout persons' closets; such difference is often found between men's pretensions and actions. The famous 'Nando Masham* used in his drink to curse him for writing psalms (as he termed it) and not paying a debt due to him.

42 *The Lord Hatton's piety towards his desolate mother*

The good old lady gave her nephew as good entertainment as she could, that is, took him into hugger mugger[1] in her closet, where she usually had some good pie, or plum cake, which her neighbours, in compassion, sent her in, for the housekeeping was very mean, and she had not the command of anything. When her lord died, the care of her, and of the whole family and the ruined estate of it, devolved upon the truly noble man, her eldest son,* who by an unparalleled prudence and application repaired the shattered estate, set his brother (the incomparable Charles Hatton) and sisters at ease.* And his signal and pious care of his good mother is never to be forgot. For he took her, destitute of all jointure and provision, home to him, and entertained her with all the indulgence and comfort he could. And the lady was pleased to declare that the latter end of her age was the beginning of the true comfort of her life.

43 *A providential reward for it*

It may be observed by those that know much of times, and read the historical accounts given of them to posterity, that many, and perhaps the most important, passages are not to be found in the histories. As in topography, some, but not half, of the remarkables of a country are to be found.[1] Where in our most voluminous writers, to say no worse, do we find an account of the providential escape of this noble lord? I must profess that in my judgment, considering his apparent goodness and merit, and the tremendous calamity that fell upon his family from the hand of heaven, his person was almost miraculously preserved. There never was an incident more indicative of a special providence than this was. Therefore I may be excused if I give here a short memorandum of it.

His lordship was governor of Guernsey, and settled with his family in the castle. There was his mother, his then wife (the Countess of Thanet's daughter),* and divers of his children, and many servants. The castle stood upon the rocks washed by the sea, and one night when all were abed, and his lordship and his lady asleep, a

---

42:1 Concealment; secrecy
43:1 'To be found' deleted in MS, replaced with 'commonly wanting.' The revision, presumably to avoid repetition of a phrase in the preceding sentence, inadvertently introduced a confusion.

thunderstorm fired the magazine of gunpowder, and blew up the whole fabric. His mother, and wife, and some of his children, and some others, were killed right out. His lordship in his bed was carried and lodged upon the castle wall, whence was a dismal precipice among the rocks into the sea. His lordship, perceiving a mighty disorder, was going to step out of his bed to know what the matter was, which if he had done, he had been irrecoverably lost, but in the instant of his moving, a flash of lightning came and showed him the precipice, whereupon he lay still till people came and took him down. And so was this noble lord wonderfully, or rather, as I said, miraculously, preserved.*

44 Journey to his sinecure, and kind entertainment in Wales

The greatest of the doctor's travels was into Wales, to visit and be possessed of his non-cure at Llandinam. His design was to have gone incognito, but by means of an extraordinary civility he was discovered, and then he was forced to receive a great deal more, for falling among the Morgans and Mansels, who honoured him with a claim of kindred,* he could not pass without being generously entertained. He came to a Welsh village (to say no worse) in order to lodge for one night, and the gentleman that lived in the town, being informed that a genteel young parson was come to lodge at the alehouse, sent and invited him to take an hard bed (as they say) at his house. The doctor complied, and after his name, relation, and errand was squeezed out of him, he must submit to be conducted from house to house, company of the country attending, and at some he stayed a week, or less, as need required, for he made himself acceptable everywhere, conforming to the ordinary ways of entertainment in use there, and consistent with his character. Sometimes in the afternoon they went to a clean but mean alehouse, and the maid that served the Welsh ale usually made a curtsey and drank to the best in the company, then he kissed her, and the frolic went round. But once coming to the doctor, he drank his cup but omitted the ceremony that was to follow. The maid, who perhaps had more mind to the smooth-chinned parson than to any of the rest, made him a curtsey and 'Sir,' said she, 'I perceive you do like no Wels 'oman.' I remember the doctor told us that when he came to his parish, he found the humour of the people very different from what on like occasions was often found in England. For instead of grumbling and affronting at a new tithemonger come down amongst them, too often known in English villages, the parishioners came about and hugged him, calling him their pastor, and telling him they were his 'sheeeep.' After he had made his escapade from his many good landlords, he got him back to his college as fast as he could.

45 His voyage to Oxford; acquaintance and entertainment there

Whilst the doctor passed some time at his best brother's house in Oxfordshire,* he desired to make use of that opportunity to visit the University of Oxford, and to make himself acquainted with some of the eminent men there. And so we equipped, and on the road fell in with a reverend divine, one Dr Hutton,* fellow of a college, and minister of Aynho-super-Montem, who was bound for the same port. Neither he nor our doctor knew each other but by rumour, but as travellers for their pastime on the road love to acquaint, so they, and began a sort of amity as well as familiarity. This was a most propitious incident, for Dr Hutton not only entertained us most humanely, but attended the doctor in his visits of the colleges and schools, and introduced him into the knowledge of the proceres[1] (as I may call them) of the university, and particularly the great Dr Fell,* who was truly great in all his circumstances, capacities, undertakings, and learning, and above all for his super-abundant public spirit, and good will, which shined in his care of the youth, especially those of quality in the university. Oh, the felicity of that age and place, when his authority swayed. He led us about, and showed his printing office and talked of his designs there, and the discourse fell wholly upon learning, books, and learned men. But I was not capable to bring away much, and remember none, and for that reason do not take upon me to account for anything at all of it. But I am sure our doctor was much caressed, and with those persons whom we happened to converse with, seeming the most considerable, he was courted as one whose conversation they apparently affected to compass and enjoy.

46 *Removed to Collegium Trinitatis to be near the master, Dr Barrow*

The addition of this Welsh preferment, being as I take it a cure of souls though a vicar endowed exercised it, might second the doctor's desires to change his college, as being incompatible with his fellowship, on which account only I believe he stayed so long there. And thereupon he procured himself to be admitted of Trinity College, had a chamber assigned him, and removed all his effects, as they say, thither. He used to allege many reasons for his choice of that college: as that he valued much the company of that society where resided many excellent persons, and he perceived more of the humane and polite in that, than in the lesser colleges. But above all, the leading card was the value he had for the more than thrice excellent master, Dr Barrow.* He had long before contracted a familiar acquaintance, I may say friend-ship, with him, and they used each other in a most delightful communication of thoughts. The good Dr Barrow ended his days in London, in a prebend's house that had a little stair to it out of the cloisters, which made him call it a man's nest, and I presume it is so called at this day.* The master's disease was an high fever. It had been his custom, contracted when (upon the fund of a travelling fellowship) he was at Constantinople, in all his maladies to cure himself with opium, and being very ill (probably) he augmented his dose, and so inflamed his fever and at the same

45:1 Chief men

obstructed the crisis. For he was as a man knocked down, and had the eyes of one distracted. Our doctor seeing him so was struck with an horror, for he that knew him so well in his best health could best distinguish. And when he left him, he concluded he should see him no more alive, and so it proved.*

47 *After Barrow, made Master of Trinity, which proved a burthen*
After the death of this most worthy person, our doctor had the mastership of Trinity conferred upon him,* and thereby possessed, as he thought, all the ease and content he could by any means propose to himself, and from thence dated, as from an epocha, the repose he had in present and in future hoped to enjoy. He accounted himself very well settled when he lived as a common master of arts in the college without any aid from the revenues of the society he thought himself happy enough.[1] What then must the alteration be when he was master, and had so great an increase of revenue and accommodation as that station afforded? But oh, the difference of a private condition and magistracy. Before, when the doctor had no charge of government upon his spirits but of himself and his studies only, he was in all respects easy. But after this preferment, than which nothing could have more nicely suited his desires and ambition, he fell under such gnawing cares and anxieties that he had small joy of his life, and it was really shortened thereby, of which in its proper place.[2] For (to speak ironically) he was so unadvised to think of duty and justice in government, and for that reason ought to be made, as he was, an example for the terror of others who (by rare chance) may fall under the mistake of such bad maxims. But here we are a little too forward.

48 *Laboured in the Greek, and was made professor, and his sentiments*
During his former residence in Trinity College, the doctor persevered in his application to the Greek literature, and his time and pains therein was not lost, for he made such advances that he was reputed one of the best Grecians in the university. And accordingly in November 1672 he was elected *Professor graecae linguae.** That service obliged him to lecture publicly in the schools at appointed times, which he performed most punctually, and thereby confirmed the opinion [that] was preconceived of him, for he was really a prime critic in that language. He used to say that a due knowledge of the Greek tongue was absolutely necessary for a divine, and as the Grecian, so the divine. He much wondered to see that skill so much slighted and laid aside as it was by the clergy in general, as appeared manifestly by the books they seek after. For one solely Greek, though a capital author, bears little price and indeed is scarce saleable, but a worse edition counter-columned with the Latin translation, or a

47:1 The phrase 'he thought ... enough' is a later addition interlined on the MS, inadvertently introducing a redundancy.
47:2 Section 85

mere translation, is everyone's money, and (comparatively) at great rates. For his part, he did not see with what face a man could pretend to be of the clergy and not understand Greek, since not only the Bible but most ancient ecclesiastical writers were in Greek. And the idiom of that language, not justly transferable into any common speech, gives the greatest light towards clearing obscure questions in divinity. Latin and the vernaculars westward, which are almost all deduced under it, carry nearly the same idioms, but the orientals and Greek partake little or nothing of them.

49 *A flattering epigram in Dr Duport's poems translated*

There is a notable recognition of our doctor's skill in Greek left by Dr Duport, his predecessor, who was a famous Grecian.* It is a congratulatory poem upon our doctor's election, and printed with his epigrams in octavo by John Hays 1676, folio 60.* This compliment being intended for the doctor's honour, who by many was thought too young for that post, shall be here inserted. And I shall join a sorry translation, which being better than none at all, is enough for me to undertake; therefore poetic lustre is not to be expected in it.[1]

Ad Joannem Northum, Armigerum, Baronis Northi filium, Regium Graecae Linguae Professorum Cantab. nuper electum, Gratulatorium

Salve Nobilis, erudite, Northe,
Linguae nobilis, et pereruditae,
Linguae scilicet Hellados Professor;
Ante annos Cathedram occupans virilem:
Qui Graecos prope junior domasti,
Quam Persas Macedo ille magnus olim;
Non bello, aut acie, nisi ingeni; ergo
Hac fretus capis Atticas Athenas
Hac tu Dorica castra, Pindarique
Heroas, Nemeosque, Pythiosque
Victores, pugiles Olympicosque;
Hac aenigmata, quae plicat Lycophron,
Et Demosthenis, Aeschinisque, robur,
Hac et Thycydidis tonantis ora,
Cum rugit leo, sustines, fugasque:
Stagiritica nec vepreta densa,
Nicandri, nec Alexipharmaca atri,

49:1 The poem and translation appear side by side in the MS. Several minor variations introduced into North's transcription have been corrected.

Nec τὰ σκληρὰ Theocriti, Aeschylive
Grandes, nec Sophoclis, times cothurnos,
Hac lingua sapis Atticos lepores,
Hac mel Cecropium, salesque; puros:
Cunctas hac face discutis tenebras
Graecorum, et monumenta prorsa, vorsa,
Illustras, Tragicique pellis umbras
Mentis lumine, Comicique Nubes
profligas, Aquilo, facisque sudum.
Macte hac arte tua peritiaque;
Et Cum coeperis, esse perge noster
In Graecis, juvenis, senum Magister.
Spartam denique nactus, immo Athenas,
Has orna; et procerum doceto pullos
Torporem Excutere, et vacare Musis,
Exemploque tuo esse litteratos.
Sic tu, Nobilis, erudite Northe,
Graecae perpetuum Professionis
Ornamentum eris, et decus Cathedrae.

To John North Esquire, son of Lord North, lately chosen to be the Regius Professor of the Greek Language in Cambridge, a congratulation
Save you noble learned North,
professor of a noble and learned language,
that of the Greeks. Before due age
you fill a manly chair,
having subdued the Greeks younger
than the great Macedonian did the Persians,*
not with war, or armies other than of understanding.
So armed you take the Attic city,
so the Doric camps,* and those of Pindar,
Nemean and Pythian heroes,*
victors, champions, and Olympics;
so the enigmas convolved by Lycophron,*
and the powers of Demosthenes, and Aeschines;
so the thundering voice of Thucydides.
When the lion roars you resist, and repel
the Stagiritics.* Neither the thorny thickets,
nor the Alexipharmics of dark Nicander,*
nor the rustics of Theocritus,* or of Aeschylus.
nor of Sophocles the stately buskins,* do you fear.

In this tongue, you taste the Attic graces,
Cecropian honey,* and untainted wit.
With this taper you disperse the dark mysteries
of the Greeks, and their monuments every way
illuminate, and rout the shades of the tragedian,
and with the light of thought you drive away
the comic clouds,
and, oh North, turn all to fair weather.
Go on in this, the art and skill,
and once entered, proceed, though young,
in Greek, and be a tutor to us your seniors.
Having taken Sparta, nay Athens,
adorn them, and instruct the young nobility
to shake off ease, and incline to study,
and offer your example to become learned.
So honourable and learned North, you
shall be to the Greek profession a perpetual
ornament, and the honour of the chair.

50 *The translation excused*
I do not pretend the translation here, though unconfined from any rule of verse, is exact and hits the sense of the author precisely, and who but a professed master of the Greek learning, as Dr Duport was, can do it? But I verily believe that not many of our makers of verses would have done it truer, though perhaps more clinquant,[1] therefore *tale quale*,[2] this must go. The poem itself might pass, but for one Aquilonian pun. Because Boreas in Homer is a clearer of the air, North must interpret Aristophanes' comedy tituled *Nubes*, and so by the style of Aquilo, make clear weather.* The doctor (Duport) was a very little man, and inclined strangely to such little conceits. Even in the chair, when he was deputed Regius Professor of Divinity, and styled *pater*, he could not forbear saying *sum paterculus, sed non Velleius*.[3] But bating him that ace,[4] he was truly a great man.

51 *Formerly was Clerk of the Closet to King Charles* II
Our doctor, before he was Master of Trinity or had any preferment of the gift of the crown, waited as Clerk of the Closet to King Charles II.* That post was not only a sure

50:1 Glittering; tinselled
50:2 Such as it is
50:3 I am a little father, but not Velleius. Velleius Paterculus (ca 19 BC–after AD 31), author of
       Historiae romanae
50:4 Making that slight abatement

track to preferment in the church, but agreed exceeding well with his humour, for there he lived upon an hill and saw how the world went, and withal had his cell to retire to, which was a very convenient lodging in Whitehall upon the parade of the court, near the presence chamber. And his diet was provided for him, and the chaplains-in-waiting were company to his wish. At the beginning, he was in danger of being troubled with impertinent visits, which had proved cross to him whose design and pastime was reading and thinking; for at court there is always a sort of people whose day labour is having nothing to do, and are apt to say, 'Come shall we go, and spend half an hour with Mr Clerk of the Closet?' and adding 'to drink a glass of wine or ale,' who could resist? But he had a caution given by a friendly old courtier not to entertain at his chamber on any account, not so much as with small beer in hot weather, for if he did, his quiet would forsake him. All advice is acceptable to those that are inclined aforehand to take it, as the doctor was, who lived like an hermit in his cell in the midst of the court, and proved the title of a foolish French writer, *La Solitude de la cour*.*

52   *Dealt as a confessor to the devotees in Whitehall*
I have heard him say that in times before the reformation, by institution, or usage, the Clerk of the Closet was the proper confessor of the court. And when he resided there, divers persons, far from papists, especially ladies who thought auricular confession, though no duty, a pious practice, applied to him for like purposes and to ease their minds. And he as piously conformed, and did the office of a pastor or parochus[1] of the court. I have also heard him say that for the number of persons that resided in the court, a place reputed a centre of all vice and irreligion, he thought there were as many truly pious and strictly religious as could be found in any other resort whatsoever. And he never saw so much fervent devotion, and such frequent acts of piety and charity, as his station gave him occasion to observe there.* It often falls out that extremes are conterminous, and as contraries illustrate each other, so here, virtue and vice. Therefore it is not reasonable to condemn aggregates of any denomination, or the individuals separately, for the practices of some, although they may be the ruling party amongst them.

53   *Obtained a prebendary of Westminster*
During this sunshine of favour, the doctor obtained a prebendary of Westminster,* which also suited him well, because there was an house and accommodations for living in town, and the content and joy he conceived in being a member of so considerable a body of learned men and dignified in the church, as the college of prebends were. Absolutely unlike an inferior college in the university, here was no

52:1   A parish clergyman

faction, division, or uneasiness, but as becoming persons learned and wise, they lived truly as brethren, quarrelling being never found but among fools or knaves. He used to deplore the bad condition of the cathedral church, which to support was [as] much as they were able to do. It was an extensive and industrious managery to carry on the repairs. And of latter time so much hath been laid out that way as would have rebuilt some part of it. This residence was one of the asylums where he found some ease and comfort in his deplorable weakness, as I shall show when I come to that melancholy pass.[1]

54 *Accepted and greatly esteemed by the Duke of Lauderdale*

The doctor was much honoured by the countenance, or rather friendship, of the Duke of Lauderdale.* He was His Majesty's Commissioner for Scotland, and being himself a very learned man, was a great favourer and encourager of all such. The doctor came first into his cognizance by the means of his duchess. When she was a widow with the title of Countess of Dysart, she lived at Fakenham in Suffolk, not far from the doctor's relations, who neighbourly corresponded.* This lady's two sons, the Tollemaches,* and the doctor were playfellows at school and at home, and after he was grown up she desired to see him, and he often waited upon her, and most respectfully answered her severe catechizations, for she was a lady of abundant wit and knowledge of state affairs and the court. Thence the transit was direct into the conversation of the duke, who finding the doctor a well-read scholar, judicious, and in the learned languages a critic, and what at that time was too much wanted among the men of parts, of loyal principles, sustained by reasons of duty and policy inexpugnable, greatly esteemed and frequently admitted him into a familiarity of converse with him. He communicated his library, which was spacious and furnished with books that were curious and recherché, especially *in rebus biblicis*.[1] And there was opportunity of discoursing of editions and criticism, and also of (what had been much the duke's study) the subjects of popery and fanaticism.

55 *Created Doctor of Divinity in the presence of the Duke of Lauderdale*

It happened that once when the king was at Newmarket, the duke (though no horseracer) attended. And it concerned him not a little to be continually near the king, for at that time the spirit of sedition (with which the court itself was not a little infected, and pointed not only at the Duke of York and his succession, but for like ends at the king himself, but most of all at the Duke of Lauderdale who stood like a rock in the way) was rampant, and it had been a court trick, when any points of consequence and disagreeable to the ministers were to be gained by teasing, to take

53:1 Section 105
54:1 In biblical matters

the opportunity of the Newmarket meetings when the grave counsellors were at London or elsewhere far enough off. Therefore the duke, knowing that the stress would light upon the affairs of Scotland, his province, and person, in order to get him if possible, removed, thought fit to be, as they say, at the shaving of his own beard.[1] The body of the University of Cambridge complimented the duke with an invitation to an entertainment, which he accepted, and nothing was wanted that could be thought of to make it agreeable to him. In the Regent House he was placed at the upper end of the table, and there saw and heard the manner and forms of creating a doctor of divinity. And as a respect to the duke, that degree was solemnly conferred upon our doctor,* as one of his favourites, and by that opportunity the doctor came into his degree easily, which in the common track had been both expensive and troublesome. Then the duke had the offer of the degree of doctor of laws, with which statesmen, as suitable to their profession, are ordinarily complimented. The duke accepted it and his *placet*[2] passed in form. Then the Orator* having made his eloquent speech, all was thought to be over, but the duke rising up, began with a loud voice, *Non conabor*,[3] etc. to answer the Orator, and concluded in a stately form with thanks to his *Alma Mater*. One thing was remarkable: the duke was one of the tallest and bulky men[4] one should ordinarily see, and the Orator the least, but whether the duke complimented the Orator with an advantage in eloquence, as he had in figure, those who saw and heard both may determine. But certainly the discourse of the professor in executing the forms of creating the Divinity Doctor, all in purest Terentian Latin, and most apt invention, was an accomplished delight and entertainment to us aliens that never heard the like before. But in conclusion of all these academic operations, we have got a finished Doctor of Divinity, and now we may with better warrant (than as hitherto, for pure compendium) give him the style accordingly.

56 *The mastership of Trinity a preferment to his heart's content at first*
After the death of the excellent master, Dr Barrow (who sat as vice-chancellor at the solemnities before mentioned), our doctor, as I hinted before, was preferred to the mastership of Trinity College.* That was a settlement beyond which his ambition had not a *plus ultra*,[1] and he was not in his nature capable of being more happy than he was at his first entrance upon that charge. But how circumstances altered to pervert his ease and content into a state of trouble, misery, and finally loss of life, I am to

55:1 The passage 'shaving ... beard': outwitting; deluding
55:2 Vote of assent
55:3 I will not attempt.
55:4 MS has man.
56:1 Anything beyond

make the conclusion of this narrative. But in the mean time, upon his leaving his attendance at court, which had made a great lacuna in the midst of his studies and caused him often grievously to complain, he was restored to his text, and might prosecute his designs in his beloved college, where he found himself posted with honour and advantage. And as it was his desire, so it was his fate, to die Master of Trinity.

57 *Apology for some excursions*

And now before we advance further, it will not be amiss to take some account of the doctor's studies, relate what we know of them and of his designs to publish, as he had surely done, if he had lived to have (or to have thought he had) finished any of the works upon his anvil. And considering I have here undertaken the life of a person who, like a flourishing fruit tree, blossomed fairly, and then underwent a fatal blight that destroyed fruit and tree altogether, for which reason there will not fall out much of action to be historically related, I may be indulged in speculation, which had been the chief work of his life. And if I digress in some short discourses dissertative upon the subjects ever agitated among philosophers, I please myself with thinking how much he would have approved such liberty, and in that rapture hope the like may be here excused.[1]

58 *Designed an history of philosophy, recommended Plato, and published some of his pieces*

The work of philology being well over, the doctor did not confine himself to the study of theology, though that was become his avowed profession, but extended his researches into the dark recesses of learned antiquities, languages, and philosophy. As for the latter, he seemed to be very inquisitive and busy about an history of the antique philosophy, and making comparisons of it in the several ages of its flourishing, noting the various sects, and the mutations of the dogmata, and the transitions from one sect to another. He took notice that such an history is much wanted, but of collectors and transcribers of sentences, *plus satis*.[1] He was partial to Plato, and recommended the reading of his works to students. He obstetricated forth an edition of some select pieces, which concerned chiefly the catastrophe of Socrates. This was published in octavo at Cambridge, 1673, and entitled *Platonis dialogi selecti*.* In a short preface the doctor shows how moral philosophy came into Greece, gives a short character of Socrates and his manner of teaching, and then the occasion of this publication, and why of these rather than any other pieces of Plato, which former

57:1 A reference to the digression on the New Philosophy, which has been omitted in this edition.
    See pp 41–2.
58:1 More than enough

pieces, he says, contain a knowledge that everyone ought to covet, whereas the others contain many dry speculations fit enough for the proper time, and now for such as covet to know everything. And hereby this choice is had at a cheap rate, which in the whole works would be a great expense. And he wonders that Aristotle had been often published in separate volumes, but never Plato. He gives a short account of each of the pieces, and why he chose the translation of Ficinus rather than Serrenus,* and of his adding a sectionary index to the whole. There are some other pieces of ancient philosophy which are published and joined in a collection of the like made by Dr Thomas Gale.* These were published in 1671. And of our doctor's share he gives this account: *Habes denique Pythagorica Fragmenta. Videre ea quidem jam saepius in lucem, transfusa in plures, credo, formas, quam ipsius Pythagorae anima. Ex iis alia nunc primo latine versa, alia autem notis illustrata debes Johanni North, V.C. qui generis sui claritudinem, (quae certe Magna est) virtute et eruditione exaequat.*[2] Nothing more of his hath come through the press to my knowledge, but by what I have heard him say, I guess he had or intended to publish more of the like, intending thereby to draw the scholars off from their rigid attachments to Aristotle into an acquaintance with Plato. And if he had lived, he might have done much more towards it, if what he did had not had a considerable effect.

59 The bad use made of Aristotle's philosophy

It seems the doctor thought Plato's[1] way of philosophizing more consonant to Christian morality than Aristotle's was. The ancient fathers inclined that way, until a known course of corruption in the hierarchy bred an occasion to abandon Plato, and to take up with Aristotle, whose discipline was apter for maintaining indeterminable disputes about anything or nothing, truth or falsity and error almost indifferently. What else could be the meaning of their pouring out of Aristotle that empty jargon of matter and form upon the holy eucharist, by which, and the many syllogistical artifices, they maintain their gainful impositions, and particularly that monstrous *ens rationis*,[2] transubstantiation, which they fortify with chimeric notions of substance and accidents out of the same nonsensical philosophy? What imports Aristotle's having had a transcendent genius if his insufferable domineering and contempt of others led him to divide from truth and to take up with certain schemes of words

---

58:2 You have, then, the fragments of Pythagoras. Indeed, I think that now they see the light translated into more forms than the soul of Pythagoras. Some of these for the first time translated into Latin, and others illustrated by notes, you owe to John North V.C. [*vir clarissimus*–a most illustrious man] who equals the glory of his family (which is certainly great) in virtue and learning.

59:1 MS has the Plato's.

59:2 Creation of the mind

that signify nothing, whereby makes all his own? But more of this subject afterwards.³

60 *His writing, especially Greek, fair and orderly*
The doctor's handwriting was very neat and clean, much resembling what nowadays they call an Elzevir letter.¹ He used a smooth and round pen, without cutting his letters, which were singularly well formed and legible, and yet not like to any other man's handwriting, which happens to many that write for themselves, and much in a solitary way. His characters were small but very black, using no abbreviatures. But above all his Greek writing was exquisite, which demonstrated that he wrote a great deal of it. I have seen many of his letters, and also notes upon authors, and do not remember to have seen a blot or obliteration in them, which argues a very considerable proceeding, and a clear understanding, which going before the pen, preven[ted] the occasion of many corrections and alterations as most ordinary writers are tormented with. And it seems that, for order of writing, he chose the pattern of printed books.

61 *He was a friend but no student in the mathematics,*
as calling for the whole man
As for arts and sciences that flourished in his time, he desired to be a stranger to none, but did not pursue them, *ex professo.*¹ Upon this account he applied to the mathematics, but as a friend and not a lover. He used to converse much with Dr Barrow (who in those sciences was *verissime adeptus*),² which one would have thought should have fired him, but it had a most contrary effect, for it cooled him, and made him abandon the study. The doctor represented to him what pains he had taken, and particularly that he had spent more time upon one proposition, which was to prove an arc of a circle equal to a straight line (in order to square the circle), than most men spend in qualifying themselves for gainful professions, and all that he got was a demonstration that it was impossible to be done. He found reason to suspect that every arc, and every straight line were incommensurable, and then *actum est*, as he observes, *de tetragonismo.** Hereby the doctor perceived that if he pursued mathematics he must adhere, and neglect all his other studies and designs in which he found himself much advanced. Sir Isaac Newton was in the college a contemporary,* and being made by nature and inclination for mathematical studies,

59:3 That is, in the omitted digression on the New Philosophy
60:1 See *John*, section 18, n.
61:1 As an expert (literally, out of a declared intention)
61:2 Genuinely skilled

had much encouragement and assistance therein from Dr Barrow who, some say, first hinted to him the plan of his great cosmographical system. But, however, it falls out oddly that to the best of my remembrance Dr Barrow is not so much as named in any of his writings. This being so, old Aristotle himself, consulting his own fame, could not have done better.*

62 *How dealt with a solitary pupil on that subject*

While the doctor lived in Jesus College and was fellow, he had but one solitary pupil,* and that youth discovered to him an inclination to know what the mathematics were. And his tutor thereupon procured him Fournier's first six books of Euclid,* and wished him to read them. And the lad fell to, and after the definitions read the two first propositions, and then remonstrated to his tutor that he found no encouragement to go on, for there was a triangle, and a straight line, and a stir to prove equalities that were plain of themselves. The doctor answered that if anyone read mathematics and was not delighted, might depend he did not understand what he read. Thereupon the scholar read further, and found that a line struck obliquely over one or two others plainly proved that the three angles of every triangle were equal to two right angles, and then mastering the forty-seventh proposition and some others, he acquired such a goût as carried him through a student's course. And though he was no great proficient, yet he was fond of the mathematic sciences ever after.

63 *Master of the (then) new philsophy, and managed disputes*

As for the new philosophy, whereof Monsieur Descartes was the celebrated author, the doctor made himself master of it so far that he could show wherein it was coincident and wherein it differed from the ancient sects, and so brought it into connection, pursuant to the design of his intended history of philosophy. But he did not set up for a dogmatist in particulars, and chose to keep the volant,[1] free to discourse and censure as he from time to time thought fit, declining all *ipse dixits*[2] or taking sides as of a sect or party. In his conversation upon these subjects, he kept to the method of the schools, where *solvit* or *non solvit*, rather than true or false, carries it, though the former are not the *criterium* of the latter, for there may be many *solvits*, but one truth, and it may happen that, according to our understandings, that one truth in our judgment shall not *solvere*.* Among his vertuoso friends and acquaintance he loved to spar questions and foment disputes, and then whip into the chair as moderator, siding as he thought the reason swayed. And they must look well to their hits, for a false or weak reasoning seldom escaped him, and they must make good their arguments, or let go their hold. His hardest task was to keep his

63:1 To hover between two sides or opinions
63:2 Dogmatic statements

disputants in due bounds, for in the most disinterested altercations heats will kindle and exasperate, till the parties can scarce understand one and other, and in this manner the Doctor and his near friends, with utmost consent and satisfaction, used to entertain their hours, when affairs permitted them to be so happy.

———

Here follows a dissertation of the new, and modern new philosophy, which may be perused or let pass to fol. 227 according as the knowledge of late authors may have given a taste, or not.[3]

———

64 *Intent to pursue certain subjects*

Here we drop our physical reflections, and as to our doctor, I have observed that men professing general learning, after they have coursed through all sciences and literate inquiries, have at length determined their thoughts towards some particular subjects as have proved to be favourites, and have become so taken up with them that their application hath been chiefly regardant to them, and from thenceforth matters relating thereto shall be more strictly canvassed and pursued than any other, and all in hopes to make some advances therein. And accordingly the doctor began to concentrate his thoughts towards certain particular subjects, and had formed the outlines of some tracts he intended to compose for the improvement of learning in those topics, which he thought had been imperfectly held forth, and not well understood. And of these, according to my best remembrance of his ordinary talk and the hints he threw out, as also a little notebook he left behind him, I purpose to give the best account I can.

65 *History of philosophy, and of heathen theology*[1]

I am well assured that he intended to compose a critical history of philosophy and philosophers, with the originations, connections, transitions, and alterations of the dogmata, and also of the several sects, how they sprung up one under another, comparing their nostrums and showing wherein they agreed and disagreed, with their squabblings and altercations. And so coming down so low as his own time, to show how the moderns had borrowed from the ancients, and what they had set up new of their own. He used to say there was of this kind of learning little to be found in print, and being once well done, would be very useful to scholars. I do not remember that Rapin's works, which tend a little that way, were then published,* but his design is more criticism than history. The doctor also intended an history of the gentile theology, which he said was almost wholly wanted. As for commentations

and notes of his own upon the Greek and Latin classic authors, he had great heaps of
them by him, but, as I think, intended not to publish any but occasionally as authors
might happen to be reprinted when they might be serviceable. And of that sort were
his notes upon some (forementioned) pieces of the Platonic school put out by
Thomas Gale.[2]

66 *Against Socinians, republics, and Hobbes*
In Christian theology he had a full intention to publish a thro[1] confutation of the
Socinians,* and some shrewd touches that way are found in his notebook, of which I
am to give an account.[2] I have heard him speak much of the importance of that
controversy, and he was so far a prophet as to declare he thought that heresy would
soon break out and openly insult Christianity itself. I do not remember he discovered
any disposition to attack the papists or sectaries, though he had considered them
well, as his notes show, but he might think there were labourers enow at that oar. In
politics he had no mean designs. I think they may be reduced to three subjects: (1) To
expose a deceitful notion of a republic, which he accounted the worst of tyrannies
under a mask of liberty, showing the diabolical oppressions, injustices, and ingrati-
tude of communities acted in course, and especially against good and just men. He
said he would go no further for this than an history of the republic of Athens, which
would show it all fully. The government of that city came nearest to a pure
democracy of any that ever was in the world. It suffered continual change (such is the
natural tendency of a populace), and at length fell under tyranny in the worst sense,
which is the proper end of all popular sway. (2) He intended a confutation of Mr
Hobbes[3] (a writer in that time much in decant),[4] and (3), as an appendant to that, a
discourse of natural justice among men, all laws positive whatsoever abstracted; that
is, how according to right reason, men are bound to live together, if no pact or law of
any kind had been ever established. This was the forwardest of any design he had. I
have cast an eye glancing at a large folio book of his own handwriting (and very fair)
upon that subject, but might not read any part of it, so nice was he of even his friends'
censure of what he did; how much more of the public. I neither know nor believe that
he made any person living acquainted with his scheme, but he hath often in discourse
proffered divers of his notions, which I thought very singular. I do not know of any
other writing design he had, but am sure his mind was always full of various matters,
which often in discourse broke from him, and were such as, if he had lived, might

65:2 See *John*, section 58, n.
66:1 Zealous; earnest
66:2 Sections 70–5
66:3 See sections 74, 75.
66:4 Much discussed (presumably from *decantate:* to sing or speak over and over again)

have proved subjects of useful treatises. And as to his tenets and opinions in those he was at work upon, I shall from the light of his little notebook, give some faint account.[5]

67 *Complained of the drudgery of composing*
By what is said, it appears that he was extremely nice in all his compositions, and however it fared with the subject-matter, he was sure never to be pleased with his own composition and style. He never used an amanuensis, therefore he might justly, as he often did, complain of the drudgery of composing and of the great difficulty of writing well. He was much taken with the penning of *The History of the Royal Society* by Dr Sprat,* and said that if he might so acquire the style of that writer, he would read no other book for an whole year. He used also to say that study and invention were his pleasures, but penning his greatest labour and pain. It is thought that the Lord Verulam invented and suggested, but then, as to the transcribing and even methodizing his matters, he rested himself upon others.* The Romish interest have numerous learned societies, and not a few of the same order, witness the Jesuits, who communicate in any great work that is to be published by sending out tasks to their brethren as they think will be best performed, all which returned and composed by that college or person who sits at the helm, a stately work is launched. These are *ultra posse*[1] to a solitary author, whose heart is broke by the pains of digesting and transcribing, to say nothing of the charge of amanuenses and copiers. It is pity there is not a like communication among us.

68 *He had no assistances, and suffered by his slowness*
This niceness of our doctor, being so very severe as it was, had an unlucky turn, by keeping back the closing of any work. He never thought it complete as it should be, and would do all himself: invent, consult, compare, digest, and transcribe, and never used any amanuensis or copier. And by this means (as will be showed) the public lost the fruit, and he the credit of all his labours. He had a ready, clear, and significant style, and wanted nothing but what many have too great a share of, confidence and assurance of himself; this may appear in those scraps of his which are in print. But another inconvenience attended his labours to be exact: he found, by often iterating, his thoughts lost of their force and his pen grew stiff (as they say painters, in working up, lose the spirit of their first draught). I have heard him complain sensibly of these inconveniences, but such helps as I have mentioned would have given him great ease, but he was not disposed to favour himself that way. This slowness of his pen-work was prejudicial to him in other respects, for his mind was full and wanted a

66:5 In sections 70–5
67:1 Beyond possibility

discharge, and that drew a weight upon his spirits. Sorrow they say is eased by complaining, though to the winds; so a learned man that gathers for writing may be so full charged that, until he hath unloaded his thoughts upon paper, and to his satisfaction, finds little ease.

69 *Surprised by a fatal sickness, and by his order all his books etc. went to the fire*

But the worst of all was that, while his writings were in this manner retarded, young as he was, a fatal sickness overtook him, whereby all at once he was utterly disabled to pursue or finish anything he had at any time in his life given a beginning to. And under this infliction, finding himself, as to all future study and composing, in a desperate condition, he adjured his best friend and trustee of all his concerns (whom he had in his will made sole executor), immediately after his death, to burn every writing of his own hand left behind him.* And he would not be entreated to the contrary nor satisfied without a solemn promise of him, *in conceptissimis verbis,*[1] that he would faithfully do it. It is probable he had done it himself, but life is scarce ever without hopes of better than utter extremity, and it was possible for God to restore him to his strength of body and mind. But it fell out otherwise, for his condition was languishing to the time of his death, of which the melancholy account is at hand, and he was so far desperate as to all study that if he attempted anything tending that way it brought epileptic fits upon him, which tortured and exceedingly dispirited him. So that his friend could not deny what he so fervently asked. And accordingly, not long after his death, all his critical notes, lectures, sermons, animadversions, treatises, and discourses of all kinds, perfect (if any were so) or imperfect, useful or not, went altogether in lumps as innocent martyrs to the fire.

70 *A petit notebook escaped the flames*

But it hath fallen out that one of his pocket portfolio books in octavo containing some of his extemporaneous thoughts upon various subjects, out of all order, some with ink but most with red chalk or black lead, clapped down there, *ex improviso,*[1] lay out of the way and escaped this general conflagration. And these notes coming to my hands, that lay under no such obligation, instead of destroying, I transcribed them, but in a kind of order under heads, and in that manner purpose to preserve them.* In doing this I was satisfied that there was much in them, if not fit to appear in a rude dishabille, yet of too great value to be lost. And though set down in his solitudes *raptim,*[2] when he was abroad or in court-waiting and absent from his books and

69:1 In the most binding words
70:1 As they came
70:2 As they happened; suddenly

papers, for his remembrance afterwards, they show that his reaches were not short nor his flights low. And upon a little attention to his sense, it seemed to be marrow and drawn from the penetralia of each subject touched upon, and where was a *jugulum causae*,[3] his point was at it. And however I am suspended as to the communicating these notes in any way public or private as I have digested them (for such *extempore* scraps must needs carry many defects), I shall nevertheless give a short account of the chief of them, and thereby also demonstrate the tendency of his designs and studies.

71 *Notes of theology, criticism, philosophy, and policy*
The subjects may be ranged under these general heads: (1) *theologica*, (2) *crittica*, (3) *philosophica*, and (4) *politica*. Under the first, theology, it appears the doctor was prepared to batter the atheists, and then the Arians and Socinians. After having laid open their strengths, he meant to attack them with their own arms (as they pretend), right reason. And in order to this he hints somewhat of the rationale of the Christian religion and the holy sacraments of it, and finally to sustain the authority of ss (his mark for the holy scriptures), and that done, *actum est de Socianismo*.[1] There are some remarkable touches concerning Arminius* and Calvin; he is manifestly of opinion with the former, but looks upon the other, with respect to ignorant men, to be more politic, and thereby in some respects fitter to maintain religion in them, because more suited to their capacity. But that is referred to art, and not to truth, and ought to be ranked with the *piae fraudes*,[2] which seems no good character of presbytery. It hath been known that the worst of heresies have been popular. There are some remarks about the Roman Catholics and latitudinarians, but not so copious as upon other heads. There is also many touches about the heathen theology, a learning he much affected, tending to improve and clear the history of the heathen idolatry.

72 *Criticism*
There is little of (2) criticism, but enough to show he was not a little concerned about style and language. The account given of Aristotle's logic is with more freedom than the humour of the university, among the seniors at least, would patiently have allowed. He chargeth it to be not only useless but pernicious to all true philosophy and knowledge, and proves it by the vain offspring it had, meaning the schoolmen and scholastic disputation. What I found of books and literature, which among scholars is termed philology, is placed here.

70:3 Vital point of an argument
71:1 He is finished with Socianism.
71:2 Pious frauds, i.e., deceptions committed for a good object

73 *Philosophy*

The third head, *philosophica*, which is large and various, may not well be contracted, and stands referred to itself, when it may be perused. But I must observe that there is a manifest track of the aforementioned design of writing the history of the antique philosophy,[1] with a comparison of the ancients one with another and of all with the moderns, which had been a work the greatest scholar might have been proud of. It appears here that he was not a sectator[2] of Aristotle or of any other, but according to the justness of his thoughts doth right to all, and impartially to prefer truth. He gives his eulogies and correptions[3] clearly, and (after his way of thinking) according to merit. He was not wonderfully instructed in the minute particularities of Cartesius' mundane system, nor (for reasons before touched)[4] was it very material for him, or any one else, so to be.

74 *Politica. Against Hobbes's origin of right*

The last head is (4) *politica*, and deals most in the state of nature and the original foundations of right and wrong amongst men, from whence, as I touched before,[1] he intended to derive his principles of government and law. This is chiefly levelled against Mr Hobbes,* and shows some sparks of that fire he was kindling to cast a better light upon nature's primordial laws than that author had set up. He slighted confuting that author, whose frame leaned upon two or three dogmata, which enervated, down comes the whole structure which that author had with a world of wit and plausibility erected thereupon. As, for instance, against the opinion that the state of nature is a state of war, he opposeth demonstration that it is otherwise, being a state of pure amity and innocence. And against the having no right to anything, or (which is the same) that in the state of nature every man hath right to everything, he opposeth that, if right be not the first thing in nature, there can be no right at all in the world, for laws cannot bind unless it was right before they were made, that, when made, they should bind. And against that all right hath a beginning by pact, he demonstrates that upon like account as before that opinion is *felo de se*,[2] for if it be true that men are bound by pact, that truth must be antecedent to pact, so that if it be not admitted in the first place that pacts bind, it is impertinent afterwards to enter into any. And upon this original scheme of right, which he so much studied and

---

73:1 See section 58.

73:2 Disciple; partisan

73:3 Reproofs

73:4 That is, in the omitted digression on the New Philosophy. John North distrusted Descartes' 'elementary descriptions, which could not be made good by any discoveries' (f 62v).

74:1 In section 66

74:2 Self-contradictory (literally, a crime upon himself)

insisted upon, depends all the force of laws and agreements in the world, and if any were made inconsistent therewith, he made no scruple, with Tully, to say there[3] might be force, but no obligation.*

75 *Against power from the people*

He is much *emporté*[1] against that Hobbianism that the magistrate's power is derived from the people, and for that reason a supreme magistrate can do no wrong, or, as Mr Hobbes says, right and irresistible power are all one.* The doctor shows that under laws the magistrate can do no more rightfully than a private person might justly do by the law of nature. As when the magistrate kills for theft, it is not by virtue of a power derived from the thief as one involved in the common submission, but he doth it in the right of the injured party, who in the state of nature might rightfully have done the same. Therefore as particular persons in the state of nature may do wrong, so when the magistrate (though enabled as to force under laws) doth the like, he is equally a wrong-doer. And for this reason the chief magistrate, under laws, may be as wickedly unjust as a private person in a natural state can be. Therefore it is a pernicious opinion that the supreme power can do no wrong, and countenanceth tyranny, and especially that of assemblies who are most apt to call themselves the people. The doctor derided the opinion that the estimate of pure nature was to be taken from any persons adult and educated in corruption and confirmed by practice, howsoever lawlessly jumbled together, all which *cacoethes*[2] reflecting upon pure nature, vanisheth, leaving only innocence in the room. And even his terrigenal[3] men would be void of ambition, or knowledge of wants, for even appetite is a result of experience. I do not remember much in his notes of the patriarchal or theocratical schemes of government; perhaps they lay out of the way of his inquisitions. He thought that adult persons were free from the duty of filial obedience, which is against the *patriarchia*,[4] and, as I take it, right reason, which makes that duty coeval with life itself, for he that hath a life lent him is a debtor for it all the days of his life.

76 *Some singularities in his humour*

I shall next touch upon some singularities of the doctor's fancy and humour, and some other circumstances relating to his character and studies, and so, passing over the divers stages of his life as my memory serves, defer what will be very melancholy

74:3 MS has they.
75:1 Carried away by anger
75:2 Evil habit; malignant disease
75:3 Earth-born
75:4 System of government by the father or eldest male of the family

as near the catastrophe of this design as I may. In the university he was taken notice of in his public exercises for venting of new notions, as they are called, of which many are to be found in his notes, but that is a sorry appeal, which I make not without a discontent that all his books and papers fell not into my hands as those did. It had been a shrewd temptation to have snapped a parole or trust, to no account prejudicial but of the fire. But his humour was to hold all within himself till he was entirely satisfied that no slip or oversight might give disadvantage to his cause or himself, lest any less guarded words or expressions should escape him. Nothing could have secured him in that point better than the participation of his friends. In a critique of works, an author upon his own hath but one eye, but upon another's he hath two, and often spectacles to boot. He was so deeply concerned for his cause, as well as his own esteem, that he durst not trust even a friend with either. And he had a dread lest this petit notebook of which I have given an account might happen to stray and fall into unknown persons' hands who possibly might misconstrue his meaning. In contemplation of which contingent, he wrote upon it this pleasant imprecation: 'I beshrew his heart that gathers my opinion from anything he finds wrote here.'

77 *Perpetual thoughtfulness, and withal diffidence*
He was always exceeding thoughtful and full of notions. He could not rest from working on his designs, and at the same time so diffident of the event that, between impulse and despair, he was like Mahomet in his tomb, or as they say Erasmus hung.* Despair had the greatest influence, and it sat so hard upon his spirits that he desired rather to be utterly forgot than that any memorial of his dealing in literature should remain to show that such a one as he ever existed, which should not be proof against the teeth of the next ages. After he had the government of himself, he would not endure that a picture should be made of him, though he was much courted, and invited by Sir Peter Lely to it.[1] And what was very odd, he would not leave the print in his bed where he had lain remain undefaced. And he could not bear the thought of being laid forth when he should be dead. I have heard him say that when he went first to Cambridge he had a severe fever, and his good mother came over to nurse him, and she seeing his legs, as commonly with young folks, said 'Fye, John, what makes your legs so dirty? What will they say if you should come to be laid forth?' That speech, which was indeed a little coarse, as he said, sunk so deep in his imagination that he never after could endure the thought of that same laying forth. Some years after, at his father's house, he had another acute fever, and his mother was his tender nurse. I have heard her say that he had fancies so extravagant that she concluded him to be delirous. Once he desired her to come and hear two notions, very fine notions. His mother snapped him up and bid him go to sleep with his notions.

77:1 See section 5.

No, she must needs come and hear them, 'Well, what are they?' 'Beer and beer, madam, the finest notions in the world, beer and beer.'

78 *Florid visage but weak constitution*

As to his person and constitution, excepting only the agreeable air of his countenance and florid head of flaxen hair, I have little to produce that may be commended. His temperature of body and austere course of life were ill matched, and his complexion agreed with neither. For his face was always tincted with a fresh colour, and his looks vegete[1] and sanguine, and as some used to jest, his features were scandalous, as showing rather a *madame en travestie*[2] than a bookworm. But his flesh was strangely flaccid and soft, his going weak and shuffling, often crossing his legs as if he were tipsy. His sleep seldom or never easy, but interrupted with unquiet and painful dreams, and often nocturnals,* of which (to his intimate friend)* he sometimes complained. The reposes he had were short and by snatches; his active spirits had rarely any perfect settlement or rest.

79 *Inclined to the stone and addicted to forebode extremes*

The distempers which most afflicted, or rather frighted, him were gravel and rheums. The former held him in sad expectations most part of his life, and the other was most urgent towards his latter end and in truth were the occasion of his death, as will be showed afterwards.[1] His worst indisposition lay in his mind. That is, an unhappy tendency to believe that in all incidents and emergencies the worst that in possibility might happen would fall to his share, and accordingly his mind always lighted upon extremes. He never had a fit of the stone in all his life, but voided plenty of red gravel, which he was told was a sympton that no stone gathered. But that weighed little with him, but every morning he speculated his night's urine, and as the use of splenetic folks is, called witnesses to see what quantities of gravel he voided. But such are the failings of sedentary persons, and those who pass most of their time alone; a life of action allows not leisure to dwell upon such reflections. But this excuse the doctor had, his father died a miserable martyr of the stone, and many think that disease, as well as the gout, often falls *ex traduce*.[2] But the doctor's humour in these respects was so extreme that his foreboding of evils to come often put him into real passion. I have heard him in an almost agonizing concern say that it was not death that he feared, but a painful life. I hinted his corporal infirmity at first;[3] he had not the

78:1 Healthy; flourishing
78:2 A woman in man's clothing
79:1 In sections 93–6
79:2 Propagated
79:3 Section 11

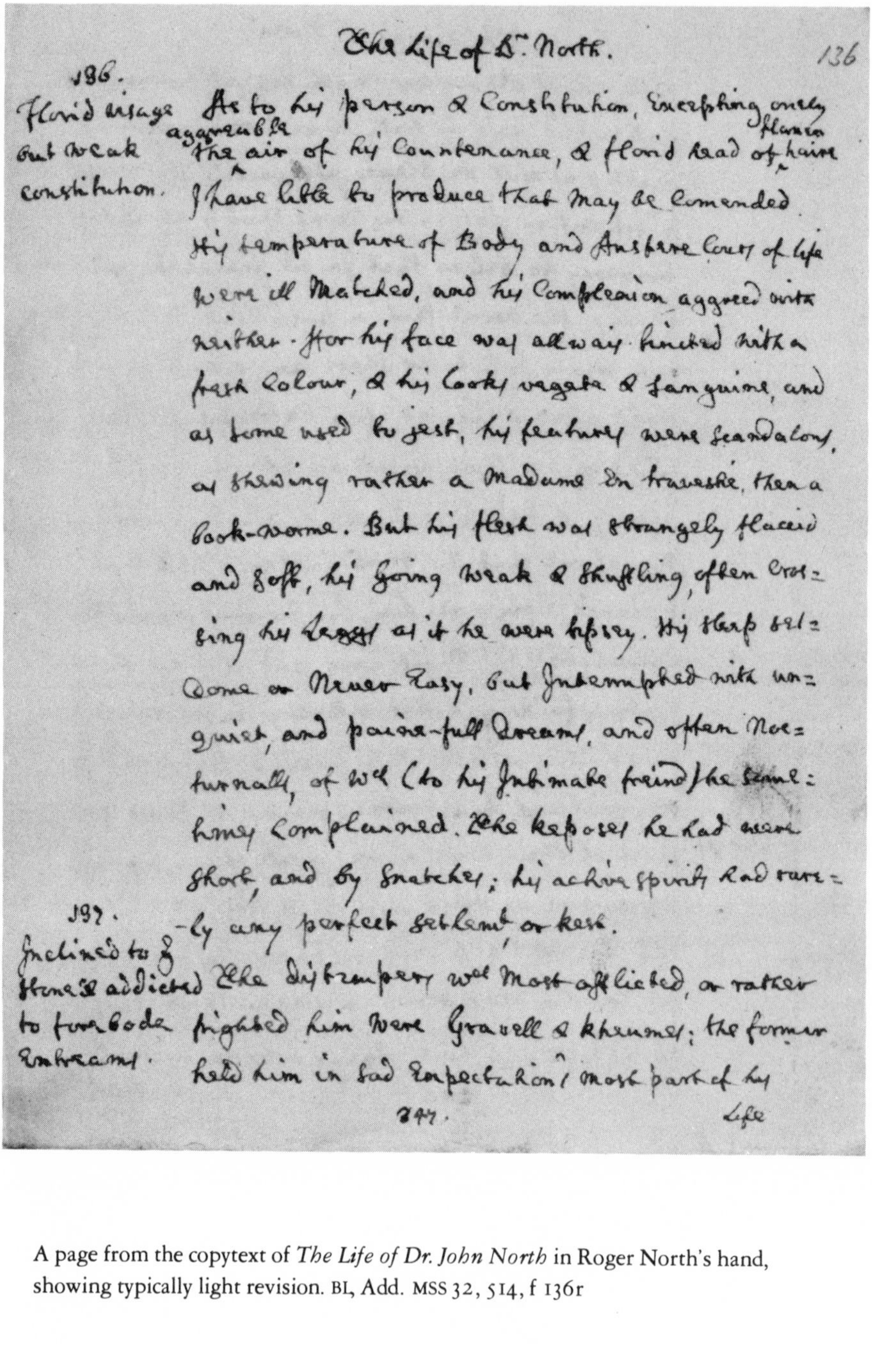

186.

Florid visage
but weak
constitution.

As to his person & Constitution, excepting onely the air of his Countenance, & florid head of haire, *agreeable* *flavin* I have little to produce that may be comended. His temperature of Body and Austere Cours of life were ill Matched, and his Complexion aggreed with neither. For his face was allway tincted with a fresh Colour, & his looks vegete & sanguine, and as some used to jest, his features were scandalous, as shewing rather a Madame en travesti, then a Book-worme. But his flesh was strangely flaccid and soft, his going weak & shuffling, often Cros= sing his leggs as it he were tipsey. His sleep sel= come or Never easy, but Interrupted with un= quiet, and paine-full Dreams, and often Noc= turnally, of wch (to his Intimate freind) he some= times Complained. The reposes he had were short, and by Snatches; his active spirits had rare= -ly any perfect settlemt or rest.

187.

Inclined to ye
Stone & addicted
to forbode
Entreams.

The distempers wch most afflicted, or rather frighted him were Gravell & Rheumes; the former held him in sad Expectation most part of his

247. *Life*

spirits of a good constitution, such as support men in actions of personal valour and contempt of danger, though staring them in the face. He had a good share of philosophy, but not enough to fill up that blank in his nature. If there be a state wherein brutes have an advantage over humankind, it lies in their nescience of evils to come, which protects them from anticipating calamity, or like men, whether certain or uncertain, make them present by imagination.

80 *Suspected he should be blind*

Another great trouble the doctor had upon his spirits – which was an opinion he should certainly live to be blind. He was indeed short-sighted and looked near upon his books. He did not distinguish anything well at a distance, and was told that such character belonged to lasting eyes; but after his way of anticipating evils, he soon lost all that imagination could deprive him of. He reflected much on the case of Milton, who was a wit, and lived to be blind.* In his *Paradise Lost* he inserted a poetical contemplation of his blindness, thought to be one of the chief flowers in his poem.* And the doctor for his comfort often read that passage, and had his eyes been out, he might [have] had it read to him, which was time enough. The doctor once travelled with his best friend* and some other company, and his friend thought fit to take a merry opportunity to make him better conceited of himself. 'Mr North,' said he, 'is not that a very fine windmill?' (when none was in sight). The doctor looked about, and seeing none, 'I protest and as I am a living man,' said he, 'I verily believe I shall now soon be quite blind, for I cannot discern so much as that windmill,' at which his friend and the company made a stout laugh upon him. And at all times in company he met with raillery enough to have created in him a better opinion of himself. And if he had lived much amongst them, such free conversation would have had its effect, but retiring to his studies at the university, the black veil came over his fancy as if it had never been clear, which will be more fully demonstrated in the sad story of his fall.

81 *Great cares about small matters charged on his nature*

It is certain that he was overmuch addicted to thinking, or else he performed it with more labour and intenseness than other men ordinarily do, for in the end it will appear that he was a martyr of study. He scarce ever allowed himself any vacation; what he had was forced upon him. There was no undertaking or occurrence how trivial soever whereof all the circumstances or emergencies that possibly might concern him were not volved and revolved in his mind, lest he should be so unhappy to oversee any, as if mere trifles had been cardinal to the interests of his whole life. If he was to ride to his father's house, walked to church, or made any visit in town, he was in pain about the contingents, and so low as to fret at the fancy he had that the people in the street looked on him. He was, in a word, the most intense and passionate thinker that ever lived and was sane. I may here be told that if I think by these descriptions to exhibit the portrait of a great man I am out of the way, for what is less consistent with such a character than such timidities? I answer that I am not giving the portrait of a perfect man, and whoever pretends so to do is a foul flatterer. And yet the character I give is not a small one because of a single infirmity, natural and unavoidable. If any man, however in name and truth great, did not labour under some unhappy crasis[1] of body of one kind or other, which inclined him to transgress in the decorum of his actions, the doctor had much to answer for in being so singular. But if it be (as certainly it is) otherwise, then all that can be required of a wise and good man is to know his foible and strive to correct it, and if he holds himself firm against all manner of corruption which might grow up under it, and keeps down scandal, he is completely absolved.

82 *His continual art and practice to amend himself*

That our doctor was well intituled under this apology I am fully satisfied, for first he understood himself and all his peculiar frailties perfectly well. And his friends could not show him more of himself than he knew, and if there was any difference, the weight fell on his side, who was sensible of more foibles in his nature than his friends could observe. But they could perceive him often struggling with himself to curb excesses growing upon him, and he was either much overseen or surprised, when he showed any extraordinary concern or passion. And in this *autarchia*[1] he performed so well that strangers seldom or never perceived his disorders. But among friends he was more solute,[2] and gave some advantages against himself which served for raillery; and that never displeased him. And he used his friends as spies upon himself to discover his own failings, and for that end used to be very sharp upon the company, and if anyone that he might be free with had a sore place, he was sure to give it some rubs, and harder and harder till they must needs feel, and then they fell to retaliating, which was his desire; often saying that he loved between jest and earnest to tell people of their faults, that they might pay him in specie telling him his own.* A small degree of acquaintance gave him an inlet to this kind of sport, and he managed his freedoms with such fluent wit and respect and with decency of behaviour, that nothing was ever on that score taken ill of him. But what imports all this to the character of a person honourable by birth, and not only studious, but politely learned, and for his religion, justice, sobriety, and good manners unblameable? And one that laboured all his life to make himself in all respects better, and to

---

81:1 Combination of elements or humours
82:1 Self-government
82:2 Free

amend whatever he found amiss in himself, wherein he was not unsuccessful? And that carries more of merit than virtue itself, when there is no natural impulse or temptation to the contrary.

83 *His religious and moral character*
It will not be amiss to relate what I know of his character more particularly. As to his religion, his being in priest's orders speaks him to be of the Church of England established by law, although that rule hath of late undergone many scandalous exceptions. But he was critically orthodox and sincere, as the whole series of his life and actions plainly demonstrated. And his zeal was never more exasperated than against men busy in disturbing the orderly exercise of pure Christianity among men, especially in our church, within the pale of which iniquity itself could not find a plausible scruple, either on account of doctrine or discipline, for the sustaining of which his mind was chiefly at work. And to show his conscientiousness therein, I shall relate one passage. Sir John Cutts of Childerley, a relation of his,* knowing that the doctor sometimes used to touch an organ, and for that purpose had one in his chamber but it was borrowed and not his own, very generously offered to make him a present of one that had stood in his house, but never to anyone's knowledge made use of. The doctor positively refused it, although in a free circumstance he would have been most glad of a present so seasonable to him as that was. And he told me his reason was that the room where the organ stood was called the chapel, and he supposed the instrument had been intended for religious service, and probably at some time made use of accordingly. And he said to me that others might think of those matters as they pleased, but he had and ever should have a great regard to them. He was so very nice, that he could not bear that any religion, no not a false one, should be ridiculed, and scarce allowed the prophet's discretion in deriding Baal's priests.* For false religions are evidences of the true, and if derision be put in common practice against the one, it will soon be perverted upon the other. I need not, to complete his character, add anything of his personal virtues, such as probity, temperance, chastity, common honesty, and justice. His enviers (for enemies he had none) had never any colour to insinuate anything to his disadvantage. In short religion, justice, probity, and humanity were his study, delight, and practice.

84 *Averse to faction, and preferred absolute monarchy to a democracy*
As to the public, which in his time began to be muddled with faction that through the supinity of our government had got ground, and the artificial cry against popery and arbitrary power sounded loud in all corners, he showed an utter detestation of the faction and their rabble, and could not but be angry when he heard what troubles they created to the state at that time. He was well apprised of the history of the (then) late troubles, and thought the like in danger to be reiterated. He declaimed

against all the proceedings (however popular) tending that way, as no less mad than the actions of stolid brutes, void of thought and foresight of consequences, that hurry hurry themselves into perdition and ruin. Brute beast indeed, meaning the populace, but it hath horns and houghs,[1] therefore stand clear, but neither eyes nor ears to any purpose but finding the shortest cut to confusion and destruction of itself and everything else that stands in its way. And the case is not at all mended by a set of fine appellatives, for hypocrisy is commonly varnished with the like. The doctor, as I showed,[2] had been a notable student in the qualities of powers in government, and really thought that of the two extremes – absolute monarchy or pure democracy – the former was incomparably to be preferred. And since exorbitancies will grow up in all governments, the rule of one hath fewer, and those less oppressive, than that of many. The great fault of monarchy is that it cannot be pure monarchy, but must be assisted in government by many, as councillors, ministers, etc., and still of those the fewer the better, even to a single viceroy if he can well act the monarch. Solemn councils are formal and hypocritical, and the best counsel is taken *ex improviso* and *ex re nata.*[3] He used to say that the arguments against monarchy were taken from the examples of bad kings, but who called up the examples of bad republics? To the little finger of one of them, the loins of a monarch are light. And weighing the happinesses of people in general, there is no comparison between those which have been under monarchies, and those under republics, so much do the former exceed. And the grievances under monarchy fall mostly upon ambitious troublesome grandees, who are made amends by the advantages they have in high places, but all that while the people have their ease and quiet, and in that one single article of suppressing civil war, the people (who are seldom undone any other but most frequently that way) are more than adequately compensated for all the evils of monarchy that speechmakers can suggest. The doctor was often copious in his discourse upon these subjects, and used to toss and tumble over his Grecian republics, under which no honest good man could serve and not be ungratefully used and finally destroyed. He had a just value for the temperate government of his own country, and abhorred, as he did the devil and his angels, all those troublesome folks that laboured by altering to make it worse, and so finally to enslave the people.

85 *His most rigid and austere course of life as Master of Trinity College*
But now I must withdraw from speculation into actual pratique of government, I mean that of our doctor as Master of Trinity College. This preferment took him partly from his studies but almost entirely out of those advantages which by a few

84:1 Hocks; heels
84:2 See sections 66, 74, 75.
84:3 Without premeditation and in the actual situation

friends he enjoyed; that is from a frequent, easy, free, and pleasant conversation, into an anxious, solitary, and pensive course of life, which, with his austere way of ordering himself, drew upon him a most deplorable sickness, and that proved the decadence of all his powers of body and mind, and then by a slow and painful gradation laid him down in the arms of everlasting rest. This track will lead me to consider the doctor now, not as a private person but as a magistrate, and in the exercise of no slight charge. He wanted the nervous capacity of his immediate predecessor Dr Barrow, who was moulded for indefatigable labour, but on the contrary the doctor was frail and infirm and of a nature that needed recruits, and, to reinstate its forces, some measures of indulgence. He was temperate and regular, and at chapel and meals lived by the rule of his college. He kept a good table with some wine, and always invited some of [the] fellows and gentlemen of the college to dine with him, and all was well but as touching the bottle, which he would not suffer to be too many for them. But if his line had been a little extended that way, it would have produced freedoms and dispersed those cloudy formalities which will fall between a superior and inferiors, unless the nerve is cut with the glass and humour hath a free play. He wanted nothing more than a free society. The state (if I may so term it) of a master of a college in Cambridge is such that he can scarce look out or make a visit but with attendance and form, and in his college all are upon their guard where he is, and very few if any were thought capable of a true and familiar friendship, that is, clear of all design or project. He was always disposed to be free enough, but that never works well *inter sub et supra.*[1] He had not learned the art of some persons well preferred, I mean to be careful of himself and use the means of long life in order to make the most of what is fallen to their share. Nor is it expected that one in his place should have put himself, as he did, under all the severities of a college life. But he considered that having the charge of maintaining the discipline and order of the college, his demeanour there was not his own to dispose of, but dedicated for example to others, and that he ought to perform strictly in his own person all that, by a common rule, he required of the scholars under him, especially in keeping chapel, wherein he never (willingly) failed, not in winter nor summer, whatever the season or early the time was. Nothing but a sense of duty could have made him so swerve from the interests of his health, and I am very well assured that he laid to heart, as they say, the good of the society and his duty regarding it, against which he slighted all considerations relating to himself.

86 *His solicitude for good order and justice in elections*
There are some I have known who make such trusts no encumbrance at all, but let things pass as they may, and take little care but of their profits. But our doctor's

85:1 Between inferior and superior

principle was very different, and that being derived upon a strict integrity, could not be reconciled to the perfunctory, but he thought himself bound to be active, as well in keeping down disorders, always apt to rise under him, as also to see justice done to all the scholars. And in particular he was resolute in adhering to the college statutes, and to see that elections went fairly; and in the business of fellowships that created him no small trouble. Everyone knows that the pupil-mongers, often senior fellows who were his coadjutors, would favour good pupils though perhaps no good scholars, in order to get them into fellowships, when others had better pretensions. And this bred interest-making, and for the most part brought importunity upon him, as if by teasing and urging points might be gained. All which partialities were fastidious and hateful to him that had none, and whatever impetuosity he endured, he never would consent to prefer a dunce to a good scholar when the standing was equal, but always declared to do justice to whom upon account of better merit it belonged. These were not slight cares to him, that used to create great ones out of slighter occasions.

87 *Trouble about mandates obviated by pre-elections*

The court mandates for elections were very irksome to him.* He knew well how those favours by means of courtiers were obtained, and often suspected that some of his seniors, when they could not compass their will of him another way, were instrumental in obtaining them. And he used to inveigh bitterly against that practice, declaring that whoever of them was guilty of it did not consider their duty and their oaths and that it must in time bring the college to nothing; for if elections are for favour, and not merit, who will think of rising by any means but courtship or corruption? And then assentation[1] or money must supply want of parts, learning, and sobriety, and the college once so filled will continue and avow the same methods, whereby gentlemen's sons in the college, under the influence of such a regiment, [will] be exposed to the mischiefs of idleness, expense, and debauchery spreading in the university, as bad as in any lewd corporation town.* It is a common unhappiness that whoever opposeth growing corruptions and abuses in societies shall have enemies enow, and no vexation of him be left uninflicted that might be raised up against a common enemy, and so hornets, when disturbed, become impertinent and endeavour to sting. As for the mandates, I believe they were too hard for him that had as good an appetite to disobey them as to his meals at high noon. But instead of that, and to ease his mind a little (for he lived in perpetual dread of mandates), but principally for the good of the college, he found out a way by pre-elections to obviate an inconvenience he could not resist. And thereupon out of the several years, four or five, one under another, he caused to be pre-elected into fellowships scholars of the best capacities in the several years, which made it improbable another election

87:1 Obsequious assenting to the opinions of others

should come about in ten or twelve years then next ensuing, for until all these elections were benefitted there could be no vacancy. And that broke the course of mandates while he lived. The doctor was solicitous about nothing more than the business of elections, which he thought the spring of good and evil to the college, and (as he thought) in some degree to the public.

88 *Thought over-rigorous, became unpopular and affronted*

He had occasion enough to exercise all his philosophy, for without anything else to make him uneasy, a disposition in the scholars to be disorderly had been sufficient. He had first laid down his own example of regularity and sobriety before them which ought to have inclined them. And after that done and continuing, he thought it his duty to be informed as well as might be of what was outrageously amiss amongst them. He never connived at any thing whereof by the duty of his place he was bound to take notice, but either by admonition, or otherwise (statutably), he did his best to amend it. And he endeavoured also to make the discipline of the college as light and easy to the scholars as he could, by using private intimations and friendly advices tempered with mild reasoning and persuasion. But for all that he grew unpopular amongst them. They took him to be over-officiously rigid and strict, saying it had not been so before. Youth will always mistake manhood to consist wholly in disorderly living, and that order and discipline belongs only to boys. And to show how much men they are, they behave themselves (as some did to him) contumaciously, and many of them contrived to affront him. I have heard it said, but not credibly, that one night as he was walking in the cloister, some lads merry-making in an opposite chamber, and fancying he came there to spy what was doing, came down and used him ill, but I never heard him speak of it, as he did of most things that concerned him, nor did make any inquiry about it, as he would have done, to discourage such affronts, therefore I do not believe the story to be true. This I was a witness of: one winter night, while we sat in his diningroom by the fire, the chimney being opposite to the windows (looking into the great quadrangle), a great stone was sent from the court through the window into the room and fell but a little short of the company. He seemed to take little notice of it; we guessed him to be inwardly vexed, and soon after the discourse fell upon the subject of people's kicking against their superiors in government who preserve them as children are preserved by parents, and then he had a scroll of instances out of Greek history to the same purpose, concluding that no conscientious magistrate can be popular, and in lieu of that he must arm himself with equanimity.

89 *The building of the library, and the occasion*

When the doctor entered upon the mastership of Trinity College, the building of the Great Library, begun by his immediate predecessor, Dr Barrow, was advanced about three-fourths of the height of the outward wall. And the doctor most heartily and sedulously applied his best forces for carrying it on. And besides his own contributions, most of his friends and relations, upon his encouragement, become benefactors, the particulars whereof will appear in the accounts of that noble structure.* The tradition of this undertaking runs thus. They say that Dr Barrow pressed the heads of the university to build a theatre, it being a profanation and scandal that the disputations and speeches should be had in the university church, and that also be deformed with scaffolds, and defiled with rude crowds and outcries. This matter was formally considered at a council of the heads, and arguments of difficulty and want of supplies went strong against it. Dr Barrow assured them that if they made a sorry building, they might fail of contributions, but if they made it exceeding magnificent and stately, and at least exceeding that at Oxford, all gentlemen of their interest would generously contribute, it being what they earnestly desired, and *tantum non*[1] required of them, and money would not be wanted as the building went up and occasion called for it. But sage caution prevailed, and the matter at that time was wholly laid aside. Dr Barrow was piqued at this pusillanimity and declared that he would go straight to his college and lay out the foundations of building to enlarge his back court, and close it with a stately library, which should be more magnificent and costly than what he had proposed to them, and doubted not but upon the interest of his college in a short time to bring it to perfection. And he was as good as his word, for that very afternoon he with his gardeners and servants staked out the very foundation upon which the building now stands.* And Dr North saw the finishing of it, except the classes,[2] which were forward but not done in his time, and divers benefactions came in upon that account, wherewith, and the liberal supply from the college, the whole is rendered complete. And the admirable disposition and proportion on the inside is such as touches the soul of anyone who first sees it.

90   *The differences between the doctor and his eight seniors. And how*
I mentioned before some uneasiness between the doctor and his seniors about elections, and since those matters sunk deep in his mind, and some have thought fit in print to refer to them,[1] I shall relate all I know or have credibly heard of that matter. There was much of contingency in what happened, for two masters, Pearson and Barrow,* preceded our doctor, and both being more addicted to books than business or government, were contented the eight seniors should determine affairs, and at meetings readily joined in what they agreed. This nonchalance had bred a sort of expectation that what the seniors had predetermined about elections, leases, etc., should pass current, it being enough to make the master acquainted or to show him

89:1   Not only
89:2   Stalls (singular, classis)
90:1   See *John*, section 108, n.

their opinions. But our doctor did not understand this method of proceeding, and consulted his own reason, and would be guided by that and that only, whatever the rest thought, for he looked upon himself as one entrusted and bound by duty and oath to act for the good of the college, and for that was answerable to his own conscience. And nothing but reasoning and convincing his judgment would induce him to comply. This behaviour seemed a little new to them, who having been used so much to dictate as scarce to endure contradiction. And they used all means, civil and uncivil, to reduce this master under the like reglement as the former. It is hard to allege this extraordinary conduct and to rest it upon pure parole; therefore I shall add one instance of fact, which the doctor himself told me. Once at a meeting the seniors had agreed a business, but the master did not think fit to join with them to establish it. They most importunately urged, as if their unanimous accord were reason enough to satisfy him. But it was all one, he thought it unreasonable, and positively refused to concur. At last one of them said, 'Master, since you will not agree, we must rise and break up the meeting.' 'Nay,' said the Master, 'that you shall not do, for I myself will rise and begone first.' And accordingly he rose and went into his chamber, leaving them in a sort of consternation, for they knew that without their master they could do nothing at all. After a while they thought fit to drop their huff, and in a proper manner sent and desired him to return to them, which he did, and they went on with other business.

91 *By weakness disabled to contend*

I never heard him mention any other sort of affront done to his face but this, and it seemed to grieve him because it was during his weakness, of which I am about to give an account. For while he was vegete[1] and strong, he could contend, and sustain his authority by the force of his reasons, and those he never failed to bestow fluently. But after his decadence, his body was weak and his utterance imperfect, and what was worst of all, passions apt to rise in him, which caused his epileptic fits to return, whereby he was disabled as to all serious debate or contention. And I do believe too much advantage was taken of his weakness, for being near his end, he ordered that he should be buried in the outward chapel, that the fellows might trample upon him dead, as they had done living.[2] This was spoke in the anguish of his mind, when he could judge and would be just. But wrangle he neither could, nor would, because of the hideous consequences, and possibly some things might pass in his absence contrary to his mind, and on such occasions he used to throw out such tragical speeches. But we are a little too early for these melancholy notes.

91:1 Healthy; flourishing
91:2 See *John*, section 106, n.

92 *His severities to himself increased, and society wanted*

I am next to give in the history, of the doctor's fatal sickness, so often touched upon, with the (presumed) occasion, accession, and conclusion, and what should that be but the end of all things, death? I have already accounted for his thoughtful and studious course of life, and habitual fullness of business and care in his mind. But after he came into a post of magistracy all his solicitudes exasperated, and the ordinary refreshments, which he sometimes met with before, failed. And I must add that as his course of life, so his diet was severe to himself, for he was always sober and temperate, and scarce spared the time of eating from thinking. After morning prayer and a solitary dish of coffee, he retired to his study at the end of a gallery and there he was fast till noon, unless college or university affairs called him out. After his meals, a meagre dish of tea, and then again to his post till chapel and supper, and then if he had any friendly conversation, it was still in a studious way, that is, discoursing of abstruse matters, which however pleasant to him, kept his head at work. His chief remissions were when some of his nearest relations were with him or he with them, and then, as they say, he was whole-footed. But this was not often, nor long together. Some of them used to be free with him, and in his own way, between jest and earnest, tell him he must indulge a little, go abroad, and be free with a glass of wine with good company in his college as he used to be with them, that his self-denials would endanger his health, and the like. To which sort of discourses I have heard him return a tradition of Bishop Wren,[1] who when he was told he must not keep Lent, his body would not bear it, 'Will it not?' said he, 'then it is no body for me.' And the doctor, by his life of perpetual thinking, had settled his mind in resolutions so stiff that he often seemed rather morose and humoursome than, as his constant profession was, to be governed wholly by reason. When his friends have been importunate with him, to say (in the common forms of free converse) why? and for what reason? he hath answered, 'Reason is to govern me, but my will's a reason to everybody else.'

93 *Afflicted with rheums and his uvula swelling*

It was very remarkable that nothing of any evil which the doctor at any time in his life feared came upon him, but somewhat else, and of what he had no imagination or dream, and indeed the worst I think that could befall human kind, that is to be paralytic, and epileptic. If in his anticipating mind a thought had entered that he had been obnoxious[1] to those distempers, I cannot say how he would have comported under it, for nothing could come near[er] the quick with him than a distemper that insulted his faculties of reasoning and judgment, wherein his mind must suffer as

---

92:1　See *John*, section 16, n.
93:1　MS has onoxious.

well as his body. The distemper came upon him by these steps: first a cold, then an unusual quantity of rheum discharged at his throat, and the tonsil glandules tume-fied, and at length his uvula. And as the course of these colds is, a deal of spitting and venting of rheum at his mouth followed. Here is nothing extraordinary, but what often happeneth in colds, and being assisted with warm humectations[2] and repose, the disease itself, allowing time for it, makes the cure. And what could be done more reasonably than to encourage that proper discharge of a peccant humour, which nature itself, and in the way of a common catarrh, had found out? But that which most concerned the doctor was the swelling of his uvula, which continuing overlong gave him (that always anticipated extremes) an apprehension that he must at length submit to have it cut off. And this operation was so dreadful to him that to prevent it he must needs apply to the most noted physicians in the university. And they considered the case and prescribed as they thought most proper. But their endea-vours succeeded not, but in all appearance (if any judgment may be made by events) proved the ruin of their patient. And this may be a warning in ordinary cases not to seek extraordinary remedies.

94 *Remedies: Amber smoke and astringent powders*

I fear that in my report of this case I may offend the medical faculty. But I am not free to suppress or palliate matters of fact which were of the last concern to my subject. If one may be so free to interpose a censure, their fault (if any was) lay in meddling at all, and not sending the good man home to his mother to be nursed. But instead of that, partly as I guess to humour him, and partly to put in practice their university learning, fell in pell-mell with their prescriptions to divert this flow of rheum from discharging at his throat and mouth, and to send it another way. But first the cause, as they said, must be removed, which was to be done by rectifying his digestions, that rheums might not breed so copiously, and then they might safely stop the vent. And in order to this, a circulatory course (as they called it) of physic was prescribed, enough to have purged a strong man from off his legs. And the doctor most scrupulously conformed, for he had a great regard to all kinds of university learning, and believed that of physic to have more logical conclusions in order to cures than their own faculty elsewhere will allow them. After this career performed, the prescription was to take amber as tobacco in pipes, and to have certain astringent powders in quills blown into his mouth upon his uvula. The unctuous smoke of the one joined with and held the other fast, so that nothing might pass in or out that way. It was not considered all this while that the patient, with his cathartic courses, was grown so weak and feeble that in all likelihood rheums must breed in his body rather than abate.

93:2 Moistenings

95 *Went to London reduced to a skeleton*

But they had a resigned patient to themselves, than whom a tamer subject to make experiments upon could not have been found. It is certain that by these methods of physic, smoke, and powders, the doctor was reduced to extreme weakness, and, finding no amendment, ventured to come up to his friends in London. They knew nothing of his having been ill, for in his letters he had complained of nothing but a cold he had got. They were amazed to see him come helmeted in caps upon caps, and meagre as one newly crope out of a fever. *Quantum mutatus ab illo!*[1] His regimen was no less changed than his habit and countenance. He must stir little abroad, and for the world not after sunset, though it was July (which was the only time of his friends' refreshment abroad), for fear of increasing his rheums. He must drink nothing small,[2] nor much of anything. Grapes and peaches, being full of humidity, were poison, but nuts and dry bread toasted without stint. And all the while at fit periods the pipes and powders came, and one or other must blow for him. His friends had no notion of this latter medicament, nor, as I guess, his physicians, otherwise they had not prescribed, nor we suffered the continuance of it. After the doctor's death I told this case and method to Dr Lower,* the prime physician of his time, and he said that he would undertake by only the smoke of amber to put the soundest man in the world into convulsion fits.

96 *By diet and friends wonderfully recovered in a month*

The doctor's friends, having all this wonderful alteration before them to observe, concluded him gone of the spleen and the best physic for him was society, plentiful diet, and turning abroad in the air, when we could get him so to do, and not without perpetual raillery at his caps and new discipline, so contrary to what he was always used to. Upon this account he was taken down to Hammersmith, a villa of his best brother's, and in the space of a month from his first coming up, purely by his coming into his friends' way of living, between London and the country, a cure of him was perfectly made, and he came to make no scruple of eating, drinking, and airing as they did. His volumes of caps were disbanded, his countenance grew florid, and his ordinary briskness and good humour returned to him. Thus (*sub Deo*) by pure relaxation and diet (all medicines apart) this egregious cure was wrought. In this state he was returned to his college, with good counsel enough to indulge as he had done with us, and, for doctors, to use only the famous three: Diet, Quiet, and Merriman.* But as to his amber and powders, which he cared not to leave wholly off, his friends pretended not to judge of them, but thought them to be whims of the physicians, and as chips,[1] neither evil nor very good.

95:1 How much changed from that [Hector who wended homeward, clad in the spoils of Achilles]:
    Virgil, *Aeneid*, 2.274, a common quotation
95:2 Diluted liquors
96:1 An addition that does neither good nor harm

97 *Upon an admonition of two contumacious scholars,*
he dropped apoplectic

After the doctor was returned to his college, his rigours to himself and austere course of life also returned, and his rheums beginning again to flow, by like advice as before, cathartics, amber, and powders were reiterated in full force, and all without the least regard to the successful experiment that was made upon him about London; till his body growing weaker, and his disease stronger, the humour, having no vent at his mouth as it naturally tended (for all those pores were closed), broke out in his brain, and threw him down all at once in a desperate apoplexy. The manner of the access was this. The master and seniors thought fit to revive an antiquated discipline, according to the statutes, of admonishing disorderly scholars, in order (without amendment) to expulsion. And in the morning the doctor came out from the meeting (where probably he had been a little roiled) to perform his duty upon two scholars then brought to be admonished. And it was observed that he admonished with more than usual earnestness and acrimony in his speech, for the lads were much to blame, and behaved themselves very contumaciously. When the body is weak, passion is usually strong, and divers things concurred to stir it up in him, which probably touched the trigger, and *inter loquendum,*[1] he dropped down. It is possible that, without these circumstances of emotion of his spirits, this had not happened at that time, but then it is more than likely that on some more unhappy place or occasion, as preaching, or in some other solemn presence, the like had happened, but here it was almost at his bedchamber door. He was immediately taken up (wherein the two scholars were very assistant), and carried to his bed, there being little hopes of life in him. But the physicians were immediately sent for, and due methods were used as in cases of apoplexies.*

98 *Not dead, kept from sleep; his mother extorted it to a lively effect*

After the ordinary tormenting operations performed, he recovered a little sense, but was excessive drowsy, and it was judged that unless that symptom could be conquered, he must drop from them, whereupon by direction followed perpetual noise and clangour of one sort or other to keep him awake. There was consort of tongs, firegrate, wainscot-drum, and dancing of curtains and curtain rings, such as would have made a sound man mad. It was presumed that if he fell asleep he would never wake more, so his instruments were plied until his good mother (who was immediately sent for) came to take care of him. She was a magnanimous lady that had nursed a large family old and young for divers years, and in experience was more than a match for a college of physicians.* She saw in what torment her son lay, drowsy to death, and gave attention to what the physicians said, but all the while admired the music they made. She desired of the physicians that her son might have a little sleep. 'No Madam,' said they, 'for if he sleeps yet, he will never wake again.' The good lady had no longer patience, but set up her maternal authority, and told them flat and plain that her son should have rest, and that quietly, for full two hours, and she would answer the consequences. He was her son, and she would have the nursing of him. Thereupon she dismissed the musicianers, and desired the learned and unlearned (for there were many eavesdroppers and newscarriers in the room) to withdraw and leave her. She kept with her only the maid she brought, and they two went to work, ordered the bed, and laid the poor patient in such a posture as she thought most proper for his taking rest, and then, sending her maid to wait without, she sat her down at the bed's head and all was hush for the full time. Sometimes she peeped in upon him, and found no reason to retrench any part of it. After this she opened the curtains and called in the physicians and the rest that had a mind to be there, and showed them how easy and quietly he lay, and breathing as nature required. His countenance had a good colour, and his face was composed, which before was distorted in divers manners, with his eyes staring like one of the furies. 'Now Doctors,' said she, 'what think ye?'

'But Madam,' said one, 'will he wake?'

'You shall see,' said she, and gently jogging his arm as he lay, he waked, and opening his eyes, knew several there and spoke to them. The physicians were exceedingly surprised, for they expected great difficulty to have waked him, and had been consulting of methods how to do it.

99 *Left in a numb-palsy, and his notions*
Now the mine was fired, and all the fracas it could make upon a poor mortal bulwark of animated earth determined, and what remained was only ruin and confusion as the blast had left it, never to be recovered into its former order and strength again. The fit went off, but left the doctor under the infliction of a desperate numb-palsy all one side of him which the learned call an hemiplegia. He kept his bed for some considerable time before he ventured to rise, and then he was able only with help of a friend and a crutch to crawl a little about the room. His mouth and face was drawn up on the lame side, and his left arm and leg altogether enervous,[1] and neither did him much service as long as he lived. But in time the weak leg served just to lean on, while the other got a little forwards, but itself was dragged after. He dropped his crutch, but never ventured to walk far without help at or near his elbow. He told me the images in his mind during this infliction, as far as he could remember them. First, during his admonishing he perceived himself to lean towards his left side, and the leg that should have sustained him seemed enossated[2] and to be like the finger of a glove, by which it was plain to him he must fall, and accordingly he gave way to it.

99:1 Bereft of nerve and strength; powerless
99:2 Boneless (perhaps North's coinage)

After this he remembered nothing at all of what happened to him, until by help of his mother he had taken a little repose. And then in a dreaming manner his conceit was that he had got a strange leg in the bed with him, and was much perlexed which way to get rid of it, whether he should call to have it taken away or not. And it was a great while before he could bring himself, even awake, to own it.

100 *The prodigious declination of the doctor's mind to levities*

It is an uneasy task, but (according to the profession I make of truth, for better or worse) necessary, to show the miserable decadence of the doctor's thinking and memorial capacities. What is the difference between manhood and puerility but that the former hath a large stock of useful memories, and also strength habituated to action, which the latter wanting, runs after levities and anything for variety, without choice, unless appetite or inclination (and even that flows from experience) draws it. Suppose an hurricane falls upon a sound man's memory and obliterates great part of his collections and confuseth the rest; as one may imagine a fine poem wrote upon the sand, and much ruffled by the wind, there might be enough left to show it had been good sense, but the dignity of the verse was lost. So the man would lose his judgment of true values, and relapse into a sort of puerility, but still his moral character, that is will to good or evil, remain unaltered. This was the case of this good doctor. The seat of his memory was ruffled by the disease falling upon his brain and nerves, which had made such havoc that he had no firm notion of himself or of anything, but had his experience to gather and his understanding to frame over again. After he could lie awake and think, I guess he had some reflection that he had been over-severe with himself by too much assiduous study and abstemiousness, which possibly had brought that disease over him, and then fancied to cure himself by a course directly contrary, and accordingly thought that now he must be merry and jolly. Pursuant to this (conjectured) model, the company that assisted about his bed to entertain him must find merry tales to tell, and if a little smutty, the mirth paid for it. The lighter sort of books and frivolous comedies were read to him, and he heard them with notable attention, and at the quaint passages was unusually affected, and often laughed, but (as his visage was then distorted) most deformly. He fancied to admit a young gentleman of the college, one Mr Warren,* to be his reader in ordinary, who was very useful during his weakness to help forward his tedious hours, and deserves to be remembered with much respect.

101 *That continued some time after he left his bed*

After he was enfranchised from his bed, and had the entertainment they called walking about his chamber, and divers friends and acquaintance came and stayed with him, he gathered some little strength, but his levities still continued, and he used to please himself with rehearsing paltry rhymes and fables. And what with difficulty of utterance (for his speech was touched, and never perfectly recovered), and what with his unseemly laughing, it was long before he could get anything well out, and at last made but broken stuff of it. All this was inexpressible grief and mortification to his friends, seeing that dismal alteration. They had known his genius bright, and in his health, solemn, grave, and instructive, and his mirth, when it happened, not without a *copia*[1] of pleasant wit and, as it ought to be, ever decent and without offence, far from all suspicion of a possibility that such levity of humour and discourse should ever appear in him. He seemed as an high-flying fowl with one wing cut. The creature offers to fly, and knows no cause why he should not, but always comes with a side-turn down to the ground. The doctor had some remembrances of his former forces when he could mount up and fly; now his instruments on one side failing him, he was forced to deal in low concerns and reptile conceits that scarce rose from the ground.

102 *The fatal infirmity of epileptic fits that destroyed him*

The doctor lived to recover his faculties of mind and powers of his body in some measure, and had it not been for one immense malady that attended the palsy, and held him down, there had been hopes of a competent recovery, and that malady was epileptic fits. These appeared soon after the apoplexy went off. They were gentle at first, but continually invigorated, and every one of them gave him a twitch nearer his grave. And these were esteemed the result of amber smoke; there happen many apoplexies and palsies but few, if any, come off with an epilepsy. It is said of Conradus Lycosthenes: *continuis laboribus fatiscente primum paralisi correptus sit, quae illi et linguae et dextri lateris usum tempore ademit donec septennio post apoplexia graviori accidente ex hac vita opere nondum perfecto.*[1] This learned man's case being exactly like the doctor's, saving only the epilepsy, that I thought fit to transcribe it out of Bierling.* These fits came nearly after a month's interval, but were not strictly periodical or lunar (as old women dream). Any disorder or intention of thought, a little anger, cold, or disappointment, brought them, which made him seek to be as quiet and still as he could. They dejected his spirits to a very great degree and deprived him of all comfort. And a great unhappiness was that in his fits he could not help biting his tongue, and that kept back the recovery of his speech. He found that strong wines helped to put off a fit, which made him, when he

101:1 Abundance

102:1 Exhausted by continuous work, he was first seized by paralysis, which took away for some time the use of his tongue and right side, until in the seventh year afterwards, the apoplexy getting worse, he departed this life, his work not yet finished. Conrad Wolffhart, known as Lycosthenes (1518–61), German theologian and classicist suspected one, to desire it as a condemned malefactor doth a reprieve, and accordingly used the strongest sherry, glass after glass, which formerly he would have thought more than a cup too much; but it was a reasonable recruit of his spirits, which by such fits are of course overthrown.* As the doctor's strength of body decreased, so these malignant fits returned thicker, but more languid, for there was scarce pabulum left to sustain the rancour of them. And after they had brought him almost to forget the world, and to spend most of his time upon a couch, which was after near five years from the first stroke, there was very little left for them to do.

103 *During all his weakness, his religion and moral virtues rather increased*
I must here do a piece of justice to the doctor and his memory by affirming upon my own knowledge that during the extremity of his mental weakness, his religious principles, resolution in justice, and good will to the world, which I may call universal charity, continued as integral and intemerated[1] as they were in the strongest moments of his life, and, respecting his external behaviour, much more zealous than before. Such a trial coming over a man as this was, if he had worn a mask, or had had the least tinct of hypocrisy, it had gone off, and the pure man appeared as he was. Here the *cons[c]ientia vita[e] bene anteactae*[2] was of service to him, else, as happens to weak women and others in like case, he might have fallen into melancholy dejections, misconstructions of providence, despair, and the like extremes of weak minds. But as I said, whatever the state of his body was or his capacity of study, his will and moral determinations were not in the least vacillatory. There never fell a word from him tending to complaint or discontent at his condition; he would freely relate what he felt, and how, and no more. He governed himself as well as he could, his submission was absolute, and his patience exquisite.

104 *With weakness his judgment recovered. Strength hath nothing to do with will*
I have had two observations upon the doctor's case. One is that in the progress of his disease, as his body grew weaker, his judgment grew stronger, so that his levities wore off, and he became again sociable. And after he retired to the college, he dealt in the college affairs with a sense clear enough, though he could not debate or contend because of his fits, which any earnestness brought upon him, and continually left him weaker. After the first year of his illness he behaved himself with great gravity and respect, and the chief failing that appeared in him was an over-iteration of gratulatories and compliments, and more inclined to silence than formerly he was. The other

103:1 Inviolate
103:2 The consciousness of a life well lived

observation is that strength or weakness of body hath nothing to do with the will and morality in relation to duty and honesty. Nay, further, that strength of parts or understanding, which in itself is not free, doth not control the will, which is free.* And we are not to argue moral honesty or knavery in any man on account of his strength of body or mind. For it is found that the best parts are often joined with the most corrupt natures, witness the famous heretics, politicones,[1] and malefactors. Therefore they are much to blame that argue against anything of duty from the examples of any persons strong in wit and invention, who with all their sophistry may have a corrupt will. Every man hath wit enough to be upright. It may be said that providence hath dispensed strength of mind unequally, and the like may be pretended of form, beauty, and wealth. But no man can complain for want of free will, whereby he is justified. Men may be forced to act, but never by any human power to will, ill things. And according[ly] the doctor to his last behaved himself in his college in maintaining the statutable order, steadily doing justice to the deserving scholars and discouraging others. Nor was it possible by any means, fair or foul, to move or corrupt him to any act against his judgment or conscience.

105   *His attempts to preach or study stopped by his fits*

But now, before we part, I shall add a few words about the doctor's manner of passing his time in his weakness. After he was able to go abroad and to use his coach, which he did not without much trouble and assistance, he went sometimes to visit his mother, near Bury,* where he passed his time most easy, and to his content, because it was defecate[1] of all manners of business. He there made the proofs of his ability to preach, and with much ado was got into the country pulpit. His matter was very plain and pious, but he laboured under such an invincible want of utterance, and what he did speak was with so much pain and deformity, as rather mortified than edified the congregation, and at length he was forced for fear of his fits, which he found coming, to leave off abruptly. He desired also to resume a little study and the use of his pen, but his fits said nay, and finding that all preparation towards any actual exercise of his duty threw him into fits, he was forced to be contented with having had a good will and made his utmost proffers towards it. His mother parted with her woman to be his constant attendant and nurse,* and she commonly travelled and went abroad with him. And without so good a servant and friend he had passed his time very painfully. He often went to London and resided at his prebendary, which was a pleasing variety to him. In conversation he was apt to throw out tragical and odd sentences: as once he was overturned in a chariot with his mother, and it was his turn to be uppermost. 'Now madam,' said he, 'you have borne me twice, once in your

104:1 Politicians (contemptuous)
105:1 Clear and pure

belly and now on your back.' One Sir Anthony Irby,* a goer-about-to-complain-of-the-times, came to visit him, and 'Dr North,' said he, 'are not these sad, sad times?' (which, by the way, to the doctor was the most fastidious discourse that could be used). 'Aye indeed,' said the doctor, 'they are sad times, for I am sadly, sadly sick.' All the service his friends could do him was to visit and indulge, and conversing merrily and freely with him. He did not well bear long visits, especially of those whom he did not much like. If he found a disposition to fits, he called for wine, which reinvigorated his spirits. His best diversion was variety, and he had most of that in London, for he could creep about the cloisters to prayers and to visit his neighbours.

106 *Charities, and devotion constant. Retired to Cambridge and died;*
his epitaph J.N.
In these marches the beggars had found him out, and marked him for their own; he always carried a cash on purpose for them. They knew his motions as if they had been his domestics; he scarce ever failed of giving everyone that asked something. Always at his taking coach and lighting, his attendance was great, and whoever was with him must stay till the dole was finished. Sometimes if he fancied them good people, in a garb of humility he would ask their prayers, which they plentifully bestowed, in his hearing at least, and probably with a true zeal, for he was the best master they had. These charities were public, and besides what must necessarily be so, he affectedly concealed. By his last will* he gave a full fourth part of all his estate to be distributed to poor people, which by his best brother, whom he made his sole executor, and those that came under him, was done. His devotions, besides the public service of the chapel and churches where he was (which he never failed if he was able), were no less affectedly secreted that his charities, for they were always in perfect privacy and by himself. He had certainly *mens sana, o si fuisset in sano corpore*![1] And about three or four years after his first illness, he made his last retirement to Cambridge and seemed to bid all his friends adieu.* And there he passed the sorry relict of his life. It was most alone by himself, for his mother was dead,* and his most esteemed friends engaged in great dealings above. He declined college business, which because of his too sensible incapacity he found he could not administer to his mind, took most to silence and (however seldom) yet when he did speak, it was to the purpose, and often very pathetic and perhaps, being offended, resentingly sarcasmous. He frequently wrote to his best brother, which he could with his sound hand do, at times, and as he found himself easy. I have seen some of those letters, which as I remember were in a fervent or rather flaming style, upon the subjects of his friendship, esteem, value, and his own wretched unworthiness; but they are all gone after his works to the fire, or swept aside and out of my

106:1 A sound mind, oh that it were in a sound body! (a variation of Juvenal, *Satires*, 10.356)

Letter from John North to his brother the Lord Keeper, dated 29 June 1680. Bodleian, MS North c 5, f 89 reach.* His weakness of body continually increased, and his fits accelerated. His chief ease was his couch, where he usually lay expecting fits and wishing for death, the only means to free a limpid soul, as his certainly was, from that dungeon of flesh in which he lay stuck fast as in a mire. And at length, in one of his fits as was supposed, without discovery of any pain, about April 1683, he went out rather than died.* He lies interred in the outward chapel as he directed in his lifetime, and (as was noted) nothing significative but *J.N.* upon a small stone over him.* He was desirous that if he could not leave somewhat behind him worthy to be remembered, of which (as I have shown)² he never was satisfied, not to be remembered at all.

107 *Marriage, to which not averse, might have preserved him*
It may be conjectured that if he had married it would have preserved him longer, for the cares of a family are frequent and importune enough, but interrupted and passant. These, compounded with studies, had relieved both. And he was not at all averse to it, for he used to say a rich wife was a good benefice, and he found no topic more for his purpose in rallying his friends than that. Once he observed that at one of his best brother's christenings there was a grievous clatter about gossips,¹ entertainments, nurses, etc. He comes to his brother, and 'Seriously,' said he, 'and as I am a living man, brother, there is more than one would imagine in that saying: "anything for a quiet life".' In a word (however the doctor pleased himself with whetting his wit upon his married friends to such a degree as they scarce bore, and yet were pleased, for his girds were oblique and touched to the quick, but not directly exceptionable, and commonly brought a shower of the like hail upon himself), his conclusion was in the vein of Erasmus: *ut magis gaudebis, et minus dolebis, et ut minus gaudebis, et majus dolebis.²*

108 *The Doctor's integrity integral and unimpeached to the last*
I know nothing of exception justly taken to him during his whole life, although he was a scholar almost universally known and observed, unless it were after he came to the government of the college, and then only for his rigorous exacting of duty and order in the scholars, and severe justice in elections. As to the former, he was taken for an innovator but by the disorderly only, and those carried it so far as to say his passionate severity (they called malice) to the scholars brought his disease upon him. And for the other, although the seniors were much piqued at him for not always agreeing with them, it was only among themselves, and in the particular cases

106:2 In sections 67–8
107:1 Godparents; female friends invited to be present at a birth
107:2 As you will have more happiness and less sorrow, so you will have less happiness and more sorrow. (I cannot find the passage in Erasmus.)

neither side carried it further into malice and rancour, whence open faction and party-making might flow. The doctor contented himself with the ordinary allowances, and never made any encroachments upon the rights and revenues of the college, nor squandered their monies in decorations or otherwise, after his own fancy or advantage, to the oppression of the fellows. If any have done otherwise since, let them go away with the honour of it.* And as to the late controversies between the master and his fellow[s], in which they have on both sides alluded to our doctor's case, it is certain it signified no more to the questions of right depending amongst them than to the monarchy of Spain. For what was it to the purpose if Dr North vexed the fellows or they him, and in some particular instances only, and those not referred to profit of either, but only to government in the college? But so people in difference are apt to scold. I might here insert their several prints, but having declared the whole matter in itself impertinent, and withal not touching our doctor in any respect, I hope it may be excused.* And here I leave the good doctor freed from his unhappy case of flesh, but withal a bright example of orthodox religion, learning, justice, and good will, to his eternal rest and assurance of the rewards of well-doing.

Notes to the *General Preface*

The numbers in the left margin refer to the text pages.

51 the Jesuits] The following notation appears in the margin of the MS, apparently intended to amplify the reference to Jesuit historians: '*Baronius Bellarmine Maimburg etc.*' Caesar Baronius (1538–1607), cardinal and founder of the Oratory of Italy, wrote the polemical *Annales ecclesiastici* (Rome 1588). Saint Robert Bellarmine (1542–1621), Italian controversialist, was the author of *Disputationes de controversiis christianae fidei* (Ingolstadt 1586–93) and many other polemical and devotional works. Louis Maimbourg (1610–1636) wrote *Histoire de Lutheranisme* (Paris 1680) and *Histoire du Calvinisme* (Paris 1682).

52 hedge] 'If we once conceive a good opinion of a man, we will not be perswaded he doth any thing amiss; but him whom we have a prejudice against, we are ready to suspect on the sleightest occasion': John Ray, *A Collection of English Proverbs* (1670), quoted in *Oxford Dictionary of English Proverbs* (Oxford: Oxford University Press 1970), p 772.

52 knave] 'Nor can weak truth, your reputation save, / The Knaves, will all agree to call you Knave': John Wilmot, Earl of Rochester, *Satire LXIV*, lines 164–5.

53 not one] Ps. 14:3.

54 tutor's fault] This rather surprising outburst against tutors was no doubt prompted by a personal experience. In the *Autobiography* North bitterly recounts the perfidy of a governor appointed to care for his ward, Sir Peter Lely's son (3:205–9).

54 ladies ... cart] Derived from the practice of using a cart for the public exposure and chastisement of lewd women.

55 Their groans ... process] This condensed and obscure passage might be paraphrased thus: They claim that their sufferings [actually caused by their own stupidity] are a sign of true religion, which is their way of converting evil into something holy, and

164 Notes to the *General Preface*

so they hide one sin by committing a worse; at the same time they dismiss the real elements of repentance and restitution as retrograde. (The term 'conscientious,' like 'perseverances' earlier, is particularly associated with extreme puritanism.) It is interesting to see how, in sections 5–8, a traditional aristocratic disdain for the mob is joined to a condemnation of religious sects, which in fact are now equated with the mob. Collectively stupid, further muddled by religion, the mob is ripe for exploitation by unscrupulous political adventurers, and represents a threat to monarchial order as well as to decent men who wish only to serve their country.

55 '41] 1641 saw the execution of Strafford, which was preceded by raucous demonstrations. The sectaries were increasingly vocal and parliament often unruly.

55 Guazzo and Capriata] Marco Guazzo (d 1556), soldier, poet, and author of several histories. Pietro Giovanni Capriata (d 1660), whose history of the wars of Italy North may have known in the translation of Henry, Earl of Monmouth (1663).

56 wise man's sense] An allusion to Prov. 11:14: 'Where no counsel is, the people fall: but in the multitude of counsellors there is safety.'

59 Guicciardini] Francesco Guicciardini (1483–1540). The reference is to the satirical *Advices from Parnassus* (Venice 1612); trans (1656; rev 1706) by Trajano Boccalini (1556–1613). Advice VI tells of 'an unfortunate Laconick ... who spun out into three words a Thought, which in the judgment of the Laconick Senate might have been fairly compris'd in two ... The sentence was, that he should read over Guicciardin's *War of Pisa*: But the very first Leaf put the poor Wretch into such a deadly sweat, that away he ran immediately and threw himself at the feet of his judges.' Apollo appears largely in the book. There is no work by Guicciardini specifically entitled *War of Pisa*, but perhaps the book that Boccalini considered so excruciatingly diffuse was Guicciardini's great *La historia d'italia* (Florence 1561).

59 An Italian ... plum cake] The 'Italian' was Alessandro Tassoni (1565–1632), author of the mock-heroic poem *La secchia rapita* (Paris 1622; trans 1710). The 'Frenchman' was Nicholas Boileau-Despreaux (1636–1711); his mock-heroic *Le Lutrin*, based on a dispute among the canons of Ste Chapelle, Paris, appeared in 1674, with additions in 1683. The war of the plum cake appears in *Gargantua*, chapters 25f.

60 P. Paolo ... work] Paulo Sarpi (1552–1623) was a Venetian theologian and author of the anti-papal *Historie of the Council of Trent*, trans Nathanael Brent (1620). Sarpi defends his method of narration at the opening of the third book. (It is not clear why North refers to Sarpi as P. Paolo, unless it is because of a confusion between Sarpi's real name and his pseudonym: Pietro Soave Polano).

61 Carolus Magnus ... quality] *Carolus Magnus*: Charles the Great, or Charlemagne (742–814). He and his paladins are the subject of numerous *chansons de geste*, of which the *Chanson de Roland* is the best known. The most fruitful period for the development of the *chansons*, at least as they have survived, was the early and mid-twelfth century; most of the best known works of romance are considerably later.

62 Hobbes ... times] Possibly a reference to chapter 21 of *Leviathan* ('Of the Liberty of
Subjects'), where Hobbes inveighs against the modern tendency to find in the
classical authors a false justification for rebellion. North picks up the theme again
in section 19 in connection with Grotius' *De jure belli ac pacis*.

62 *Lives of the Philosophers*] Diogenes Laertius (AD 3rd century) wrote a compendium
of the lives and doctrines of more than two hundred authors in which he relied
heavily on quotations and secondary sources.

62 Philostratus] Flavius Philostratus (b ca AD 170) wrote the *Life* of *Apollonius of
Tyana*, a philosophizing mystic of the first century AD. He is better known for his
Lives of the Sophists.

63 Grotius ... Greeks and Latins] *De jure belli ac pacis* (Paris 1625) by Hugo Grotius
(1583–1645) was of fundamental importance in the development of international
law. When W. Whewell edited the work in 1853, he remarked on the 'multitude of
quotations from ancient historians, orators, philosophers' and removed most of
them.

63 book ... republic] Possibly a reference to the revolt of Holland against Spain and the
eventual establishment of republics of the seven united provinces. North may also
be confusing *De jure belli ac pacis* with Grotius' *Apology* (Paris 1622) written in
defence of the state of Holland. Here North's opposition to the use of classical
precedent stems from his hatred of republicanism (cf his favourable citing of
Hobbes, *Gen. Pref.*, section 17). A more general cause was probably his enthusiasm
for the new science that rejected ancient authority in favour of a first-hand
empiricism.

64 late piece ... nonconformity] Richard Baxter (1615–1691), *Reliquiae Baxteriana, or
Mr. Richard Baxter's Narrative of ... his Life and Times*, ed Matthew Sylvester
(1696). Baxter relates national events from a personal viewpoint, and the latter
part of his book, in particular, is thick with religious controversy. As a thoroughgoing anti-sectarian North is unable to perceive the fine autobiography that exists
beneath Baxter's partisanship.

64 German reformers ... Walton] *Dignorum laude vivorum* (Frankfurt, 1653), a combination of two earlier works by Melchior Adam (d 1622). *The Mirrour of True
Nobility and Gentility. Being the Life of ... Nicholaus Claudius Fabricius Lord of
Peiresk* by Pierre Gassendi (1592–1655), trans W. Rand (1657; first published Paris
1641); North seems to have been much influenced by this book, especially in his
treatment of Dr John North (see pp 22–3). The life of Jean-Baptiste Morin
(1583–1656) appeared anonymously with a posthumous edition of his *Astrologia
gallica* (The Hague 1661). Isaac Walton's lives of John Donne, Richard Hooker,
George Herbert, and Robert Sanderson were published in 1640, 1665, 1670, and
1678 respectively.

64 pair ... Lee] Robert Nelson (1656–1715) wrote *The Life of George Bull* (1713).
According to *DNB*, Nelson also supplied materials to Francis Lee for Lee's

Memoirs of the Life of John Kettlewell (1718). North's strong non-juring sympathies led him to include these two biographies.

65 Joseph Scaliger ... known] Joseph Scaliger (1540–1609); collections of his sayings were popular in the seventeenth century. This quotation appears in editions of *Scaligerana* (e.g., Cologne 1667, and Groningen 1669) under the heading 'Histoire écclesiastique,' but with no source cited.

66 Mr Stow ... him] John Stow (1525?–1605) kept himself poor by devotion to his antiquarian research. John Strype (1643–1737), ecclesiastical historian and biographer, edited Stow's *Survey of the Cities of London and Westminster* (1720) and prefixed to it a life of Stow. At p xii Strype quotes the 'Licence, or Brief, as we now call it, from King James I. to collect the charitable Benevolence of well disposed People, for his Subsistence.'

66 Spanish *Guzman* ... *English Rogue*] The *Guzman de Alfarache*, a picaresque novel of great influence, was written by Mateo Aleman (1547–1614?) and published in Madrid and Lisbon, 1599–1604. *Histoire générale des Larrons*, a collection of nearly seventy rogue biographies, was ascribed to Sieur d'Aubrincourt, but later appeared with the initials of François de Calvi; it was published in Paris, 1623–5. *The English Rogue Described, in the Life of Meriton Latroon*, an immensely popular book with many editions and versions 1665–80, was begun by Richard Head and continued by him and Francis Kirkman. For an account of the latter two books see F.W. Chandler, *The Literature of Roguery* (Constable 1907), pp 17–18, 211–21.

66 *Cyrus* ... *Telemachus*] Both books are concerned with the education of leaders. The *Cyropaedia* of Xenophon (ca 428–ca 354 BC) is a historical novel in eight books with Cyrus the Elder as hero. *Télémaque* (The Hague 1699), by François Fénelon, relates the imaginary adventures of Telemachus and illustrates moral and political ideas.

68 the *Pantheon*] North is apparently referring to one of the English versions of *Pantheum mythicum* (Paris 1659).

69 Valerius Maximus] Valerius Maximus composed a handbook of illustrious examples for rhetoricians, *Factorum ac dictorum memorabilium* (post AD 27).

71 fine things] An allusion to act 3, scene I, of *The Rehearsal* (1672), attributed to George Villiers, Duke of Buckingham, and others: 'BAYES: Plot stand still! Why what a Devil is the plot good for but to bring in fine things?'

71 Davila ... courted] Enrico Caterino Davila (1576–1631) was the author of a history of the French civil wars, *Historia delle gerre civili de Franci* (Venice 1630). There were many continental and English editions during the seventeenth and eighteenth centuries.

73 Mr Edmundes ... English] Clement Edmundes (or Edmondes) (1566–1622); his *Observations* on Caesar's *Commentaries* appeared progressively until 1609 and were reprinted, together with his translation of the *Commentaries* and a life of Caesar, in 1655.

75 destroy them] Prov. 1:32.

77 Burnet's Lives ... turn] Gilbert Burnet (1643–1715), *Some Passages of the Life and Death of the ... Earl of Rochester* (1680); and *The Life and Death of Sir Matthew Hale* (1682). Nowhere in *Lives of the Norths* does North reveal a personal acquaintance with Lord Rochester of the Wilmot family, but he had many dealings with Chief Justice Hale and has provided an excellent character sketch of him in *Francis* (1:79–83). There is an amplified version of the sketch in *Autobiography* (3:93–102), where North is even more scathing about Burnet's life of Hale: 'and I should recommend to him the lives of Jack Cade, Wat Tyler, or Cromwell, as characters fitter for his learning and pen to work upon than him.' Such animus must have its basis in politics, and might have been due to Burnet's opposition to the Norths' ally Lauderdale (*Examen*, pp 555–6), and to his important support of William and Mary.

78 Pylades and Orestes] Orestes, son of Agamemnon and Clytemnestra, was educated with his cousin Pylades, with whom he formed a friendship so close that it has become proverbial.

78 bears] Originally a scornful proverb: a person was declared to be not fit to carry guts to a bear.

78 idiography] An interesting word that does not appear in *OED*, and which was probably coined by North. The term 'autobiography' was not available to him (*OED* gives 1809 as its earliest appearance) but, in any case, 'idiography' here appears to designate writing about oneself that includes both journals and autobiography.

78 Cardan ... *propria*] Jerome Cardan (1501–76), Italian physician, mathematician, and philosopher, wrote *De propria vita* (Paris 1643).

79 Bassompier ... life] François de Bassompierre (1579–1646) wrote *Mémoires du Maréschal de Bassompierre* (Cologne 1665) while he was in prison.

79 Edward VI] Edward VI (1537–53). *Edward's Journal*, a daily chronicle of his life from his accession until 28 November 1552, was first printed in Gilbert Burnet's *History of the Reformation* (1679–1715).

79 Laud's journal ... to do] William Laud (1573–1645), Archbishop of Canterbury, *The History of the Troubles and Tryal of ... William Laud ... Wrote by Himself, during his Imprisonment in the Tower. To which is Prefixed the Diary of his own Life*, ed Henry Wharton (1695). Once again North's judgment of a work is coloured by his political feelings.

80 What ... corrupters] A similar passage in *Examen* (p i), referring to an alleged contract between White Kennet and the booksellers, suggests that North had in mind a specific example of this general evil.

81 two-handed ... worse] The two books North is referring to are probably Laurence Eachard's *The History of England from the Restoration of King Charles the Second*, vol 3 (1718); and White Kennet's *A Complete History of England*, vol 3 (1706). Eachard's third volume covers the period from the Restoration to the

beginning of the reign of William and Mary, and is a detailed, lively mixture of the colloquial and the documentary, written mainly from a Tory point of view. Kennet's Whig history provoked North to a full-scale refutation in *Examen*. Yet again North's personal and political loyalties have distorted his literary judgment.

82 family relation] The next four sections contain a somewhat confusing account of the North family and its connections. Four separate genealogies are involved: North, Chute (with Dacres), Whitmore, and Montagu. To clarify Roger North's explanation the relevant parts of these genealogies are presented in the appendix (sections I, II, III, and IV). Roger North's own branch of the family is given in section V of the appendix. His concern to record these details is an indication of a powerful motive for writing the *Lives*: family piety.

83 Dudley also] Dudley, 3rd Baron North (1582–1666), Roger North's grandfather. In addition to the account below, there are glimpses of him in *Francis*, I: 32–6, and *Auto*, 3:67–8. See also *Gen. Pref.*, section 46, n.

83 Lord North's daughter ... Hampshire] See Chaloner Chute, *A History of the Vyne in Hampshire* (Winchester 1888). The three names appearing below in square brackets are supplied from this book (pp 78–9) and replace gaps left by North in his MS.

83 *A Forest*, etc.] *A Forest of Varieties* (1645). He also published *A Forest Promiscuous of Several Seasons Productions* (1659).

84 Sir Francis Vere] A mistake for Sir Horace Vere (1565–1635), whose expedition in 1620 for the relief of the Palatinate attracted many of the young nobility (*Cal. S.P. Dom.*, 1619–23, p 159). Sir Francis Vere (1560–1609) was his brother.

84 He served ... '40] The so-called Long Parliament sat from November 1640 to April 1653. Dudley North was Knight of the Shire for the county of Cambridgeshire from 1640 until he was excluded in 1653. It is typical of North not to flinch from relating what to him was a politically shameful fact.

85 The eldest ... Rolleston] See Augustus Jessop's note, *Auto*, 3:286–7 and 292.

85 two sons ... North and Grey] See Augustus Jessop's note, *Auto*, 3:295–8.

85 the youngest ... without issue] See Augustus Jessop's note, *Auto*, 3:295 and 304.

85 Her library ... remains] See pp 10–11 and Augustus Jessop's note, *Auto*, 3:303–4 and 309–10.

Notes to the *Life of Dr John North*

The numbers in the left margin refer to the text pages.

94 As for ... or not] A branch or bunch of ivy was hung up as a vintner's sign. Good
wine needs no bush, and North leaves it to the reader to decide whether his biography is in the same category.

97 *Parrhasiana*] Jean Leclerc, *Parrhasiana, or Thoughts upon Several Subjects, as Criticism, History, Morality and Politics ... by Monsieur Le Clerk, under the Feigned
Name of Theodorus Parrhasi* (1700), first published in French (Amsterdam 1699).
Leclerc (1657–1736) was a continental scholar and critic, an Arminian, and a friend
of Locke. While North was taken with the format of Leclerc's book, he disagreed
with many of his views. He had been particularly irritated by Leclerc's *Life and Character of Mr. John Locke*, which North knew in the English translation of 1706 and
which he thought distorted some of the events in the reign of Charles II. He
attacked Leclerc in a pamphlet entitled *Reflections upon Some Passages in Mr. Le
Clerc's Life of Mr. John Locke, in a Letter to a Friend* (1711), reprinted with
North's *Examen*, pp 674–92.

97 Dr Clarke ... philology] Samuel Clarke, DD (1675–1729), philosopher, friend and
popularizer of Newton, whose theories he defended against the attacks of Leibnitz
in *A Collection of Papers which Passed between the Late Learned Mr. Leibnitz and
Dr. Clarke* (1717); for a modern edition see H.G. Alexander, ed, *The Leibnitz-Clarke
Correspondence* (Manchester: Manchester University Press 1956)). North's own
anti-Newtonianism seems to owe much to Leibnitz. Clarke's religious philosophy
was a blend of rationalism and orthodoxy that satisfied neither deists nor conserva-
tives. His most controversial work was *The Scripture-Doctrine of the Trinity*
(1712). North was among the many who were alarmed by the Arian tendency of
this tract, and the British Library has two drafts of his 'Answer to Dr. Samuel

Clarke's Scripture Doctrine of the Trinity' (Add. MSS 32,550 and 32,551); the first is dated 10 February 1713. Despite the encouragement of George Hickes (copy of letter in Add. MSS 32,551), North's attempt at refutation was apparently never published. Despite his antagonism to Clarke, North exchanged letters with him on 'some phisiologicall matters' as F.J.M. Korsten points out: *Roger North* (1651–1734) *Virtuoso and Essayist* (Amsterdam: Academic Publishers Associated 1981), p20; n197 pp264–5.

98 Baron of Kirtling] Dudley, 4th Baron North (b November 1602), educated at Cambridge; he was MP for Horsham 1628–9 and for Cambridgeshire later (*C.P.*, 9:656–7). Roger North gives a sympathetic account of him and Lady North in an unfinished draft of the life of the Lord Keeper (BL, Add. MSS 32,523, ff 5–8). He seems to have been a kind and conscientious man but sorely tried by a tyrannical father, by the problem of supporting a huge family on a small income, and by chronic illness. Passionately fond of music and 'knowing in books of all sorts,' he was himself the author of four published works: *Observations and Advices Oeconomical* (1669); *A Narrative of Some Passages in or Relating to the Long Parliament* (1670); *Some Notes Concerning the Life of Edward Lord North* [1682]; and a devotional work, *Light in the Way to Paradise* (1682). He was also a poet of some ability, as appears from a MS discovered at Hillside House, Newmarket, and sold at Sotheby's (the Honourable Dudleya North, 14 March 1967, item 204). Lord North died on 24 June 1677 and was buried at Kirtling. See also Augustus Jessop's account, *Auto*, 3:283–4.

98 Anne...Boughton family] Lady North was born ca 1613 and married Dudley North in April 1632. She died in February 1681 and was buried, with her husband, at Kirtling (*C.P.*, 9:657). Roger North always speaks of his mother with great tenderness and respect (see *John*, section 98), and with cause, for she seems to have spent her life serving her family. Her letters reveal a lively and good-humoured woman, occupied with the trivialities of family life, and concerned to keep all members of her large family in touch with each other. There is a portrait of her by Cornelius Johnson. Jessop published eleven of her letters (*Auto*, 3:211–20), and there are more in the British Library (Add. MSS 32,500 and 32,501), and among the North papers in the Bodleian Library; see also Sotheby, the Honourable Dudleya North, 14 March 1967, item 206.

98 divers...younger] There were fourteen children:

Charles	became Lord North and Grey
Edward	died young
Francis	the Lord Keeper, became 1st Baron Guilford
Dudley	Turkey merchant, customs commissioner
John	subject of this biography
Montagu	merchant, imprisoned at Toulon

Roger	author of this work
Frances	died young
Katherine	died young
Dorothy	died young
Mary	married Sir William Spring
Anne	married Robert Foley of Stourbridge
Elizabeth	married first Sir Robert Wiseman and then the Earl of Yarmouth
Christian	married Sir George Wenyeve

BL, Add. MSS 32,515, ff 2–2v

98 account ... required] The account is not required because North has already provided it. See *General Preface*, sections 45–8, and appendix, sections I–IV.

98 St Edmunds Bury ... there] King Edward VI Free Grammar School. John North appears in the school list for 1656 (S.H.A. H[ervey], *Biographical List of Boys Educated at King Edward VI Free Grammar School, Bury St. Edmunds, from 1550 to 1900* (Bury St Edmunds 1908), p 278. Thomas Stephens, or Stevens (?–1677), was admitted to Jesus College, Cambridge, in 1629, and was created a DD in 1661. He was high master of the school 1638–45 and 1647–63. John North was to renew his acquaintance with Stephens at Cambridge (section 30), and when Francis North was attorney general, he tried to help Stephens to a church preferment (*Cal. S.P. Dom.*, 1673–5, p 608).

99 everybody else] BL, Add. MSS 32,515, f 4: 'the poor boys who must endure six, seven, or eight hours at a church fasting duty, under the fatigue of four or five holders-forth successively tiring one after another.'

99 Dr Boldero ... hanging] Edmund Boldero, DD (1608–79), a native of Bury St Edmunds, became a fellow of Pembroke Hall, Cambridge, in 1630. He was ejected because of his royalist sympathies and imprisoned. Later he enjoyed the patronage of Bishop Wren, who granted him several livings and nominated him to the mastership of Jesus College, which he assumed in 1663 and where he was to meet John North again (section 9); see P. Barwick, *The Life of Dr. John Barwick* (1724), pp 37–8. There is a delightful but improbable anecdote about Boldero in Gilbert Wakefield's *Memoirs* (1804), 1:80–1, quoted in A. Gray and F. Brittain, *A History of Jesus College* (Cambridge [1960], pp 92–3.

100 Mr Henry Grey] Grey eludes identification. There were several noble families of this name and Henry was a popular Christian name among them.

100 like him] The portrait is still (1983) at Rougham Hall, Norfolk, in the possession of the present Roger North; it was reproduced by Jessop in the 1887 edition of the *Autobiography* (opposite p 156). Sir Peter Lely (1618–80) was a close friend of both Francis and Roger North, who helped him in legal matters (*Francis*, 1:408–10). Roger North was one of Lely's executors and a guardian of his children, and he has left a fascinating account of how he discharged his duties (*Auto,*

3: 190–3 and 198–209). See also the executor's account book. BL, Add. MSS 16,174. Of Blemwell no trace can be found outside of North.

101 Barnadiston] See *Examen*, pp 516–27. Sir Samuel Barnadiston, a Whig, and Lord Huntingtower, a Tory, were competing for the office of Knight of the Shire in Suffolk, made vacant by the death of Sir Henry North in 1672, and Sir William Soame, as sheriff of the county, had to oversee the election. According to North, Barnadiston's supporters mobbed Lord Huntingtower's booth and made a fair election impossible. Soame, uncertain what to do, declared a 'double return' (i.e., both candidates elected) and left it to parliament to decide the issue. The parliamentary committee declared for Barnadiston, who promptly sued Soame and won heavy damages. Francis North, Soame's counsel, advised him to take the case to the Court of Common Pleas. But before the case came up, Francis North became Chief Justice of the Common Pleas (1675) and it fell to him to decide the appeal. Great interest was now aroused, especially since all along the case had been regarded as a trial of strength between the two political parties. As was expected, North reversed the judgment. Some years later, after Francis North's death, Barnadiston revived the issue in the House of Lords and, to forestall his appeal, a pamphlet was published entitled *The Late Lord Chief Justice North's Argument* (1689). For the other side Sir Robert Atkyns produced *An Argument in the Great Case Concerning Election of Members to Parliament* (1689). For a judgment contrary to Francis North's see Pollexfen's *The Arguments and Reports of Sr. Hen. Pollexfen* (1702), pp 470–8, reprinted in *The English Reports* (Edinburgh: William Green 1980), 86:615–17. Roger North's account of the case should be compared with that in *DNB* (under Barnadiston). The inclusion of this incident was no doubt prompted by the fact that Huntingtower and John North had been schoolmates; John North later became an intimate of the family. Lord Huntingtower's mother (Countess of Dysart) married the Duke of Lauderdale (*John*, section 54 and p 184n).

101 few speakers] BL, Add. MSS 32,515, f 5v: 'our doctor had passed through the whole course of this school one or two years before he went to the university, for he was too young to be removed, and his person but diminutive. And in that time he acted as a subtutor or monitor over others in the school; which was likewise a considerable advantage, because it riveted in his mind the classic learning, and so prepared him for other studies at the university.'

101 Molineus] Pierre du Moulin the Elder (1568–1658), Protestant controversialist. His *Elementa logica* (Leyden 1596) went quickly through thirteen editions. Nathanael Delawne's English translation appeared in 1624 and Joshua Ahier's in 1647. Roger North received similar tuition from his father (*Auto*, 3: 13).

102 1661 ... at least] John North was admitted a fellow commoner at Jesus College on 25 February 1661 and matriculated on 13 December 1661 (Bodleian, MS Rawlinson Letters 42, f 252). William Cook (ca 1633–1707) was admitted to Jesus College in April

1648, received an LLDin 1673, and was a fellow of the college from 1653 to 1707. Henry Ferne, DD (1602–62), a writer of political and theological pamphlets, entered Trinity College in 1620. An ardent royalist and king's chaplain, Ferne preached the last sermon Charles heard before his execution. Ferne was made Master of Trinity College at the Restoration and was vice-chancellor in 1660 and 1661. North is mistaken about Boldero's mastership of Jesus, which he did not assume until May 1663 (*John*, section 3 and p 171n). For Dr Stephens see *John*, section 3 and p 171n.

102 grandfather ... nobleman] Dudley, 3rd Baron North (the first with the name Dudley), b London 1582. He succeeded to the barony young and almost ruined himself by his extravagances at the court of James I. He retired early to Kirtling, his estate in Cambridgshire, where 'his active spirit found employment with many airy entertainments, as poetry, writing essays, building, making mottoes and inscriptions' (*Auto*, 3:67). In 1645 he published a miscellany of verse, characters, letters, and reflections, *A Forest of Varieties*, revised in 1659 as *A Forest Promiscuous of Several Seasons Productions*. Roger North, who knew his grandfather only in his old age, depicts him as tyrannical and vindictive, yet he seems to have an amused admiration for this incorrigible old lord, who 'had taken a resolution never to be in the wrong' (*General Preface*, sections 45, 46, repeated in Jessop, 'Author's Preface,' I: 4–6; *Francis*, I: 21, 32–6; *Auto*, 3:67–8). According to the Kirtling Parish Register, Lord North was buried there on 9 January 1667 (letter to the present editor from Mr M.M. Farrar, county archivist, Cambridge, 16 June 1966); his will (Bodleian, MS North c 31, no.37) was proved on 31 January. Roger North is mistaken in saying that John North left the rank of fellow commoner on his grandfather's death; by then he had been a fellow of Jesus for two years.

103 the land] BL, Add. MSS 32,516, f 8: 'I cannot forget my own case in that college, having been to my face reproached by the worthy Dr Cook himself for not having such fine waistcoats as some others he used to name did. I think it is the only place where the follies and fondnesses of youth never die, which in cities and courts they manifestly do.'

BL, Add. MSS 32,514, ff 8v–9: 'It was very common for the rakish part of the college society to sconce this gentleman, as they call it; that is, send to the butteries [where butter, ale, etc. are kept] for whole bellarmines [large drinking jugs named after Cardinal Bellarmine] of ale, and then write it to his head, which being, as they made it, a very good jest, the ale went down the glibber. But when he found them out, it made woeful expostulations, for he with his fluencies of speech would exaggerate the matters, as if he never would conclude, and irritated them so much, that from jesting they came within an ace of quarrelling; and this sometimes when the sconce was not above 1d. or 1½d, still urging that by the same rule it might be £10. All which, that might as well have been passed over with a witty reprehension, as ralliation between jest and earnest, made them conclude that avarice had possession of the very soul of him. I remember once among his friends he maintained a notable thesis in philosophy, which was that laying his clothes upon his bed contributed to the sooner wearing them out because heat macerated and caused a *solutio continui* [continuous dissolving], and for that reason forbore so to do. After he was preferred, and had got a little money aforehand, his relations used to get him securities at interest for it, and sometimes for want of such keep it in their hands and pay him a moderate interest. And this course was very agreeable to him. But once it fell out that £1000 of his was paid in to him on a sudden by his best friend [Francis North] ... It is not easy to conceive how this sudden stroke concerned him; it must have been a very great mischance that should inflict such a melancholy dejection as for above a week, or rather till his money was adrift again, apparently seized his spirits.

103 brother and friend] Francis North, 1st Baron Guilford (1637–85), the 'best brother' who plays such a prominent part in Roger North's biographical writing. In his rapid climb to the post of Lord Keeper he pulled his brothers with him and became, in effect, the saviour of the family. In 1675 he tried to secure the mastership of Jesus College for John North (*Cal. S.P. Dom.*, 1673–5, p 608), and he was probably behind most of his brother's preferments.

104 old usurer] It has not been possible to identify the 'old usurer'; possibly it is Roger North's joke against himself.

104 Dr Cave ... Dr Beaumont] William Cave, DD (1637–1713), son of a clergyman made poor because of his royalist sympathies. Cave wrote church history voluminously and at one time carried on a long paper war with Leclerc. 'He was an excellent and universal scholar, an elegant and polite writer, and a florid and very eloquent preacher': John Nichols, *The History and Antiquities of the County of Leicester* (1798), vol 2, pt 2, p 774. Joseph Beaumont, DD (1616–99), son of a clothier of Hadleigh, Suffolk, was admitted to Peterhouse, Cambridge, in 1631, and became a fellow in 1636. He was ejected in 1644, but at the Restoration became master first of Jesus College, then of Peterhouse, and in 1674 Regius Professor of Divinity. Beaumont was author of *Psyche* (1648), an epic poem of staggering length allegorizing the progress of the Christian soul through the world. *A Life* by John Gee is prefixed to *Original Poems by Joseph Beaumont* (Cambridge 1749); see Hugh Pigot, 'History of Hadleigh,' *Proceedings of Suffolk Institute of Archeology* (Lowestoft 1863), 3:157–8).

104 *Admissus ... 1666*] He was admitted as a fellow of Jesus College by mandate and letter of the king. '1666' should read '1664' (see Arthur Gray's notebooks, Muniments Room, Jesus College, Cambridge; *Alum. Cantab.*). Bishop Wren's confirming mandate followed on 29 October of the same year (Jesus College, Cambridge, MS Caryl 37–14). John North, therefore, had been in the college less than four

years. The mistake originated in a letter from Thomas Baker, the Cambridge antiquarian, to his Oxford friend Hilkiah Bedford. Roger North knew Bedford and
must have asked him to make enquiries at Cambridge about John North. The
result was the letter from Baker, dated 12 February 1716, providing several useful
but not entirely accurate details of John North's career (Bodleian, MS Rawlinson
Letters 42, f 252).

104-5 the bishop ... name] Matthew Wren (1585-1667), uncle of Sir Christopher, protégé
of Lancelot Andrewes, Master of Peterhouse, Bishop of Hereford, of Norwich,
and, 1638, of Ely. As Bishop of Ely Wren was Visitor of Jesus College and so would
be called upon to arbitrate any disputed matter. This anecdote was provided by
Thomas Baker in his letter to Hilkiah Bedford (see preceding note) and is not
quite correct. According to college statutes, there had to be an equal number of
northern and southern fellows. As a Cambridgeshire man John North was a sou-
therner, but by virtue of royal mandate he had taken the place that should have
gone to a northerner. The fellows were at a loss to know how to proceed at the
next election and applied to the Visitor for guidance. The bishop ruled that, despite his origin, North should be regarded as a northerner. Only a saint could have
resisted the pun (Jesus College, Cambridge, MS Caryl 35-28; Gray and Brittain,
Jesus College, pp 154-5).

105 This Mr Scott ... loss of him] Robert Scott (ca 1633-after 1692), whose customers
included Charles II, Sir Christopher Wren, Robert Hooke, William Temple, and
Samuel Pepys. Adiel Mill was apparently an unscrupulous adventurer who bought
Scott's stock and goodwill with money entrusted to his care by his cousin Moses
Pitt. It was Pitt who had overreached himself in the atlas project and was trying to
escape his creditors by making over his assets to Mill. When Mill failed to pay the
promised instalments, Scott and other creditors made him bankrupt and he was
forced to join Pitt, who was by now in Fleet Prison. See Graham Pollard and
Albert Ehrman, *The Distribution of Books by Catalogue* (Cambridge: Roxburghe
Club 1965), pp 94-6; and Leona Rostenberg, 'Robert Scott, Restoration Stationer
and Importer,' *Papers of the Bibliographical Society of America*, 48 (1954), 49-76.
Roger North took a friendly interest in Scott and in 1692 tried to help him avoid
another fraud, this time concerning a mortgage. North appealed to his brother-in-
law Robert Foley to advise Scott, 'who hath parted with his stock, but happens to
be intrigued in it which hath given him much trouble. He never was other than an
honest man, even in his trade, though in that hard enough, but out of it never was
a more generous true-spirited man. He was absolutely the prime merchant-libraire
of his time in Europe, and hath at this time credit in all places where books are
dealt with and esteemed, and hath been in the cabinets of most eminent statesmen' (BL, Add. MSS 32,500, ff 143-143v).

106 Aulus Gellius) Aulus Gellius (ca AD 123 –ca 165). His *Noctes atticae* is a huge
 compendium of history, biography, criticism, anecdotes, and extracts from
 Roman and Greek authors. For a modern translation see J.C. Rolfe, *The Attic Nights
 of Aulus Gellius* (Heinemann 1927).

106 Gryphius] Sebastian Gryphius (1493–1556). In order to meet the new demand for
 handy editions of the classics, Gryphius remodelled his printing house at Lyons,
 acquiring several new founts of type, including the exquisite italic for which he and
 other Lyonaise printers became famous. From 1528 until his death he issued over a
 thousand works, mainly popular editions of the classics in Latin, and gained a high reputation among scholars for his extraordinary accuracy. See R.C. Christie, 'Sebastian
 Gryphius, printer [a Fragment],' in *Historical Essays*, ed T.F. Tout and J. Tait (Manchester: Manchester University Press 1907), pp 307–23.

106 old Elzevir] The compact roman type associated with the famous editions of the
 classics produced by the Elzevir (or Elzeveir) family in the Low Countries throughout the seventeenth century. The type was neat and strong, but closely set and
 uncomfortable to read. See D.B. Updike, *Printing Types* (Cambridge, Mass.: Bel-
 knap Press of Harvard University Press 1962), I: 15.

106 Guilford] Francis, 2nd Baron Guilford (1673–1729) (*C.P.*, 6:212). When his father
 died in 1685, he became the ward of his three uncles, Dudley, Montagu, and Roger
 (*Francis*, I: 110).

106 that time and ours] The 1670s and 1680s, as opposed to the time of writing, the
 1720s.

107 Bateman, Innys] Christopher Bateman dealt first in Middle Row, Holborn, and
 then at the Bible and Crown, Paternoster Row, and was active until ca 1730. Swift
 was one of the book-lovers attracted by Bateman's large stock of new and second-
 hand books: *Journal to Stella*, ed H. Williams (Oxford: Clarendon Press 1948),
 I: 157, 178–9, 310; 2:601. Other accounts of Bateman are in J. Nichols, *Literary
 Anecdotes of the Eighteenth Century* (1812), I:424n; J. Dunton, *The Life and
 Errors of John Dunton* (1818), p 217; H.R. Plomer, *A Dictionary of Printers and
 Booksellers* (Oxford: Oxford University Press 1922), pp 2–25; F.A. Mumby, *Pub-
 lishing and Bookselling, a History*, rev ed (Jonathan Cape 1954), p 142. Probably
 Innys is William Innys who dealt from the Prince's Arms, St Paul's Churchyard,
 during the first quarter of the eighteenth century (Plomer, *Dictionary*, pp 167–8).
 Hume referred to him as 'the greatest bookseller in Paul's Churchyard': S.C.
 Roberts, *A History of the Cambridge University Press 1521–1921* (Cambridge:
 Cambridge University Press 1921), p 91 n.

108 served] BL, Add. MSS 32,516, ff 18–18v: 'That worthy person is famous in the college
 for his insensate behaviour in the college hall. He would stand at the hearth, and
 warm his hands at midsummer; and if one changed his meal for a dry bone, he
 would be satisfied, thinking he had dined, and the like.'

108 name, T.P. ... pun] Timothy Puller (1638?–93), fellow of Jesus College 1658–76 (North reveals his full name in BL, MSS 32,516, f 18v). Judging from his book, *The Modera-tion of the Church of England* (1679) (rev Robert Eden, 1870), he was not so fatuous as this anecdote might suggest. John North officiated at Puller's wedding to Alice Codrington in December 1676 at Westminster Abbey: *Registers of ... West-minster*, ed J.L. Chester (Harleian Society 1876), 10:14n.

109 music ... family] For a full account of the family addiction to music see John Wilson, ed, *Roger North on Music* (Novello [1959]).

109 master of arts] 'One Mr. Parnell,' according to BL, Add. MSS 32,515, f 31. Probably Robert Paynell (d 1677), admitted to Jesus College in 1656. 'He had an extraordinary gift of sleeping, and once after dinner, being about the time of his rising, the fellows went into his chamber to visit him; he was abed and by him lay Baxter's *Saints' Ever-lasting Rest*': Add. MSS 32,515, f 31v.

110 act-keeping suppers] Act-keeping was the public defence of a thesis by a candidate for a degree. The supper was probably the entertainment mentioned in W.W. Rouse Ball, *Cambridge Notes*, 2nd ed (Cambridge: Heffer 1921), p 285. It was given by the moderators to the proctors and others on the night before publication of the degree results.

111 Mr Wagstaffe ... gentleman] John Wagstaffe (1633–77), an Oxonian. Anthony à Wood described him, unkindly, as 'a little crooked man, and of a despicable presence,' and when his book on witchcraft appeared, he was 'laughed at by the wags of this univer-sity, because, as they said, he himself look'd like a little wizard.' He died 'in a manner distracted, occasion'd by a deep conceit of his own parts, and by a continual bibbing of strong and high tasted liquors' (*Athen. Oxon.*, 3:1113–14).

111 book of witchcraft] *The Question of Witchcraft Debated, or a Discourse against their Opinions that Affirm Witches* (1669; 2nd enlarged ed 1671). Perhaps the reason North remembered Wagstaffe is that he was later to gain firsthand expe-rience of witches as a lawyer accompanying his brother on the Western Circuit. His enlightened and compassionate attitude (possibly influenced by Wagstaffe) relieves the otherwise sad reading (*Francis*, 1:166–9; *Auto*, 3:130–2).

111 Dr Sherman's ... Dr Stephens'] John Sherman, DD (d 1671), was appointed a fellow of Jesus College in 1650 and became president (a senior position among the fel-lows) in 1662. He is the author of *Historia Colegii Jesu, Cantabrigiensis*, ed J.O. Halliwell (1840), one MS copy of which was presented to John North and is still preserved at Jesus College (MS. ANT. I.2); see Gray and Brittain, *Jesus College*, p 84. For Dr Stephens see *John*, section 3 and p 171n.

112 old Silenus] The name humorously applied to Socrates because of his resemblance to the satyr Silenus (Plato, *Symposium*, 215B).

112 Mr Walpole, Sir Edmund Bacon] Robert Walpole (1650–1700) of Houghton, Norfolk, father of Robert Walpole the statesman. He was admitted to Trinity

College in 1667. Highly esteemed by the Whigs, he was elected deputy lieutenant of Norfolk and colonel of the militia; he was also MP for Castle Rising. Roger North became a neighbour of the Walpoles when he retired to Rougham and appears to have been on very friendly terms with them (*Auto*, 3:305). Sir Edmund Bacon (ca 1652–83) of Gillingham, Norfolk, succeeded his father as 2nd baronet in 1666, the year he was admitted to Caius College. He entered Lincoln's Inn in 1669: John Venn, *Biographical History of Gonville and Caius College 1349–1897* (Cambridge 1897), 1:426. The names are given in skeleton form in the copy text, but appear in full in BL, Add. MSS 32,516, f 23 v.

112 Sir Christopher] Sir Christopher Hatton (ca 1651–1720) of Long Stanton, Camridgeshire, admitted at Jesus College in 1669, entered the Middle Temple in 1670. He became 5th baronet in 1685.

112 the Capels] Arthur Capel, Earl of Essex (1631–83), and Sir Henry Capel, Baron Capel of Tewkesbury (d 1696). Essex became Monmouth's main adviser, and at the discovery of the Rye House Plot was imprisoned in the Tower where, in July 1683, he was found with his throat cut, an apparent suicide. The Norths were related to the Capels on the maternal side: B. Burke, *Dormant ... and Extinct Peerages* (1883).

112 Mr Sydney Godolphin ... Middle Temple] A slip on North's part, also appearing in an earlier MS version (BL, Add. MSS 32,516, f 24) but corrected there. Sydney Godolphin, the lord treasurer and 1st Earl of Godolphin, was never a member of the Middle Temple and did not die until 1712. North means Francis Godolphin, an older brother of the lord treasurer, who was admitted to the Middle Temple in 1667–8: H.A.C. Sturgess, *Register of Admissions to the ... Middle Temple* (Butterworth 1949), 1:176. He died in 1675 while travelling to Dublin on government business: H. Elliot, *The Life of Sydney, Earl of Godolphin, K.G.* (1888), p 61.

112 Mr Charles] Charles Godolphin was admitted to the Middle Temple in January 1670 – nine months after Roger North himself – and was called to the bar in 1677: Sturgess, *Register*, 1:180.

112 fire ... counsumed] The fire occurred in January 1679 and North has left a vivid account of it in his *Autobiography* (3:37–44).

112 Sir John King ... Westminster Hall] Sir John King (1639–77), Queen's College, Cambridge, was admitted to the Inner Temple in 1660 and called to the bar in 1667. A man of spectacular talent and industry, he soon controlled a huge and lucrative chancery practice. He became king's counsel and attorney general to the Duke of York and was knighted in 1674. Roger North gives a character sketch of King in *Francis* (1:380–1); Tully is a familiar name for Cicero: hence, an outstanding orator. Westminster Hall is part of the old Westminster Palace built by William Rufus, the principal seat of justice from the time of Henry III until the nineteeenth century.

112 Mr William Longueville] William Longueville (1639–1721) was called to the bar of
the Inner Temple in 1660. He made a large amount of money in conveyancing and
was able to restore the ruined family fortunes. He was a friend of Samuel Butler,
often helped him towards the end of his life, and finally paid for his burial. Both
Roger and Francis North thought highly of Longueville and employed him in
family business (*Auto*, 3:237–9). There is a character sketch of him in *Francis*
(1:379–80).

113 the ladies ... to be carved] That is, to carve for him. The implication is that, since
the women could not occupy the honourable places at the upper end of the table
in their own right, they must be there in the capacity of servants.

113 sinecure ... Llandinam] Llandinam, Montgomeryshire. The certificate of subscrip-
tion, signed by Sheldon, is dated 18 November 1670 (Bodleian, MS North c 25, f
11).

113 Dr Sheldon] Gilbert Sheldon (1598–1677), Chancellor of Oxford, Archbishop of
Canterbury 1663. He was a firm anti-puritan, an able administrator, and a munifi-
cent man – the Sheldonian Theatre at Oxford was built at his expense and was
merely the most spectacular of many benefactions.

113 Canterbury] BI, Add. MSS 32,516, f 26: 'He [Sheldon] had been a cavalier in the
rebellious times. When excluded from his posts at Oxford, he retired, and during[?] the wars lived eremitically [as a recluse or hermit] in or about Nottingham-
shire. The Trent was a great delight to him, for he loved fishing, and so also the
other common recreations in the country, as coursing, etc.'

114 in the place of them] BI, Add. MSS 32,515, f 19: 'It is pity there is not a power in the
university to transfer the revenues to uses more diffusively profitable to the students in general. And if one may have leave to suggest in such a case, it should be
for the purpose of erecting and maintaining of public lending-libraries for the use
of the bachelors and undergraduates, who are denied access to all the libraries
within or without the colleges in the whole university ... As it stands now, the most
pregnant lads, sons of ministers and others not able to buy for themselves, are
lost for want of a little early access to books.'

115 Kirk] Kirk's coffee-house was in the parish of Gt St Mary although its exact location is uncertain. In 1664 one H. Kirke paid hearth tax in that parish on seven
chimneys, and in 1674 on fourteen, so that his business seems to have thrived:
W.M. Palmer, *Cambridge Borough Documents* (Cambridge: Council of the
Borough of Cambridge 1931), 1:140–1. Kirk also paid poor rates from 1660 until
1691, his Christian name appearing as Henry from 1663. The coffee-house was
apparently still in existence in 1749, when it is recorded as paying tax (Palmer,
Cambridge Borough Documents, 1:73). H.P. Stokes, 'Topographical Notes on the
Hearth Tax Records [1664 and 1674],' *Cambridge Antiquarian Society Proceed-
ings* (Cambridge: Cambridge Antiquarian Society 1915–16), 20:91, mentions a

coffee-house between Great St Mary's Church and the University Library, and if this was Kirk's, then it stood on the west side of what is now King's Parade (formerly High Street), on the site at present occupied by the Senate House, or the lawn in front of the Old Schools. A search among university property deeds, however, has failed to confirm this location. (I am indebted to Mr J.M. Farrar, Cambridgeshire county archivist, for most of the above information).

115 Muddiman] Henry Muddiman (1629–92) was important in the founding of the official government newspaper that started in November 1665 as the *Oxford Gazette*, changing its title to the *London Gazette* twenty-four issues later. His main achievement was the production of an enormous number of newsletters sent regularly from London to various centres in the provinces during a period of over twenty years. Two examples, addressed to 'Mr. Kirke, Cambridge,' have been printed, one dated 16 August 1670 (*Cal. S.P. Dom.*, 1670, pp 378–9), the other 9 May 1671 (*Cal. S.P. Dom.*,671, pp 224–5). For an account of Henry Muddiman see J.G. Muddiman, *The King's Journalist 1659–1689* (John Lane 1923).

115 din ... coffee-house] Roger North's objection to coffee-houses was originally political. In 1676 Francis North was involved in the court's arbitrary measure to close coffee-houses on the grounds that they were being 'used to nourish sedition, spread lies, scandalize great men and the like.' Roger North strains to defend the action in *Francis* (1:197–8) and *Examen* (pp 138–41).

115 more publicly] BL, Add. MSS 32,515, ff 19v–20: 'He bent his endeavours much towards extemporary preaching, and always, when the congregation was such as he might venture in, offered somewhat at it. But either want of memory or diffidence of himself hindered his attaining that perfection."

115 The sermon ... 1671] *A Sermon Preached before the King at Newmarket October 8 1671 ... Printed by His Magisties Special Command* (Cambridge 1671). There was a special edition (partly from standing type but the greater part a page-by-page reprint) dated the same year. John Evelyn mentions another sermon by John North, at Whitehall, March 1676. The preacher struck him as 'a very young, but learned & excellent person': *The Diary*, ed E.S. de Beer (Oxford: Clarendon Press, 1955), 4:87.

115 The text ... that way] Ps. 1:1: 'Blessed is the man that walketh not in the counsel of the ungodly.'

116 his father's house] Probably Tostock in Suffolk, rather than Kirtling, Cambridgeshire.

116 Sir Roger Burgoyne] Probably Sir Robert Burgoyne, Bt (1618–77), of Sutton, Bedfordshire, about eighteen miles from Cambridge. He was a member of Lincoln's Inn and an active politician: G.E.C., ed, *Complete Baronetage* (Exeter: Pollard 1900–9), 2:104.

116 her sister] Elizabeth, eldest daughter of Sir Charles Montagu of Boughton and niece of Henry, 1st Earl of Manchester (*C.P.*, 6:396).

116 old Lord Hatton] Christopher Hatton (1602?–70), descendant of Lord Chancellor
    Hatton, Queen Elizabeth's favourite. An ardent royalist, Hatton joined Charles II in
    exile and was created Baron Hatton of Kirby in 1643 (*C.P.*, 6:396–7). For a further
    indication of Hatton's unkindness see Lady Hatton's letter of 22 September 1666 in
    Correspondence of the Family of Hatton, ed E.M. Thompson (1878), 1:50.

117 Hatton's *Psalms*] *The Psalter of David with Titles and Collects According to the Mat-
    ter of Each Psalme* (Oxford 1644). It went through many editions, continuing into
    the eighteenth century. The authorship is disputed (see *Athen, Oxon.*, 1:583–4n).

117 'Nando Masham] The copytext reads: 'Nando M----m. The full name appears in an
    earlier MS version (BL, Add. MSS 32,516, f 30) where North refers to 'Ferdinando
    Masham, the denominator of 'Nando's coffee-house.' 'Nando's was a famous
    coffee-house at no. 15 Fleet Street and a favourite haunt of lawyers: B. Lillywhite,
    London Coffee Houses (Allen and Unwin 1963), p 381.

117 her eldest son] Christopher Hatton, 2nd Baron (1632–1706), Governor of Guernsey,
    created Viscount Hatton of Gretton in 1683 (*C.P.*, 4:397).

117 brother ... sisters at ease] Hatton had three sisters, Mary, Jane, and Alice (Burke,
    Extinct Peerages). Of Charles Hatton only a little is known. There is a brief note of
    him in *Hatton Correspondence*, ed Thompson, 1:60, and from his letters there he
    emerges as an alert, well-read man, an arboriculturist, and a friend of Evelyn and
    Pepys. It is not clear why North bestows upon him the epithet 'incomparable.'

117 Countess of Thanet's daughter] Lady Cicely Tufton, whom he married in February
    1667. He married three times altogether (*C.P.*, 6:397).

118 miraculously preserved] Cf the more circumstantial accounts of the explosion in J.
    Jacob, *Annals of ... the Bailiwick of Guernsey* (Paris 1830), pp 116–17; and *Regis-
    ters of ... Westminster*, ed Chester, 10:178–89, n 5.

118 Morgans and Mansels ... kindred] It was a very slight kinship. One of John North's
    great-uncles, Sir Walter Montagu, married Anne Morgan, daughter of Henry Mor-
    gan (Burke, *Extinct Peerages*, p 374) and one of his mother's cousins married Sir
    Lewis Mansel (G.E.C., *Complete Baronetage*, 1:4).

118 brother's house ... Oxfordshire] Wroxton Abbey, near Banbury. Francis North came
    into possession of the estate through his marriage with Lady Frances Pope, daugh-
    ter of the Earl of Downe. Roger North describes life at the house in *Francis*
    (1:346–52) and *Dudley* (2:242–5). See *Victoria History of the County of Oxford*
    (Oxford: Oxford University Press 1969), 9:171–88.

119 Dr Hutton] Matthew Hutton, DD (1639–1711), fellow of Brasenose College, rector
    of Aynho (Northamptonshire) from 1677 until his death. Although Hutton does
    not appear to have published anything, he was an industrious antiquarian and left
    behind him many volumes of historical matter in MS.

119 Dr Fell] John Fell, DD (1625–86), Dean of Christ Church, Bishop of Oxford, and
    Vice-Chancellor of Oxford University. A man of unrelenting energy, he modified

almost every aspect of the university's life. Perhaps his most important work was with the University Press. He helped in setting up the first regular type foundry at Oxford and the paper-mill at Wolvercote and was the moving force behind the production of many fine works of scholarship. See S. Morison, *John Fell, the University Press and the 'Fell' Type* (Oxford: Clarendon Press 1967).

119 Dr Barrow] Isaac Barrow (1630–77), classical scholar, mathematician, controversialist, and preacher. He became Greek Professor in 1660, Geometry Professor at Gresham College in 1662, and the first Lucasian Professor of Mathematics in 1663. He resigned this last post in 1669 in favour of Isaac Newton, whose transcendent abilities he was one of the first to recognize (see *John*, section 61). Barrow succeeded Pearson as Master of Trinity in 1673.

119 The good ... day] North contradicts Walter Pope on this point, for, according to Pope, Barrow died 'in mean Lodgings, at a Sadlers near Charing-Cross, an old, low, ill built House, which he had used for several Years': *The Life of ... Seth* [*Ward*] (1697), p167. W. Whewell's attempt to reconcile the two accounts in 'Barrow and His Academical Times,' in *The Theological Works of Isaac Barrow*, ed A. Napier (Cambridge 1859), 9:xIv, is not entirely convincing, especially since in the earlier MS versions Roger North is even more explicit on the point (BI, Add. MSS 32,515, f 23; and 32,516 ff 33–33v, where he specifies Westminster).

120 it proved] BI, Add. MSS 32,516, f 33v: 'The doctor never spoke of this friend of his without passion, so great did he esteem the loss by his death. And I have known him relate the passage of the master's being once attacked by an huge mastiff in the country before any of the family (where he was) were stirring (for every morning at about four he went to the pump to wash his face and hands), and with what danger of his life he fought with and subdued the dog. I could perceive that all the while he talked, he trembled, such a terrible image he had as his friend's case were to have been his own in earnest.'

120 death ... upon him] Barrow died on 4 May 1677 and was buried in Westminster: *Registers of ... Westminster*, ed J.L. Chester 10:191. John North's warrant for the mastership is dated from Whitehall, 5 May 1677 (*Cal. S.P. Dom.*, 1677–8, p 113).

120 Professor graecae linguae] North assumed the professorship on 1 November 1762, succeeding Thomas Gale, and resigned it on 6 April 1674 (Camb. Univ. Lib., MSS Mm.2.25 and Mm.1.42).

121 Grecian] James Duport, DD (1606–79), fellow of Trinity College and Master of Magdalene, became Greek Professor in 1639 but was deprived of the post in 1654 by the Commissioners for Reforming the University. Reinstated at the Restoration, he immediately resigned in favour of his former pupil Isaac Barrow. According to Bishop Monk, Duport 'appears to have been the main instrument by which literature was upheld in this University during the civil disturbances in the 17th century': J.H.

Monk, 'Memoir of Dr. James Duport,' in *Museum Criticum, or Cambridge Classical Researches* (Cambridge 1826), 2:672-98.

121 poem ... folio 60] *Musae subsevivae, seu poetica stromata* (Cambridge 1676), pp 60-1. In his poem Duport insists on John North's ability despite his youthfulness. He celebrates both the breadth of North's reading in Greek (the writers he has mastered represent many different areas in ancient Greece, and include poets, dramatists, orators, and historians), and his skill (the poets include two of the most linguistically difficult).

122 younger ... Persians] Alexander the Great (356-323 BC) was 25 in 331, the year of the second defeat of Darius, King of Persia. John North was 27 when he became Professor of Greek.

122 Attic city ... Doric camps] The Attic city is Athens, the capital of Attica. The Doric Camp: associated with Doris, a small country south of Thessaly; in literature Doric signifies rustic, especially as opposed to the pure and polished Attic style.

122 Nemean and Pythian heroes] Presumably the winners of contests at the Nemean games (an important Panhellenic festival by 527 BC, held at Nemea), and the Pythian games (a festival at Delphi, next in importance to the Olympics).

122 Lycophron] The imputed author (b ca 320 BC) of the *Alexander* which, because of its recondite material, its blending of inconsistent myths, and its unusualness of language has claim to be the most obscure poem in Greek.

122 the Stagiritics] Of, or pertaining to, Aristotle, known as the Stagirite because he was born in Stageira.

122 Alexipharmics ... Nicander] Nicander (fl prob. 2nd century BC), author of two didactic poems about poisons and their antidotes, *Theriaca* and *Alexipharmaca*. Scholars are drawn to him by the obscurity of his language and style. An alexipharmic is an antidote.

122 rustics of Theocritus] The bucolic poems of Theocritus (ca 300-ca 260 BC?).

122 Aeschylus ... buskins] The tragedies of Aeschylus (525/4-456 BC) and Sophocles (496-406 BC).

123 Cecropian honey] The sweet arts of Cecropia (Attica), named after Cecrops, the legendary first king of that region.

123 Boreas ... weather] Aquilo, like Boreas, is a north wind. As the wind clears clouds from the sky, so North clears up the obscurities in Aristophanes' comedy *Clouds* (*Nubes*).

123 before he was ... Charles II] The Clerk of the Closet 'is commonly some Reverend, discreet Divine, extraordinarily esteemed by his Majesty whose Office is to attend at the King's Right Hand during Divine Service, to resolve all Doubts concerning Spiritual matters, to wait on His Majesty in his private Oratory or Closet': E. Chamberlayne, *Angliae notitiae* (1682), p 145. There is no mention of John North

as Clerk of the Closet either in the Lord Chamberlain's roll (*Notes and Queries*, 173 (1937), 8–9) or in *Angliae notitiae*, but that he held the position is confirmed by John Evelyn in his *Diary*, ed de Beer, 4:97n, and by à Wood, *Fasti Oxonienses*, ed P. Bliss (1815), 2:311. The date of North's appointment is uncertain. In an earlier MS version (BI, Add. MSS 32,515, ff 28–28v) Roger North says it was before John became prebend of Westminister, i.e., before 11 January 1673, but a letter from Bishop Carleton, referring to 'Lord North's son, that is to be, as reported, Clerk of the Closet,' is dated September 1674: *Cal. S.P. Dom.*, 1673–5, p 359). North is often vague about dates, so that it is safer to rely on those provided by Carleton and Evelyn and to place the appointment between September 1674 and September 1676. John North held the post, according to another MS version of the *Life*, 'for divers years': BI, Add. MSS 32,516, f 38.

124 title ... *la cour*] The 'foolish French writer' has eluded all attempts at identification.

124 piety ... there] Such piety, perhaps, as that of the remarkable Margaret Blagge (Mrs Godolphin), John North's third cousin. See H. Sampson, ed, *The Life of Mrs. Godolphin* (Oxford: Oxford University Press 1939), pp xix–xx.

124 During ... Westminster] John North gained the prebendary some time earlier in fact. He was installed on 11 January 1673: J. Le Neve, *Fasti ecclesiae anglicanae*, ed T.D. Hardy (Oxford 1854), 3:361.

125 Duke of Lauderdale] John Maitland, 2nd Earl and 1st Duke of Lauderdale (1616–82), adviser and close friend of Charles II. A ruthless, determined, and able man, he worked himself into a position of great power and was a target for his many enemies. For reasons of policy he needed an English peerage and so in 1674 he was created Earl of Guilford. it was apparently as a compliment to the duke that Francis North later adopted the title which had become extinct at the duke's death (*Francis*, 1:363). Lauderdale figures greatly in Gilbert Burnet's *History of My Own Time* and the famous character appears in O. Airy's edition (Oxford 1897–1900), 1:184–5. For Francis North's relations with the duke see *Francis*, 1:231–2.

125 Countess ... corresponded] Elizabeth, Countess of Dysart (ca 1627–98), daughter of William Murray, 1st Earl of Dysart. Her first husband was Sir Lionel Tollemache, and John North's school friends (see next note) were the children of this marriage. She married the Duke of Lauderdale in March 1672 (*C.P.*, 4:563). The estate of John North's father, Dudley, 4th Baron North, was at Tostock, close to Fakenham.

125 the Tollemaches] Probably Lionel Tollemache, Lord Huntingtower and Earl of Dysart (1649–1727), and Thomas Tollemache (ca 1651–94), a distinguished soldier: Hervey, *Biographical List*, pp 391–2.

126 degree ... doctor] There is no mention of John North's DD in the published Cambridge records, but since the ceremony took place while Dr Barrow was vice-chancellor (see *John*, section 56), it must have been between 1675 and 1676. C.H. Cooper places it in 1676, but perhaps on the same evidence: *Annals of Cambridge*

(Cambridge 1845), 3:573. The king was at Newmarket on two occasions in 1676, at the end of March and in October (*Cal. S.P. Dom.*, 1676-7, p v).

126 the Orator] Henry Paman, MD (1623-95), Public Orator, 1674-81. North supplies his name in BL, Add. MSS 32,515, f 30. One of Paman's eight Latin letters published in John Ward's *Lives of the Professors of Gresham College* (1740) is addressed to Francis North (pp 136-7). That he was on friendly terms with the family is further indicated by *Francis* (1:108-9) and *Auto* (3:111) and by his letters in the Bodleian Library, two of which are to Dudley, 4th Baron North (Dep. *c* 280, f 30). He attended at the last illness of Sir Dudley North (BL, Add. MSS 32,500, ff 139-40).

126 mastership of Trinity College] May 1677.

127 *dialogi selecti*] *Platonis de rebus divinis, dialogi selecti graece et latine* (Cambridge: Joann. Hayes 1673; 2nd ed 1683). John North had help with this work; Thomas Baker wrote to Hilkiah Bedford in February 1716: 'Mr. Billers had no acquaintance with him [John North], but upon the Doctor's being taken ill, he was desired by the bookseller to perfect the edition, which he did by taking care of the press, and adding a preface, and further says not' (Bodleian, MS Rawlinson Letters 43, f 252). John Billers was a fellow of St John's College from 1671 until his ejection as a non-juror in 1717.

128 Ficinus ... Serrenus] Marsilio Ficino (1433-99), Italian philosopher and linguist, began his translations of Plato in 1463 under the patronage of Cosimo de Medici. Jean de Serres (ca 1540-98) is a French historian and theologian; his translation of Plato appeared in Geneva in 1578.

128 pieces ... Gale] Thomas Gale (1635?-1702), John North's immediate predecessor in the Greek professorship. John North's translation of Pythagoras was in Gale's *Opuscula mythologica, ethica et physica, graece et latine* (Cambridge 1671). It reappeared in J.A. Fabrici's *Bibliothecae graecae* (Hamburg 1724), 12:617-35, and in J.C. Orelli's *Opuscula graecorum veterum* (Leipzig 1819-21), 2:209-33.

129 *actum ... tetragonismo*] He is finished with squaring the circle. The problem exercised some of the best mathematical minds of the time, including the British scholars Wallis (see *Biographia Britannica* [1747-66], vol 6, pt 2, pp 4120-1), Gregory, and Newton. For a history of the subject see J.E. Montaclu, *Histoire des recherches sur la quadrature du cercle* (Paris 1831; first published 1754); A. de Morgan, *A Budget of Paradoxes* (1872); W.W. Rouse Ball, *Mathematical Recreations and Problems*, 2nd ed (1892), pp 162-73.

129 Sir Isaac Newton ... contemporary] Sir Isaac Newton (1642-1727) matriculated at Cambridge in 1661, the same year as John North, and when North migrated to Trinity College in 1672, Newton had been a fellow there for about five years. As a fellow of the same college, and then as master, North was in a position to know the great scientist fairly well. When Francis North produced a pamphlet proposing a theory of harmony (*A Philosophical Essay on Music* [1677]), John North wrote

to Newton about it. The reply, dated Cambridge, 21 April 1677, is printed in *The Correspondence of Isaac Newton*, ed H.W. Turnbull (Cambridge: Royal Society 1959–61), 2:205–8 (also in *Hinrichsen's Musical Year Book 1945–46*, ed R. Hill and M. Hinrichsen [Hinrichsen Edition Ltd. 1946], pp 400–3).

130 better] BI, Add. MSS 32,515, f 34: '[Sir Isaac Newton] was a contemporary with the doctor in the college, and greatly esteemed by him. And it is not to be doubted but the great Sir Isaac was much assisted by Dr Barrow in his mathematic studies, if not obliged with important hints from him which he hath improved to his own very great fame; yet, however, it happens nothing of that nature is recognized in any of his books published since the Master's death.

BI, Add. MSS 32,516, ff 44v–45: 'Sir Isaac Newton was a contemporary with these and made by nature for the mathematics; notwithstanding and some have pretended that his choicest speculations are derived upon hints given him by Dr Barrow, especially those of his grand cosmography. But if so, it falls out oddly that the Master (Dr Barrow) is not so much as named in any of his writings, so far from any acknowledgment of any assistances of that kind to be found there.' North's remarks are interesting in view of D.T. Whiteside's contention that, at least during Newton's early years at Cambridge, Barrow's influence was negligible: *The Mathematical Papers of Isaac Newton ... 1664–1666* (Cambridge: Cambridge University Press 1967), I:10. Whiteside mentions that the tradition of Barrow's influence was already established at the time of Newton's death, and the question arises whether Roger North's remarks, by virtue of his kinship with the Master of Trinity College, carry more authority than those of his contemporaries. On the whole, I think not; North appears to be repeating what was perhaps a longstanding rumour among the virtuosi.

130 solitary pupil] Roger North. For a detailed account of his studies at Cambridge see *Auto*, 3:15–17.

130 Fournier's ... Euclid] Georges Fournier (1595–1652), author of *Euclidis sex primi elementorum geometricorum libri* (Paris 1644). Roger North might have used the Cambridge edition of 1665.

130 method of the schools ... *solvere*] The effectiveness of an argument was judged, not on the basis of whether or not it was true, but on whether it followed certain technical rules of reasoning. *Solvit*: it proves, resolves.

131 Rapin's works ... published] René Rapin (1621–87), Jesuit theologian and critic. North must be thinking particularly of his *Réflexions sur la philosophie ancienne et moderne* (Paris 1676). An English translation appeared in 1678, well within John North's lifetime.

132 Socinians] Followers of the doctrines of Laelius and Faustus Socinus, Italian theologians of the sixteenth century, who taught that, while Christ rose from the dead and ascended into heaven, he was not divine.

133 penning ... Dr Sprat] Thomas Sprat (1635–1713), Bishop of Rochester, *The History of the Royal Society of London, for the Improving of Natural Knowledge* (1667). Sprat's style was not unlike that required of all members of the society: 'a close, naked, natural way of speaking; positive expressions; clear senses; a native easiness' (Part II, section 20).

133 Lord Verulam ... others] Francis Bacon, Baron Verulam (1561–1626). That he relied on an amanuensis, at least for dictating his ideas, is confirmed by John Aubrey (*Brief Lives*, under 'Bacon').

134 executor ... behind him] The executor was Francis North. 'I enjoin my executor, according to his repeated promises to me, that he burn all books and papers whatsoever that are of my own handwriting': John North's will, P.C.C. 1683, I Drax 372, f 48. But some letters survived (see p 191n).

134 these notes ... preserve them] The British Library has Roger North's rough copy of the transcription (Add. MSS 32,517), and his fair copy arranged under headings as described in section 71 (Add. MSS 32,514, ff 167–227v).

135 Arminius] Jacobus Arminius (1560–1609), a Dutch theologian, whose humane views on predestination were the foundation of a liberal reaction, in the early seventeenth century, to the severe doctrines of Calvin.

136 against Mr Hobbes] Thomas Hobbes (1588–1679). The following passages seem to refer particularly to chapters 13, 14, and 15 of *Leviathan* (1651). John North's strictures are typical of the widespread opposition to Hobbes's theories: see J.E. Bowle, *Hobbes and His Critics* (Jonathan Cape 1951); and S.I. Mintz, *The Hunting of Leviathan* (Cambridge: Cambridge University Press 1962).

137 Tully ... obligation] See, for instance, Cicero, *De officiis*, 3.92: 'Agreements and promises must alway be kept, provided, in the words of the praetors, they "were not elicited by force or criminal fraud"'.

137 all one] Presumably a reference to chapter 18 of *Leviathan*.

138 Mahomet ... Erasmus hung] According to the fable, Mahomet's coffin was suspended in mid-air by loadstones: *Oxford Dictionary of English Proverbs* (Oxford: Oxford University Press 1970), pp 498–9. I cannot find the origin of the reference to Erasmus.

139 nocturnals] Night-hags or incubi. According to Robert Burton, the victim of nocturnals 'suppose an old woman rides, and sits so hard upon them, that they are almost stifled for want of breath': *Anatomy of Melancholy*, 6th ed (Oxford, 1651), pt I, section 2, memb. 3, subs. 2, p 93.

139 intimate friend] Francis North.

141 to be blind] BL, Add. MSS 32,515, f 56v: 'He used to consider the case of Milton, who was a learned man and a wit, but of very depraved principles and corrupt, and happened to be stark blind, and in that state dictated his *Paradise Lost*, which being pure fancy needed no consulting with books.'

Dr Johnson was to say much the same thing about the composition of *Paradise Lost*, half a century later, in his *Life of Milton*: '... he naturally solaced his solitude by the indulgence of his fancy ... He would have wanted little help from books, had he retained the power of perusing them': *Lives of the English Poets*, ed George Birbeck Hill (Oxford: Clarendon Press 1905), 1:124.

141 blindness ... poem] *Paradise Lost*, 3.1–55.

141 best friend] Francis North.

142 his own] BL, Add. MSS 32,516, f 86–86v: 'And it being my good fortune to be one of those he used to practise upon, and lying a little open to his play, his snapps sometimes smarted a little too much, and then he would excuse himself, saying he did it because he would have me be as free with him. And I had no reason to be very angry with him having, maugre all his good husbandry, felt his generosity, and in one instance most obliging, for he gave me a commission to send what books I would to him at Cambridge, he would return them new bound by Dawson, the best workman in that place where also bookbinding is generally best, and I think I plied him sufficiently, and have in my small library the evidence of many books whereof the binding is the best character.'

Thomas Dawson the elder (d 1708) married Elizabeth Musset on 9 October 1662 (W.P.W. Phillimore, et al., *Cambridgeshire Parish Registers. Marriages* [1907], 1:54) and had two sons, Thomas and John. Thomas junior carried on the business after his father's death, and John entered Christ's College in 1693 and wrote *Lexicon Novi Testamenti* (Cambridge 1706). There is confusion among the authorities about the identity of the various Dawsons. I am indebted to Mr J.C.T. Oates of Cambridge University Library for clarification of this matter in a letter of 31 October 1967. See G.J. Gray and W.M. Palmer, *Abstracts from the Wills ... of Printers, Binders and Stationers of Cambridge, from 1504–1699* (Bibliographical Society 1915), pp 115 and 117; Plomer, *A Dictionary of Printers and Booksellers ... 1668–1725* pp 101–2; G.D. Hobson, *Bindings in Cambridge Libraries* (Cambridge: Cambridge University Press 1929), p 168; J.B. Oldham, *Shrewsbury School Bindings* (Oxford: Oxford University Press 1943), p 134; D.F. McKenzie, *The Cambridge University Press, 1696–1712* (Cambridge: Cambridge University Press 1966), index. McKenzie and Plomer are in error.

143 a relation of his] Sir John Cutts (ca 1634–70) of Childerley, Cambridge (G.E.C., *Complete Baronetage*, 3:45). Cutts's mother was related to the Weld family, who in turn were related to the Norths. See *Francis*, 1:76–7; H.W. King, 'The Descent of the Manor of Horham, and of the Family of Cutts,' *Transactions of the Essex Archaeological Society*, vol 4, 1st series (Colchester 1869), p 31.

143 Baal's priests] 1 Kings 18:27.

146 court mandates ... to him] For a court chronically short of money the granting of vacant fellowships was a painless way of satisfying suitors. Charles II was a

frequent offender, but James II, it is said, filled every vacancy that occurred at Trinity College during his reign: W.W. Rouse Ball, *Notes on the History of Trinity College, Cambridge* (Cambridge 1899), p 106. When one John Cooper was granted a fellowship by royal mandate in 1680, John North resisted and was firmly put in his place by the Earl of Sutherland (letter of 29 November 1680, *Cal. S.P. Dom.*, 1680-1, p 94). But John North kept up the fight. In a letter to Roger North, 30 September 1682, he eloquently explains his objection to the royal mandate that would place Charles Montagu over the heads of worthier candidates (Bodleian, MS Tanner 35, f 96). However, he owed his own fellowship at Jesus to a royal mandate (*John*, section 16).

146 corporation town] A town holding a charter granting it certain rights, especially in the area of self-government. The governing corporations were often negligent or corrupt: see J.H. Sacret, 'The Restoration Government and Municipal Corporations,' *The English Historical Review*, 45 (1930), 232–59). Roger North stoutly defended the crown's sustained attack on the charters (*Examen*, pp 624–7; *Francis*, 1:277–80).

148 the particulars ... structure] A copy of the printed report on the library and appeal for funds, *Concerning the New Library Now Building in Trinity College, Cambridge*, signed by John North, 10 July 1677, is preserved by the library. John North donated £100 (Robert Sinker, *The Library of Trinity College, Cambridge* [Cambridge 1891], p 8) and £100 more by his will (W. Whewell, 'Barrow and His Academical Times,' *The Theological Works of Isaac Barrow*, ed A. Napier [Cambridge 1859], 9:xliii). The North arms appear on the ceiling of the vestibule. For an authoritative account of the library see *The Architectural History of the University of Cambridge*, ed R. Willis, rev J. Willis Clark (Cambridge 1886), 2:531–51, 686.

148 now stands] Whewell, 'Barrow and His Academical Times,' claims that North's account of the building of the library cannot be correct because Barrow's exhortation to build a theatre was made at commencement, June 1676, whereas college records show that the library was begun in February 1676. But it is a good story, and there is always the possibility that the commencement oration was a public repetition of an earlier and more private appeal.

148 Pearson and Barrow] John Pearson, DD (1613–86), was Master of Trinity from 1662 until he became Bishop of Chester in 1673. Barrow succeeded him and held the post until 1677.

152 Dr Lower] Richard Lower, MD (1631–91), best known for his work on the brain and on blood transfusion. About 1666 he left Oxford for London where, 'being much resorted to for his successful practise, especially after the death of Dr. Willis, an.1675, he was esteemed the most noted physician in Westminster and London, and no man's name was more cried up at court than his' (*Athen. Oxon.*, 4:297).

152 Diet ... Merriman] A proverbial saying.

153 apoplexies] There was more to the incident than Roger North knew, according to
the Cambridge antiquarian Thomas Baker, who has left this shocking account: 'He
endeavoured to restore the discipline of the college, but not being assisted by the
fellows, and being affronted by the scholars, who frequently broke his windows in
the night, did not succeed. When some of the scholars were taken in the fault, and
the seniors called together in order to pass a public and solemn censure, they
dropped away one by one, and left the Master in the hands of the scholars, who
was therewith so affected, that he was taken with a fit of vomiting, sunk away, and
fell down, the scholars calling out and repeating it, "He is drunk, he is drunk." He
was never after the same man. This account I had from Mr. Laughton, Trinity
College' (Cambridge Univ. Lib., MS Mm.2.25., p 283).
John Laughton (1650–1712), librarian and chaplain of Trinity. Baker suggests that
Roger North was discreetly kept in ignorance of the truth which was 'such as was
not to be communicated to so dear a friend as this author was to the Doctor'
(Cambridge Univ. Lib., MS Mm. 1.48, p 235). For further accounts of the affair see
p 192n.

153 magnanimous lady ... physicians] In a letter of 1 April 1689 to his sister Ann Foley,
Roger North recalls his mother's courage as a nurse: 'I think there was never such
an example in the world as our mother, who was no Hector, but never appeared
disturbed during all her painful nursings which she had with many of us, and more
with my father, so that although she was as tender as was possible, one would have
thought she had an heart of brass. I have heard that upon terrible wounds made
up, after the work was done, she would swoon, but rubbed through the work like a
lion' (BL, Add. MSS 32,500, f 93).

155 Mr Warren] John Warren entered Trinity College in 1671 and became a fellow of St
Catherine's in 1681. He was afterwards rector of Boxford, Suffolk (BL, Add. MSS
32,515, f 81).

156 out of Bierling] Caspar Gottlieb Bierling (d 1693), German physician, author of
several popular medical books. The quotation does not appear to be in any of his
published works, but a passage very like it is found in the preface to Theodore
Zwinger's *Theatrum humanae vitae* (Basel 1586–7).

157 overthrown] BL, Add. MSS 32,516, f 111: 'To show what small things men will catch
at hoping to help themselves, or rather, how vain medical traditions in gross cases
are, I must remember that the physicians advised him to eat mustard, as
specifically good for him in this distemper. He was so infinitely desirous of help,
that he took in with the advice and eat mustard by spoonfuls, and never thought he
eat enough.'

158 Nay, further ... free] This observation is probably intended, somewhat obliquely, as a
defiance of Locke and his argument that the terms 'Will' and 'Understanding' are

semantic conveniences and do not represent actual agents. According to Locke, 'Will' is merely the power to decide to act or not to act, which might follow a motion of the 'Understanding' – which is merely the power to perceive ideas and their connections. For Locke, therefore, the concept of 'free will' involves a semantic absurdity. See John Locke, *An Essay Concerning Human Understanding*, ed Peter H. Nidditch (Oxford: Clarendon Press 1975), bk 2, chap 21, esp sections 5, 6, 14, 17, 18, pp 236–42.

158 he went ... near Bury] At Tostock, an estate five miles from Bury St Edmunds, bought by Dudley, 4th Baron North, in 1638 (Bodleian, 'Calendar of the Papers of the North Family,' p iv).

158 attendant and nurse] Identified as 'A grave gentlewoman, one Mrs Coldham of a Norfolk family' (BL, Add. MSS 32,515, f 83). John North's will gives 'my servant Anne Coldham' £50, and it seems likely she is the same person (P.C.C. 1683, 1 Drax 372, f 48).

159 Sir Anthony Irby] Probably Sir Anthony Irby (d 1681) whose daughter Elizabeth married into Lady North's family, the Montagus (*Burke's ... Peerage* (1956), under Baron Boston). Irby's name appears in a letter from Francis North to his mother, 13 January 1669 (Bodleian, MS North c 10, f 43).

159 his last will] P.C.C. 1683, 1 Drax 372, f 48.

159 about three ... adieu] It is not clear whether by the 'first illness' Roger North means the stroke or the distemper that preceded it. The stroke itself probably occurred some time in 1678. A letter from John North to Francis North, dated 1 July 1679 (Bodleian, MS North c 5, ff 77–78 v), referring to 'my lameness and weakness all on one side, the convulsion fits,' places the stroke before that date. Thomas Blomer in his pamphlet *A Full View of Dr. Bentley's Letter* (1710) asserts that John North lived five years after the stroke (p 36), thus placing it in 1678.

159 his mother was dead] Lady North died in February 1681 (*C.P.*, 9:657).

161 those letters ... my reach] Some twenty of John North's letters have survived. Most are with the North family papers in the Bodleian; others are in Trinity College Library, Cambridge, and the British Library (Add. MSS 32,500, ff 16, 63).

161 died] John North died on 13 April 1683, 'Fryday morning about Five of the clocke': E. Foster, ed, *The Diary of Samuel Newton, Alderman of Cambridge* (Cambridge 1890), p 85. A mistaken report of his death had been circulated earlier, in 1680 (*Cal. S.P. Dom.*, 1679–80, pp 609, 610).

161 nothing significative ... over him] The grave is now indicated by a stone bearing an inscription slightly less terse:

J.N. **Mr** Coll.

April 14. 1683

162 If any ... of it] Almost certainly a dig at Richard Bentley. See the following note.

162 controversies ... be excused] North is referring to the memorable feud between the

fellows of Trinity College and their master, Richard Bentley. See J.H. Monk, *The Life of Richard Bentley*, 2nd ed, 2 vols (1833); R.C. Jebb, *Bentley* (1882). At one point Bentley had seized on John North's case as an example of the fellows' habitual recalcitrance: 'Dr. North, my last Predecessor but one ... when he endeavour'd to restore a little Discipline, was so affronted and provok'd by these Men or their Contemporarys, that the Passion threw him into an Apoplexy, and not long after cost him his Life': Bentley's pamphlet *The Present State of Trinity College* (1710), p 12. One of the replies came from Thomas Blomer, a Trinity don: 'There was no Affront offer'd, nor any Provocation given the Master in that Affair; The Seniors were withdrawn; and Dr. North had afterwards sent for the Two Offending Scholars, to give them good Advice ... And, as he was pursuing his Exhortation, he fell suddenly into a fit of an Apoplexy; out of which the Two Scholars bestirr'd themselves, and got proper Assistance, to recover him; and he actually did recover; and so well, that he liv'd Five Years after it': *A Full View of Dr. Bentley's Letter* (1710), pp 35–6. These two versions should be compared with those of Roger North himself (section 97) and of Thomas Baker (p 190n).

Appendix

Dudley, 3rd Lord North (1582–1666) = Frances (d 1677), daughter Sir John Brocket

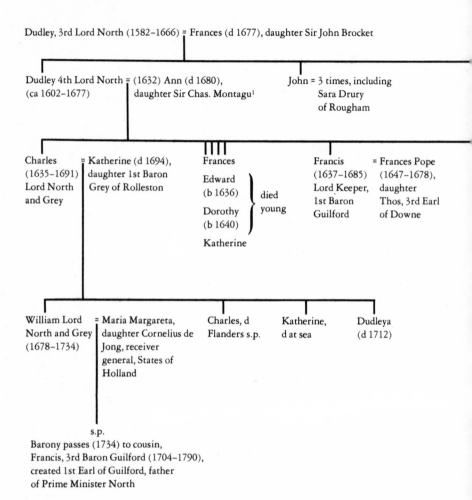

Dudley 4th Lord North = (1632) Ann (d 1680),
(ca 1602–1677)   daughter Sir Chas. Montagu[1]

John = 3 times, including
       Sara Drury
       of Rougham

Charles   = Katherine (d 1694),   Frances   Francis   = Frances Pope
(1635–1691)   daughter 1st Baron   (1637–1685)   (1647–1678),
Lord North   Grey of Rolleston   Edward   Lord Keeper,   daughter
and Grey   (b 1636)   } died   1st Baron   Thos, 3rd Earl
                                            Dorothy   } young   Guilford   of Downe
                                            (b 1640)
                                            Katherine

William Lord   = Maria Margareta,   Charles, d   Katherine,   Dudleya
North and Grey   daughter Cornelius de   Flanders s.p.   d at sea   (d 1712)
(1678–1734)   Jong, receiver
                   general, States of
                   Holland

s.p.
Barony passes (1734) to cousin,
Francis, 3rd Baron Guilford (1704–1790),
created 1st Earl of Guilford, father
of Prime Minister North

Based on Roger North's account in *Gen. Pref.*, sections 45–8; Bodley, MS North c 25, f 3;
Complete Peerage.

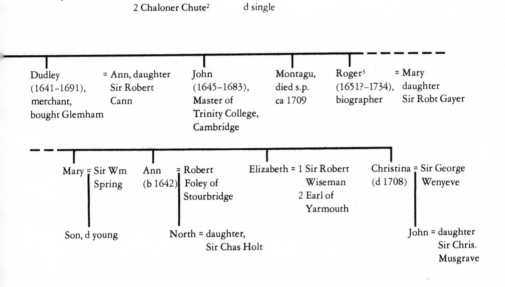

Dorothy (1605–1698) = 1 Lord Dacres
                      2 Chaloner Chute²

? Daughter,
d single

Dudley   = Ann, daughter   John   Montagu,   Roger³   = Mary
(1641–1691),   Sir Robert   (1645–1683),   died s.p.   (1651?–1734), daughter
merchant,   Cann   Master of   ca 1709   biographer   Sir Robt Gayer
bought Glemham   Trinity College,
                                   Cambridge

Mary = Sir Wm   Ann   = Robert   Elizabeth = 1 Sir Robert   Christina = Sir George
       Spring   (b 1642) Foley of   Wiseman   (d 1708)   Wenyeve
                          Stourbridge   2 Earl of
                                                    Yarmouth

Son, d young   North = daughter,   John = daughter
                              Sir Chas Holt   Sir Chris.
                                                                            Musgrave

1 See appendix, section IV.
2 See appendix, section II.
3 See appendix, section V.

II THE CHUTE AND DACRES CONNECTION

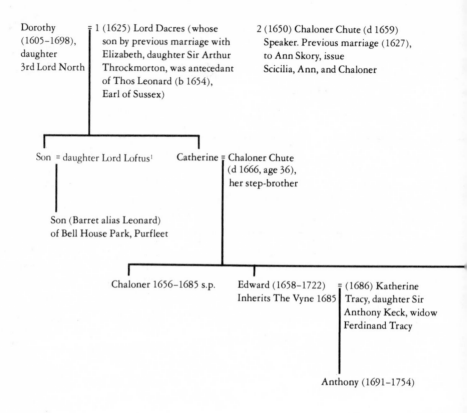

Dorothy (1605–1698), daughter 3rd Lord North ╤ 1 (1625) Lord Dacres (whose son by previous marriage with Elizabeth, daughter Sir Arthur Throckmorton, was antecedant of Thos Leonard (b 1654), Earl of Sussex)

2 (1650) Chaloner Chute (d 1659) Speaker. Previous marriage (1627), to Ann Skory, issue Scicilia, Ann, and Chaloner

Son = daughter Lord Loftus[1]

Son (Barret alias Leonard) of Bell House Park, Purfleet

Catherine ╤ Chaloner Chute (d 1666, age 36), her step-brother

Chaloner 1656–1685 s.p.

Edward (1658–1722) Inherits The Vyne 1685 ╤ (1686) Katherine Tracy, daughter Sir Anthony Keck, widow Ferdinand Tracy

Anthony (1691–1754)

Based on Roger North's account in *Gen. Pref.*, section 45; Chaloner Chute, *A History of The Vyne in Hampshire* (Winchester 1888), pp 78–9; *Complete Peerage*; DNB

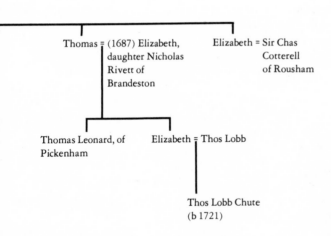

Thomas = (1687) Elizabeth,
daughter Nicholas
Rivett of
Brandeston

Elizabeth = Sir Chas
Cotterell
of Rousham

Thomas Leonard, of
Pickenham

Elizabeth = Thos Lobb

Thos Lobb Chute
(b 1721)

1 According to *Complete Peerage* (5:63) Lady Dacres's son married the daughter not of Lord
Loftus but of his son Sir Robert Loftus. The same authority spells Leonard as Lennard, and Bell
House as Belhouse or Belhus.

III WHITMORE

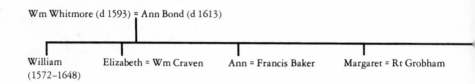

Wm Whitmore (d 1593) = Ann Bond (d 1613)

William (1572-1648) Elizabeth = Wm Craven Ann = Francis Baker Margaret = Rt Grobham

William Charles George Elizabeth = Sir John Weld

Based on Roger North's account in *Gen. Pref.*, section 46; Burke. *Extinct and Dormant Baronetcies: Whitmore of Apley Park: Visitation of Shropshire ... 1623* (Harleian Society 1889), 29: 499; Will of Sir George Whitmore, P.C.C. 1654 f 402; Receipts in Bodley, MS North c 20, f 89; *DNB*

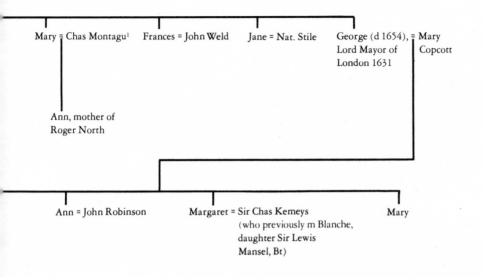

Mary = Chas Montagu[1]   Frances = John Weld   Jane = Nat. Stile   George (d 1654), = Mary
                                                                          Lord Mayor of   Copcott
                                                                          London 1631

Ann, mother of
Roger North

Ann = John Robinson   Margaret = Sir Chas Kemeys   Mary
                                        (who previously m Blanche,
                                        daughter Sir Lewis
                                        Mansel, Bt)

1 See appendix, section IV.

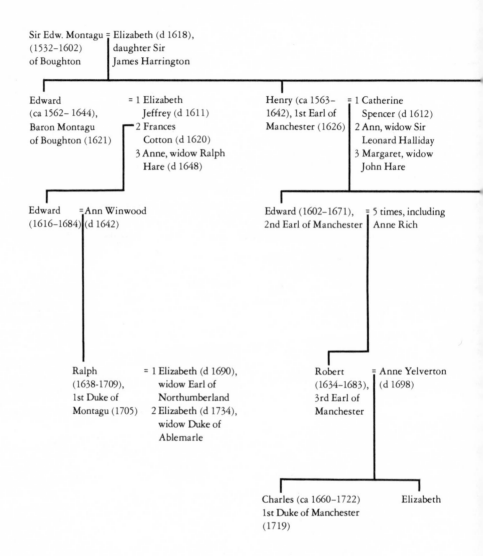

Sir Edw. Montagu = Elizabeth (d 1618),
(1532–1602)   daughter Sir
of Boughton   James Harrington

Edward   = 1 Elizabeth   Henry (ca 1563–   = 1 Catherine
(ca 1562– 1644),   Jeffrey (d 1611)   1642), 1st Earl of   Spencer (d 1612)
Baron Montagu   2 Frances   Manchester (1626) 2 Ann, widow Sir
of Boughton (1621)   Cotton (d 1620)   Leonard Halliday
                     3 Anne, widow Ralph   3 Margaret, widow
                        Hare (d 1648)   John Hare

Edward   = Ann Winwood   Edward (1602–1671),   = 5 times, including
(1616–1684)   (d 1642)   2nd Earl of Manchester   Anne Rich

Ralph   = 1 Elizabeth (d 1690),   Robert   = Anne Yelverton
(1638-1709),   widow Earl of   (1634–1683),   (d 1698)
1st Duke of   Northumberland   3rd Earl of
Montagu (1705)   2 Elizabeth (d 1734),   Manchester
                     widow Duke of
                     Ablemarle

                                                      Charles (ca 1660–1722)   Elizabeth
                                                      1st Duke of Manchester
                                                      (1719)

Based on Roger North's account in *Gen. Pref.*, section 46; *Complete Peerage*; DNB

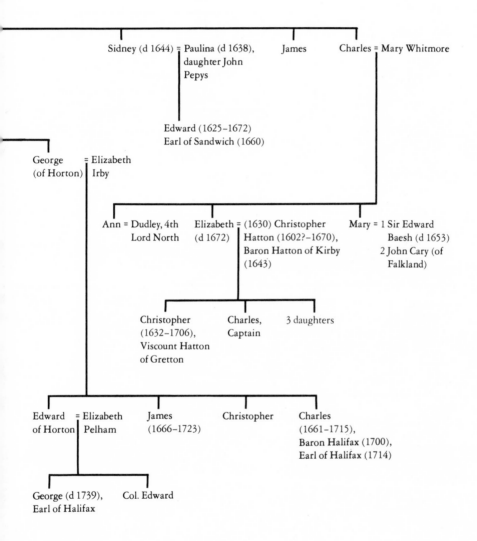

Sidney (d 1644) = Paulina (d 1638), daughter John Pepys

James

Charles = Mary Whitmore

Edward (1625–1672)
Earl of Sandwich (1660)

George (of Horton) = Elizabeth Irby

Ann = Dudley, 4th Lord North

Elizabeth (d 1672) = (1630) Christopher Hatton (1602?–1670), Baron Hatton of Kirby (1643)

Mary = 1 Sir Edward Baesh (d 1653)
2 John Cary (of Falkland)

Christopher (1632–1706), Viscount Hatton of Gretton

Charles, Captain

3 daughters

Edward of Horton = Elizabeth Pelham

James (1666–1723)

Christopher

Charles (1661–1715), Baron Halifax (1700), Earl of Halifax (1714)

George (d 1739), Earl of Halifax

Col. Edward

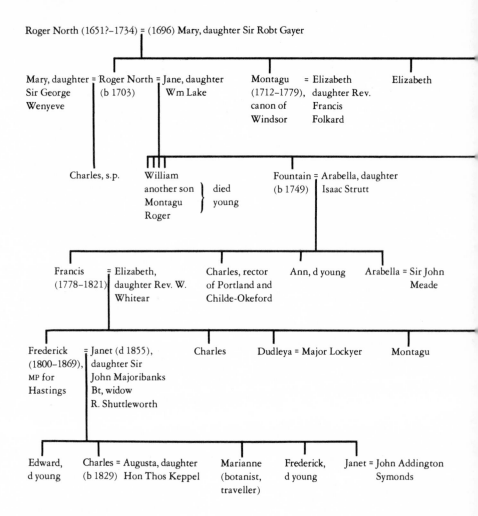

Roger North (1651?–1734) = (1696) Mary, daughter Sir Robt Gayer

Mary, daughter = Roger North = Jane, daughter   Montagu = Elizabeth   Elizabeth
Sir George   (b 1703)   Wm Lake   (1712–1779), daughter Rev.
Wenyeve   canon of   Francis
                                                 Windsor   Folkard

Charles, s.p.   William   Fountain = Arabella, daughter
                another son } died   (b 1749)   Isaac Strutt
                Montagu   } young
                Roger

Francis   = Elizabeth,   Charles, rector   Ann, d young   Arabella = Sir John
(1778–1821)   daughter Rev. W.   of Portland and   Meade
              Whitear   Childe-Okeford

Frederick   = Janet (d 1855),   Charles   Dudleya = Major Lockyer   Montagu
(1800–1869),   daughter Sir
MP for   John Majoribanks
Hastings   Bt, widow
                R. Shuttleworth

Edward,   Charles = Augusta, daughter   Marianne   Frederick,   Janet = John Addington
d young   (b 1829) Hon Thos Keppel   (botanist, d young   Symonds
                                            traveller)

Based on Bodley, MS, North c 25, f 73; BL Add. MSS 32, 502, ff 241–2; Augustus Jessop, *The Auto-biography of ... Roger North* (1887), pp xlii–xliii

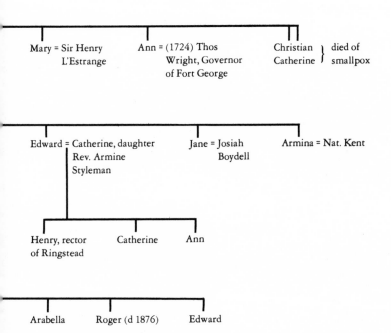

Mary = Sir Henry
       L'Estrange

Ann = (1724) Thos
       Wright, Governor
       of Fort George

Christian ⎫ died of
Catherine ⎭ smallpox

Edward = Catherine, daughter
         Rev. Armine
         Styleman

Jane = Josiah
       Boydell

Armina = Nat. Kent

Henry, rector
of Ringstead

Catherine

Ann

Arabella

Roger (d 1876)

Edward

Index